OUR

Sandra Koa Wing studied life history research at the
University of Sussex, where she was Mass Observation's first
Development Officer. She died in May 2007 at the age of
twenty-eight.

OUR LONGEST DAYS

A People's History of the Second World War

Edited and introduced by
SANDRA KOA WING

P

PROFILE BOOKS

Published in Great Britain in 2008 by
PROFILE BOOKS LTD
3A Exmouth House
Pine Street
Exmouth Market
London EC1R 0JH
www.profilebooks.com

First published by The Folio Society Ltd in 2007

10 9 8 7 6 5 4 3 2

Typeset in Garamond 3 by MacGuru Ltd
info@macguru.org.uk
Printed and bound in Great Britain by
CPI Bookmarque, Croydon, CR0 4TD

A CIP catalogue record for this book is available from the British Library.

ISBN 978 1 84668 088 5

CONTENTS

FOREWORD

In December 1936 a turbulent amateur anthropologist called Tom Harrisson became incensed at the arrogance of the London newspapers, which regularly pronounced that the British public thought this or that about the abdication crisis. They had no idea what the British public thought about anything, he concluded – nor, for that matter, did anyone else, but he, Tom Harrisson, would find out. From that somewhat presumptuous ambition grew Mass Observation: a ramshackle, triumphantly unscientific organisation which, in spite of its weaknesses, gave the world a fuller picture of what the British were really thinking and feeling than had been available at any time before or, some would claim, has been since.

In her introduction Sandra Koa Wing describes how Mass Observation became established and, by 1939, had achieved a remarkably wide coverage of national life. One of its most important elements was the collection of diaries kept by volunteers which provides the material for this book. As Tom Harrisson's publisher, I worked with him on these diaries while he was writing *Living Through the Blitz* (1976). They gave me a salutary lesson on the frailty of human memory. More from curiosity than because of any direct relevance to the book, we wrote to some of the diarists who had recorded particularly vivid accounts of incidents during the blitz. Would they, we asked, without referring to any records of the period, be kind enough to give their version of what they remembered of that incident today? Some half-dozen responded. Any relationship between the incident they had described in their diary and the story they told in 1975 was almost entirely coincidental. They got *everything* wrong: dates, places, the sequence of events. In every case they moved themselves closer to the centre of the action: the bomb that had fallen in the next street now fell in *their* street; the blast that had caused such freakish damage to a nearby house now affected *their* house. The experiment convinced me that, though oral testimony might be of value in recapturing atmosphere, it was worthless or worse than worthless if hard facts were wanted. At least, I think it did ... The papers disappeared after Tom Harrisson's death, I read the letters more than thirty years ago, who knows what tricks my memory may not have played?

These diaries, however, are the real thing – or at least the real thing as it appeared to the writers at the time. That is a significant qualification. The diarists strove for objectivity but it would be astonishing if they invariably achieved it. As Sandra Koa Wing points out, they were for the most part literate, middle-class and inclined to be left-wing. They were not, and did not pretend to be, representative of the British people as a whole. But they were part of that people at a moment when the nation was more nearly united than at any other time in the twentieth century; their hopes and fears were to a great extent those of their fellow citizens. In their immediacy, their occasional cantankerousness, their underlying patriotism, these diaries truly speak for Britain.

They show that, as is so often the case in moments of great crisis, people were more concerned with the trivia of survival than with world-shaking events. 'It's really astounding how little I *do* think of war,' wrote Nella Last. 'I'm often amazed at my "limited vision" and wonder if others have it too.' They did. As Greece and Yugoslavia crumbled before the German assault, Len England remarked that such disasters seemed 'of little more importance than the fact that the lance-corporal next door has lost his stripe for pissing outside his hut'. Food was a far more common subject for discussion than war aims or grand strategy. Henry Novy's family was lucky enough to be sent a pheasant by a friend. As they ate it the Japanese were surging triumphantly through Malaya, capturing Manila, invading Borneo. 'We talked about it all just a little, but more of our comments were reserved for the cider and how nice the bird tasted.'

The British were too busy, too tired, too concerned with the problems of daily life, to spare much energy for wider issues. 'For most fellows here, the real war scarcely exists,' wrote the RAF corporal Peter Baxter. 'Their whole life is choked up with drill and polishing floors and scrounging another helping of pudding.' Yet some issues did emerge strongly. One was the status of women. Year by year, one can feel the self-confidence of women growing as they realised that they could hold their own in a world that had previously been predominantly male-oriented. Muriel Green was a gardener, whose employer complained about the inadequacy of unskilled labour. 'In fact I am sure he really prefers the work of the women,' she wrote with some satisfaction, 'as they are more adaptable, quicker and less dogmatic than his former men under-gardeners.' Women were breaking through to fields where previously their presence would have been unwelcome or inconceivable. In April 1944 for the first time there were two women on a *Brains Trust* programme. 'Hope they do that more often,' wrote Edie Rutherford, 'must break down the idea women haven't as much sense as men – many haven't, but then many men haven't as much sense as many women!'

There is endless grumbling – by the diarists themselves and in the overheard comments which they record. There is criticism of the nation's leaders – much of it justified. There is boredom and frustration. 'I am sick of the war,' wrote Maggie Joy Blunt in March 1944. 'Sick of everything, the waiting and the sound of bombers, of my work and my clothes and the general dullness of my complicated and unfruitful existence.' And yet the overall impression the diaries leave is one of astonishing resolution, an acceptance of the inevitable, a determination to make the best of it, a conviction that, however much the war might sometimes seem to be mismanaged, the cause was a just one and it had to be seen through to victory. Writing about

London at war I said that there was much on which Londoners could look back with pride and remarkably little about which they needed to feel shame. No one reading these diaries is likely to reach a different conclusion.

PHILIP ZIEGLER

INTRODUCTION

> Now I don't think a great deal about the 'war in general' – try
> to *only* think about day-to-day – even hour-to-hour – problems
> and now dear yesterday has flowers on its grave and the raw
> wild grief has died and tender memories of what has been.
> Tomorrow seems to merge into today so quickly – I sometimes
> pant a little in my efforts to keep up – and as for 'next week',
> 'next year' – they are in God's pocket as Gran used to say.
>
> Nella Last, 14 July 1943

The Second World War saw dramatic changes in British society.
It was a war that involved not only the troops fighting on the
front line but, as never before, the civilian population at home.
The First World War had been fought abroad: Britain's 'island
fortress' had remained unthreatened and the British navy still
ruled the waves. But the promise at the end of that war of a
'land fit for heroes' had not been realised. As politicians dith-
ered, Britain remained a land of millions living on a meagre
diet in damp, dilapidated housing. For most people, it was still
a case of 'them' and 'us'.

In the 1930s, as a new war threatened, there were indica-
tions of discontent. One of these was manifested in the British
documentary film movement, which uncovered the reality of
how people lived in the urban slums and how they worked in
the mills and mines of industrial Britain. Among these docu-
mentarists was Humphrey Jennings, who in January 1937,
with the anthropologist Tom Harrisson and the journalist
Charles Madge, wrote a letter to the *New Statesman and Nation*
outlining the aims of a new social research organisation, Mass
Observation. There was a need, the letter said, for an 'anthropology of our own people'.

Mass Observation develops out of anthropology, psychology, and the sciences which study man – but it plans to work with a mass of observers. Already we have fifty observers at work on two sample problems. We are further working out a complete plan of campaign, which will be possible when we have not fifty but 5,000 observers ... It does not set out in quest of truth or facts for their own sake, or for the sake of an intellectual minority, but aims at exposing them in simple terms to all observers, so that their environment may be understood and thus constantly transformed.

The organisation developed methods of information-gathering which included a team of paid observers and a national volunteer panel of writers, recruited by Charles Madge. The investigators watched people in various places – at religious occasions, in public houses, in cinema queues – and interviewed passers-by on the streets on such topics as holidays, home life, music and dancing. Mass Observation also collected ephemera for its library: local newspapers, church magazines, leaflets, dance programmes, advertisements for lectures and meetings. The initial contributions of the panel of writers consisted of 'day surveys' written on the 12th of each month, including the day of King George VI's coronation on 12 May 1937. The panel also responded to monthly 'directives' on themes such as jokes, eating habits, money, propaganda and marriage.

By 1939 Mass Observation was well placed to preserve the fabric of individual responses to the war: the everyday effects of rationing, the blackout, conscription, war work, along with personal comments about how the war was being waged and how it was reported in the press. In August that year, with war imminent, the organisation asked its panel to keep diaries on a daily basis giving details of their everyday lives: their routines, observations, thoughts, overheard conversations, what their friends and families said to them. The panel sent their diaries to Mass Observation's headquarters in London in weekly, fortnightly or monthly instalments.

The collection of diaries survived. It is stored in numerous archive boxes, on thin typing paper, on lined paper torn out of exercise books, in small spiral-bound notebooks, in pencil, in flowing hand in ink or on letter-writing paper in tiny handwriting. There are accounts of hearing Neville Chamberlain announcing that Britain was at war with Germany, of exhaustion during times of persistent air raids, of humorous everyday incidents, of frustration with the war news, of the difficulties of food and clothes rationing, of the excitement of D-Day and the feelings of relief and anticlimax on VE Day and VJ Day. Touching the papers today releases a kind of 'archive shiver': a direct connection to the daily lives of the past.

The Mass Observation diary is a particular hybrid of private diary and public research journal. The diarists knew that the organisation's staff might read their writing, and that extracts might be published. Mass Observation produced around 2,000 reports and published 25 books between 1937 and 1950, including *First Year's Work* (1938), *Britain by Mass Observation* (1939) and *War Begins at Home* (1940). It also for some time published a regular bulletin, *Us*, which was sent to observers. These publications included extracts from the diaries and 'directive' replies from the panel, usually attributed anonymously but nonetheless generating a genuine sense of pride and ownership, as Muriel Green records in April 1940 (p. 31):

> ... we went in the town library to ask if they had got 'our' book (we always call it 'ours': hope MO doesn't mind, but you see we've never had anything we've written in print before and claiming 14 lines and Jenny 25 lines we felt a proprietary interest in the publication, and that everybody ought to see and read it) and were delighted to see that the paper cover was pinned up inside the main entrance with other new books they had bought this month for the library.

The knowledge that the diaries were not only being read immediately, but could be published for a wider audience, was often a driving motivation for the diarists. Many new diarists were recruited through Mass Observation's publications, aware that by writing about their own experiences they too could contribute to the scientific study of everyday life. This inevitably shaped what they wrote. Often great attention was paid to detail and accuracy in an attempt at objectivity: gas masks were counted, bus passengers observed, expenditure on food and clothing noted, percentages calculated. The idea that the 'researched', the 'ordinary' person, could also be the serious 'researcher' was at the core of Mass Observation's aim to create a popular anthropology. The organisation did sometimes give brief, direct feedback to diarists: Bob Willcock, one of the full-time members of staff, was at one time responsible for acknowledging the diary instalments. It is Willcock whom Muriel Green asked for when she visited Mass Observation's London headquarters in 1941 (pp. 83–5).

Keeping a diary for Mass Observation's more obvious research purposes, however, did not preclude the diarists from writing candidly about their lives as they might have done in a purely private diary, and the line between the two is often blurred. The kaleidoscope of motivations for keeping a regular diary for Mass Observation is not dissimilar from those for writing a private diary: a need for personal therapy, a kind of confessional, a desire to document one's own life for posterity, to contribute to the historical record, to adhere to a routine, to find space to ruminate. Indeed, Mass Observation became a confidante, or witness of sorts, during terrifying air raids, at times of frustration with the war and with life in general, or when there was a need to express grief and distress over the absence or loss of loved ones.

This was an all too common need during the Second World War, when few people were untouched by personal loss. To that extent the Mass Observation diarists reflected a general

experience. It is worth noting, however, that the diarists did
not represent a true cross-section of British society during the
war. Although they came from a variety of backgrounds, and
from different regions, most of them were middle-class, well-
read and articulate. They tended to be people with a natural
capacity for observing – and for recording what they observed.
Moreover, on the whole their political leanings tended towards
left of centre; several were pacifists or conscientious objectors.
This does not mean that Mass Observation set out to recruit
diarists for their political viewpoints. But it does suggest that
the people motivated to write these private/public diaries were
more likely to be sympathetic to the left than to the right of
the political spectrum.

The immediacy of the diaries gives us an intriguing insight
into life in Britain during the war which is quite different
from (though complements) the retrospective accounts we hear
today in oral history interviews, in television reminiscences,
on websites collecting testimonies, such as the BBC's *People's
War* project. We see how the war becomes the backdrop to
the lives of the diarists: life is not seen through a retrospective
'war lens'. This immediacy is particularly highlighted when
the diarists write about their thoughts for the future, for a life
after the war. Through the diary form we get a tangible sense
of shift, of a world changing or about to change. In this, many
of the diarists reflect a widespread feeling in Britain towards
the end of the war. Revealingly, Mass Observation was one of
the very few organisations to predict the Labour victory in the
general election of July 1945. A 'people's war' had changed
the people.

SANDRA KOA WING

EDITORIAL NOTE

Some silent amendments have been made for ease of reading: spelling errors and punctuation and grammatical oddities have been corrected where necessary for sense.

Finally, a word on money. The pre-decimal sterling currency comprised pounds, shillings, and pence. There were 12 pence to a shilling (1/-) and 20 shillings to a pound. One and a half shillings was represented as 1/6d, and so on.

S.K.W.

ACKNOWLEDGEMENTS

I owe thanks to: the original volunteer Mass Observation diarists who contributed so much of themselves – I hope those who are still alive will enjoy this book; The Trustees of the Mass Observation Archive, for supporting this project and for quotation and use of the collection; Kit Shepherd, Emily Thwaite and the team at the Folio Society for commissioning this book and providing much appreciated expert guidance at all stages of the project; Dorothy Sheridan, Head of Special Collections at the University of Sussex Library and director of the Mass Observation Archive, for her friendship, encouragement and advice: she is a guiding inspiration to anyone interested in Mass Observation; my excellent colleagues in Special Collections: Fiona Courage, Karen Watson, Simon Homer, Lucy Pearson and Kate Maunsell.

I am indebted to Melinda Davies and Abigail Luthmann who so generously volunteered to copy the diaries, and to Sarah Johnson for her efficient and accurate transcribing. Many thanks to Jen Purcell for sharing her transcripts of the diaries of Nella Last and Edie Rutherford. For thought-provoking comments on early drafts and unstinting support I owe thanks to Valerie Simmons, Vicky Paine, Neil Parkinson, Jenna Bailey and Mark Harris. Particular thanks are due to my family and friends, and most especially to my husband Peter Simmons for practical, intellectual and emotional support throughout the project.

S.K.W.

1939 EXPECTING WAR

At 11 a.m. on Sunday, 3 September 1939, the British Prime Minister Neville Chamberlain announced to the nation that Britain was at war with Germany. France followed suit. The immediate pretext was Hitler's refusal to suspend his invasion of Poland, which had begun two days before. But the storm clouds, in Churchill's phrase, had been gathering for some time. The build-up of German military might, the incorporation of Austria in a 'Greater Germany', the annexation of western Czechoslovakia – all this presaged war.

By the summer of 1939 the British people were expecting war. Conscription for 250,000 men over the age of twenty had been announced in April. Many thousands of women had enrolled for 'war work' in factories and on the land, to release men for the armed forces. Gas masks had been issued, in the widespread expectation that the Germans would launch a poison gas attack. Buildings were fortified with sandbags, air-raid shelters were delivered to homes. There were rumours of spies ('fifth columnists'), and some hostility towards civilian men of conscript age, pacifists and Conscientious Objectors ('conchies'), which was to continue throughout the war.

Within minutes of Chamberlain's announcement, air-raid sirens were heard in London – a false alarm as it turned out. And for the next few months, nothing happened, or so it seemed. There was no mass aerial bombardment, no gas attack, no German invasion. On the home front at least, this was a 'phoney war'. Government plans to evacuate millions from urban areas began to seem unnecessary, and evacuees were drifting back to their homes, some of them reporting that they had been made less than welcome in their rural haven. For many urban children, life in the country was a bewildering experience: one London child was amazed to discover that cows were bigger than dogs.

Meanwhile the population got used to life with the blackout:

carrying torches at night, using dimmed lights on cars, taping windows, in response to Ministry of Information leaflets on Air-Raid Precautions (ARP). Several million people were involved in Civil Defence work. There was petrol, and then food, rationing. At Christmas, families gathered in their dimly lit rooms and listened to the radio, the 'wireless'. The nation may have been gloomy, but Tommy Handley's *ITMA* (*It's That Man Again*) could always raise a laugh.

SEPTEMBER 1939

J. R. Frier, 19-year-old student, London

Sunday, 3rd. About 9 a.m. it was announced that the Prime Minister would speak at 11.15 after the time limit for the German answer had elapsed. No one here had any doubt that it would be war. We all went on with household work till 11.15, and had our fears confirmed. The speech was accepted as the inevitable conclusion. But the air-raid warning which followed was totally unexpected. There were doubts as to whether it really was a warning. Mother was very flustered – several women in the neighbourhood fainted, I learnt afterwards, and many ran into the road immediately. Some remarks – 'Don't go to the shelter till you hear the guns fire.' – 'The balloons aren't even up yet.' – 'The swine, he must have sent his planes over before the time limit was up.' When the All Clear sounded, there were more doubts as to whether it might not be another Take Cover signal. Within a minute everyone was at the gateways again; the women talking quickly to each other in nervous voices. More talk about Hitler and revolutions in Germany. 'Hitler's going to leave the Poles and start on us now.' – 'Huh, if he can get here!' Discussion on whether warning was real or only a practice. Tempers were frayed, and irritated by petty things, such as an extra loud note from the wireless. Much indignation when it was learnt that warning had been given because of a single machine, afterwards recognised as friendly.

Most peculiar thing experienced today was desire for something to happen – to see aeroplanes coming over, and see defences in action. I don't really want to see bombs dropping and people killed, but somehow, as we *are* at war, I want it to buck up and start. At this rate, it will carry on for God knows how long.

Sunday, 3rd. Customer tells us of declaration of war. Feeling of hopelessness followed by annoyance at same. Think through friends who will eventually be called up. Decide to think of them as killed off and then it will not be such a blow if they are, and will be great joy if at the end they are not.

Spend the afternoon preparing for blackout. Stick brown paper over back door glass panel, etc. Bring out Public Information Leaflets and ARP book and read through the lot. Decide bathroom to be refuge room in air raid because it is downstairs and has only one small 18½in. sq. window, and has outside walls 18½in. thick. It already has most things in ARP book: washing things, disinfectant, bandages, etc. We take in a tin of Smiths potato crisps, three bottles lemonade, several packets of chocolate from business stock, and some old magazines to read.

During the afternoon a friend from next village comes to see us. Says he has volunteered for the navy for the duration, as he is twenty-one and says he would far sooner drown than sit in a trench for days on end.

Muriel Green, 18-year-old garage assistant, Snettisham, Norfolk

Sunday, 3rd. Bedtime. Well, we know the worst. Whether it was a kind of incredulous stubbornness or a faith in my old astrological friend who was right in the last crisis when he said 'No war', I *never* thought it would come. Looking back I think it was akin to a belief in a fairy's wand which was going to be waved.

I'm a self-reliant kind of person, but today I've longed for a close woman friend – for the first time in my life. When I

Nella Last, 49-year-old housewife and Women's Voluntary Service worker, Barrow-in-Furness, north Lancashire

heard Mr Chamberlain's voice, so slow and solemn, I seemed to
see Southsea Prom the July before the last crisis. The fleet came
into Portsmouth from Weymouth and there were hundreds of
extra ratings walking up and down. There was a sameness about
them that was not due to their clothes alone, and it puzzled me,
till I found out. It was the look on their faces – a slightly brood-
ing, faraway look. They all had it – even the jolly-looking boys
– and I felt I wanted to rush up and ask them what they could
see that I could not. And now I know.

The wind got up and brought rain, but on the Walney shore
men and boys worked filling sandbags. I could tell by the dazed
look on many faces that I had not been alone in my belief that
'something' would turn up to prevent war. The boys brought
a friend in and insisted on me joining in a game, but I could
not keep it up. I've tried deep breathing, relaxing, knitting and
more aspirins than I can remember, but all I can see are those
boys with their look of 'beyond'.

My younger boy will go in just over a week. His friend
who has no mother and is like another son will go soon – he is
twenty-six. My elder boy is at Sunlight House in Manchester
– a landmark. As a tax inspector he is at present in a 'reserved
occupation'.

J. R. Frier   *Monday, 4th.* Spent the morning doing housework and revising
first aid. Noticed that any bus starting up sounds like the first
notes of a siren, and makes people start. Heard news of torpedo-
ing of *Athenia*:[1] the first real 'war news'. Overheard neighbours
talking about it over back wall; one declared an *American* boat
had been sunk (presumably because of American passengers on
board) and that the US were bound to do something about it.

Wednesday, 6th. An air raid this morning at 6.45 but we heard
nothing but the sirens. Waited in our most sheltered spot,
behind the cellar door for a few minutes, but came out again
and all went on with day's work, having breakfast, making

beds, etc., intending to slip downstairs if we heard guns or
engines. Father walked best part of way to office, after All
Clear, owing to crowds of people on trams. Being sick of doing
nothing, I went to Employment Exchange for a job, and signed
on for ARP work. Shan't hear any more for a few days, so sat
back in the afternoon and took it easy.

Wednesday, 6th. Wakened by neighbour calling outside house   Muriel Green
that there was an air-raid warning. Dash out of bed and sally
downstairs putting on dressing-gown at the same time. Jenny
and Mother stop to dress. As nothing to be seen or heard I go
back and dress. Mother goes and stands outside backdoor and
keeps saying she cannot hear anything. All neighbours are seen
standing outside looking up and down. Then ARP warden is
seen cycling furiously down the road ringing a loud handbell.
We don't know the meaning of this and get out ARP book and
it says handbells indicate that poison gas has been cleared away!
We decide it can't be that as no sign of poison gas or people in
gas masks, not even sign of an aeroplane. Nothing happens. I
stand in back garden and watch, and see people going to work,
so decide it must be all over, then small boy goes by and tells
me that the bell was the 'All Clear' sign. The warning previously was the police constable blowing whistle. Nobody was
woken up by same but a few people had seen him and warned
others. All day general indignation in village over the air-raid
warning. The handbell was loud enough to hear which was not
so important.

Saturday, 9th. Received note from Joint Recruiting Board at   J. R. Frier
Cambridge, to which I've applied, telling me to be ready to go
up for interview. Beginning to meet opposition from parents,
who would prefer me to go up for Michaelmas term [at Cam-
bridge], until I am conscripted. Most middle-aged people to
whom I have spoken about applying for a commission have
advised me to wait until I *have* to go.

Dad had to work this morning, though he doesn't usually. He was at home at 1 p.m., with grumbles about AFS and ARP workers, who have apparently, for a large part, been playing darts all this week and getting £2–£3 a week for it. Have heard same grumbles before.

Sunday, 10th. People in evacuation area most kind and willing to help. My sister is with two other evacuees and the little girl of the house, in a bungalow. The parents have taken on more than enough to manage, but aren't grumbling in the least. They really are trying to treat the children as their own. But some children are less well off – saw several red eyes in the town, which has been flooded with parents from London all day. Some 'reception parents' apparently accept the children as an evil necessity, and don't do a great deal for them, nor do they consider that the children have a bedtime. General attitude of London parents seems to be that it's better that the children should be safe in strange hands than in danger with their families.

Frank Edwards, 33-year-old war factory buyer, Birmingham

Thursday, 14th. Quite a normal day so far as ordinary things go. At the works we are still very busy turning out blackout and camouflage paint. There is also a big demand for luminous paint just now, and this I think is likely to increase. Lighting restrictions announced to be a little easier today, by allowing pedestrians to use a torch, covered, so that light is diffused, and cars can use one dimmed headlamp. Decision also announced to open nearly all cinemas and theatres tomorrow. Read a good definition of a Nazi today – 'A Nazi is a man born within the sound of Goe-bels.'

Nella Last

Thursday, 14th. The last day of having a 'little boy' – for so my Cliff has seemed, in spite of being twenty-one at Christmas. He has been so thoughtful and quiet these last few days, and so gentle. I watched his long sensitive fingers as he played with the dog's ears, and saw the look on his face when someone mentioned 'bayonet charging'. He has never hurt a thing in his life: even as a little boy, at the age when most children are unthinkingly cruel, he brought sick or hurt animals home for me to doctor, and a dog living next door always came for a pill when it felt ill – although as Cliff used to complain, it never noticed him at other times! It's dreadful to think of him having to kill boys like himself – to hurt and be hurt. It breaks my heart to think of all the senseless, 'formless' cruelty.

Sunday, 17th. Another lovely day. Cooked the dinner and did plenty of work. Used the vacuum cleaner on the lounge, beat the stair carpets, washed the hall and landing, and bathroom, scrubbed the pantry. Not bad for a day's work.

Heard the news on the wireless that Russia had invaded Poland. What next? Also listened to the BBC new parlour game, *Proverbs*, which I thought silly, as many of the proverbs they chose I had never heard of. Enjoyed the BBC Orchestra playing some of Eric Coates's music. Had supper and went to bed.

Doris Melling, 23-year-old shorthand typist and hospital library assistant, Liverpool

Monday, 18th. Went swimming before tea. Heard news of *Courageous* sinking[2] at 6. Went out with some friends after 7. None of them has joined up yet, but one has applied for a commission. Most of talk was about a booze-up, which took place during the weekend at the Old Boys' clubhouse. A very jolly affair all round, with a large number of Old Boys present, apparently. The blackout conditions induced several of them to make water in odd places, e.g. the middle of the road near Raynes Park, and on the back wheels of a stationary taxi.

J. R. Frier

Friday, 22nd. With the blacking out of the windows I cannot tell these mornings when it is time for getting up, and this morning was especially dark as it was wet as well as cold. Have been very busy again at the offices and notice that some of our regular callers do not put in an appearance now, owing to being

Frank Edwards

on National Service. I suppose we shall get less still next week when the petrol rationing is in force. Some of them have told me that they will not be able to get round but not to forget that their firms are carrying on.

Nella Last   *Monday, 25th.* I've always had rather a 'narrow' life and my joys have been so simple. I seem to have built a home like a jackdaw – straw by straw – and now my straws are all blowing away! I'm grateful for my work at the WVS Centre and I pray I can keep well enough to 'keep right on to the end of the road'. When my sewing machine is whirring it seems to wrap me round with a rhythm, as music sometimes does, and keeps me from thinking about my Cliff in the Machine-Gun Corps. I've got a lot to be thankful for. Even the fact, which often used to stifle me, that my husband never went anywhere alone or let me go anywhere without him, has settled into a feeling of content.

OCTOBER 1939

Doris Melling   *Sunday, 1st.* Listened to Winston Churchill [First Lord of the Admiralty] on the wireless – still having trouble with his s's. Then the news – more men called up. Why on a Sunday? Pa returned home and told us that Mother didn't want to come home, her reason being that she hated to see all the people looking so frightened. Was far happier in the country. Talked about plans for the future. Could we all migrate to the country?

J. R. Frier   *Monday, 2nd.* Had a letter from borough council cancelling my application for ARP work, because I'm not the proper age. (I applied on the 6th Sept. This is the only news I've had.) I can understand that an age limit has to be fixed, but I rather think there are a number of fellows over 18 and under 20 who either have no job or are working on their own, who would have been glad to do something in the way of ARP work until called up. No other jobs, paid or unpaid, are open to them, because firms are unwilling to take people of near military age.

Tuesday, 3rd. Following remarks come from conversation with my mother. A mother of a friend of mine – roughly same age and standing – 'No, I don't mind my Ron getting called up – Anything to stop that old devil getting over here.' Another mother with a young daughter at school – 'This war's happened very nicely for us – Joan taken off our hands and kept for us – and we're getting her school fees reduced because my hubby isn't earning so much. And but for the war, he'd never have come back to me.' (He lost his job after abandoning her, and had to fall back on her help.) My own mother's comments on *Evening News* headline – 'Latvia and Lithuania to kneel now.'[3] – 'Oh, so old Stalin's started Hitler's stunts now.'

Wednesday, 4th. Went to Joint Recruiting Board at Cambridge, having been summoned yesterday. This was the procedure: About sixty of us, all undergraduates or graduates, were waiting in a room in the Old Schools at 1.30. After half an hour or so, a picture-book major in mufti came in and called us out in batches of half a dozen or so to follow him. I was in the second batch, luckily. We were called one by one into the Council Room, where there were six tables with one officer, several civilians, and perhaps a clergyman to each, to deal with applicants for commissions in the army, navy, air force and for technical posts.

At my table there was a chuckling old man, a younger don, and an army captain. They were all very friendly, and seemed to have found out most of my past record already. They pointed out that although I had applied for some work where French and German would be needed, I should have to go through a normal course of training first. They hoped I'd have no objections; and I hadn't. Then they wanted to know which section I preferred.

I plumped at random for the Artillery. This apparently needed some mathematical qualifications, but they seemed satisfied when I said I had done some trigonometry, and had got a Maths distinction in Matric [Matriculation examination]. I'd never thought that would be any use to me. They suggested I should brush up my trigonometry before being called up, as I haven't touched it for four or five years. After a few more questions about my languages, and status in college, they handed me a slip of paper stating that I've been recommended for training as an officer in the RA and sent me into another room.

Here I had to fill in the usual territorial attestation forms, in triplicate, and passed on to the medical examination room. I stripped to trousers, shoes and jacket, and waited my turn in the changing room where we could have tea at 2d a cup, biscuits thrown in free.

The extremely thorough examination finished, I filled in some more papers, had the colour of my eyes and hair noted, and went upstairs to be sworn in ... The young officer here looked at my form, and found I was an agnostic (I had suggested C of E [Church of England] when asked my religion, but so doubtfully that the inquirer said – 'You can put agnostic if you like'). His conversation went on like this – 'Oh, I see you're an agnostic – well, so am I, so you can say what you like. The point is this – have you any strong objections to swearing in on the Bible? Because if you have, it means I've got to go and fetch a notary ...' I said I hadn't any strong objections. 'It's open at the dirtiest place in the Bible,' he went on, 'if that's any comfort to you.' So with one hand on Ezekiel chapter 23, I read through the oath of allegiance and became a gunner. He filled in the rest of the form, said 'Bugger!' very loudly when he made a mistake, and turned me over to the next table with a spot of advice about buying uniform at the proper shops. The next table supplied me with 2/- pay, 2/6d ration allowance, and 10/3d fare money, and I walked out much more at ease than when I went in.

Saturday, 7th. Morning spent in blackberry and apple jam-making. We don't usually make jam but this year as we have excess of apples and blackberries we thought we had better as there is a war. I have slept in room with Mother since Father died and Mother has been threatening to move me into the spare bedroom all the summer owing to face powder being spilt on the carpet. Today she moved me because she said if a bomb hit her end of the house I might be saved up the other end. She says if we are spread out there might be one survivor to have the money left behind. Mother sent the Peace Pledge Union 5/-.

Muriel Green

Tuesday, 10th. On the way home met three school friends, two out of work: one sacked [because of] the war, the other only just left school; the third going into a bank next Monday. Go for a walk with them. The four of us arrive back at our house just as a harmless old gentleman two doors away emerges; 'four strapping louts like you,' he says pleasantly enough, 'and none of you in the army.' 'It must look pretty bad,' says one of us when he has gone, 'all of us just doing nothing.' I am reminded of the story I have just heard of a benevolent old gentleman who went up to a girl selling *Peace News* and solemnly spat, one of the few signs of absurd patriotism so far this war.

Len England, 19-year-old university student, Streatham, London

Lunchtime listen to the news on the wireless, none of it seems very vital now we have heard it all before. Over tea mother regales us with rather long but interesting stories of Red Cross work in the last war and we talk of books and authors from Fielding (whom I am reading) and Sterne (whom my friend is reading) to Auden and Isherwood and whether the news is true. Mother goes and father comes in and immediately political discussion starts for the first time in the day; a hot argument on what would have happened if the Anglo-Russian pact[4] had been signed at the expense of the Baltic countries.

Thursday, 12th. Day begins as usual with breakfast, MO diary and shopping expedition. Just after dinner a friend rings me up about the theatre but he tells me as well that another friend has just come up from his evacuated school to have an examination at the War Office as he is a holder of Cert A over eighteen; this news worries me for I also have Cert A but I am now a pacifist and have no wish for military interviews, but I am reassured when I am told that he had put his name down on a special roll.

Over supper my career was discussed. Father does not mind me getting no money but suggests accountancy and other things I am not very keen on; I counter with farming and mother objects but finally listens to reason and it is decided that father should tentatively find out about accountancy and I should do likewise about farming. Then I read the paper (*Evening Standard*) and am delighted to find a piece of information in the MO report that must have been mine.

Saturday, 14th. The usually aimlessly busy morning shopping, writing report, reading; see the news on a *Star* van that the *Royal Oak* has been sunk;[5] think that this might be the origin of the *Ark Royal* rumour as names are not very different but later the news that it was not sunk before Friday gives the lie to it; then I hope that it is not a battleship because I had insisted that a battleship with 'bulges' could not be so sunk. Came home and listened to one o'clock news and found that it was.

Tuesday, 17th. Back for tea, but before that I go to the garage to get our October ration of petrol; I tear out the tickets and he accepts them without bothering to look at the rest of the book to see whether the number on the book tallies with the number on the car. Also he filled up before asking for the tickets; what would have happened if I said I had not got them, would he have bothered to siphon the petrol out again? And isn't it easy to forge booklets?

Frank Edwards   *Thursday, 19th.* Everyone seems to have got used to the blackout now, although there was a moon shining tonight, and the cinema was full and there was a queue waiting for admission. On my journey home I was impressed with the careful and sensible manner in which pedestrians used their torches, mostly I noticed just to find their way in stepping from the pavement to the road or vice versa. One or two people used their torches when the tram approached – for the driver to stop, but they didn't shine their torch upwards but shone it downwards so that the driver could see there was someone there.

Saturday, 21st. Foggy this morning. Looking forward to playing tennis – something tangible to do. Would like to have seen Waterloo v. New Brighton rugger match at Blundellsands, but can't do more than one thing at a time. Wrote after a job in Chester. Really feel very unsettled though. Wish I had something to do, really useful, all day long, instead of just wasting time, not knowing which way to turn. Can't do anything definite until I see whether the family are going to move to Chester or not. It's damnable.

Doris Melling

Monday, 23rd. Today fetched gas mask for self and Mother and Jenny from ARP warden. Have not had one until now, surprised to find not too unpleasant to wear as everyone else had said they could not breathe. Have practised wearing it in private and think I could keep it on any length of time if necessary.

Yesterday heard a mine had washed up on our beach, but today I went to look at it and it has washed away again before naval authorities could come and explode it.

Muriel Green

Tuesday, 24th. It has been a rotten day, cold and pouring with rain all day. But this evening to brighten things up I went to the Paramount Cinema to see the film *Confessions of a Nazi Spy* which I thought was very good indeed and at the present time is indeed a topical film. It seemed to be very much enjoyed by the large audience.

Frank Edwards

Once again I have to record the marked enthusiasm of the audience during the singsong arranged by the organist. Everyone joined in songs with a vengeance and thoroughly enjoyed themselves. Since the war began these singsongs seem to have taken on wonderfully and people really want to sing. Yet I have seen a similar thing attempted at the same theatre by the organist, prior to the war, when it needed a lot of coaxing to get the audience to join in and even then only a few did, but at the present time hardly any invitation to the audience is required, so eager are they.

Muriel Green   *Sunday, 29th*. Nothing worth reporting to MO seems to happen in the country. We receive no air-raid warnings and would not know a war was on apart from radio, newspapers and people's conversation, and continuous filling in of ration coupons for petrol ...

Many evacuees returned to London because on the night of Sept. 3rd and the morning of the 6th there was an air-raid warning. They said they thought they had been sent to safety areas, but they decided they were no safer on the East Coast than in London especially as they have air-raid shelters in their gardens and in the parks. There are none here. The first bomb in England fell in this village in the last war.

Other women said that they found such difficulty in the country shops. Food was much dearer at the village grocers than the Co-ops and company grocers. Nothing can be bought ready cooked and they did not understand the coal cooking ranges of the country. They all grumbled at the inconveniences of travel now only one bus each way every two hours, and about three trains a day. They were not used to living three miles from a station and bus stop. Some said there was no cinema, and one wanted to know where she could get her hair permed ... They found the country very quiet and lacked amusement. One woman said, 'I'd rather be bombed on my own doorstep than stay here and die of depression.'

The village people objected to the evacuees chiefly because of the dirtiness of their habits and clothes. Also because of their reputed drinking and bad language. It's exceptional to hear women swear in this village or for them to enter a public house. The villagers used to watch them come out of the pubs with horror. The holiday camp proprietor said they all joined the club as soon as they were sent to his camp and said, 'You should see them mop down the drink.'

NOVEMBER 1939

Friday, 3rd. Conversation piece re rationing, overheard in train. Participants – lady about 40 and young man about 25.

Doris Melling

Lady: I see they're only going to allow us a quarter of
    butter.
Y.M.: Yes, not much, is it? We'll have to use margarine.
L.: Well, 'Stork' margarine isn't so bad.
Y.M.: Yes, but we can't get different kinds now, it's all
    pooled.
L.: Oh, I didn't know that. Well, margarine is too bad.
    I've never had any though.
Y.M.: No, neither have I. I'd sooner have beef dripping.
L.: Yes, I think I would too.

Wednesday, 8th. In the afternoon about 3, I was sitting knitting in the garage talking to elderly retired man. Suddenly there was a terrific noise just as though something very large had fallen on the garage roof. The floor seemed to bounce up and down again. For a second I was deafened. I knew it was really nothing falling on the roof as nothing could fall with such force without coming through. It was far louder than if the house had fallen down beside the garage. I instantly thought it was an air raid and a heavy explosive bomb had fallen in the

Muriel Green

neighbourhood. The elderly man said, 'Blast, what's that?' I did not know whether to rush outside and see what had happened or stay in case a second bomb fell. I found I had bit my tongue in the excitement. We waited a minute in frozen horror and then ran outside. Everything was whole. I looked to see if all the houses still stood. Our mechanic was filling up the car of a retired army general. Afterwards he told me he said, 'What's that, what's that?' The mechanic: 'I think a bomb has fallen.' 'Hell of a noise, hell of a noise.' He got out of his car and we all stood for some minutes wondering what to do. The grocer's assistants from across the road and all the inhabitants of the houses, including the policeman, had come out and were looking around. Nothing further seemed to happen so we came in. Other people were gradually going back in their houses. I thought about my mother and sister who were at Beach House and wondered if they were all right. We heard aeroplanes very high in the sky and went out but could not see them. I returned to my knitting and in the meantime my sister returned on a bicycle. She said she had been cycling along when she had suddenly heard this thundering noise, and seen black clouds of smoke issuing from about a mile along the beach. She did not think it was a bomb as she could see no planes and knew it to be in the direction that a mine had been washed up.

About twenty minutes after the first noise we heard a second minor explosion and later still a third but as they decreased in loudness we thought it was other bombs being dropped further away. About 3.40 the police patrol car came for petrol and we were told that the noise was mines being exploded about four miles away. As our mechanic said afterwards, 'I really did think that old Nasti had come this time.'

Doris Melling *Thursday, 30th.* Noticed Arthur's sister on the train this morning. Is now married but carrying on with her job although her husband is not in the army, or likely to be for some time.

Know many similar cases. How are all the married women going to be dislodged at the end of this war?

Watched arrivals at service in memory of those who lost their lives on the Dock Board pilot ship on Sunday.[6] Saw the Lord Mayor, Bishop of Liverpool, and many naval fellows. The church must have been packed, so many went in. At 9.15 a.m. Russian troops entered Finland.[7]

DECEMBER 1939

Friday, 1st. And so we start a new month today – with what in store? Well, it will soon be Christmas so why worry. I think there were some surprised people today when the 22s [22-year-olds] were called up, owing to this being sooner than was expected, especially as it was authoritatively stated after the last call up on 21st Oct. that it was not expected the next age group would be called on until the new year.

Frank Edwards

Saturday, 16th. There have been numerous articles and comments in the press recently on How Our Lives Have Changed. But I protest that, for the majority, it is just what they haven't done, yet. We have had to suffer a terrible uncertainty that they might. We have had to suffer certain inconveniences – the blackout, petrol rations, altered bus and train services, a lack of theatrical entertainment, rising cost of food, scarcity of certain commodities such as electric light batteries, sugar, butter. Large numbers of children are experiencing country life for the first time in their lives. A number of adults are doing jobs that they have never done before and never expected to do. But there has been no essential change in our way of living, in our systems of employment or education, in our ideas or ambitions.

Maggie Joy Blunt, 30-year-old architectural writer, Slough

We are adapting ourselves to the inconveniences, but our lives have not changed. It is as though we were trying to play one more set of tennis before an approaching storm descends. The storm does not descend and we go on playing tennis. Nothing happens. A local MP, addressing members of a Comforts Fund Working Party recently, remarked that he was not in favour of this 'half-asleep' war. Scattering pamphlets is no more use than scattering confetti. I am sorry to have to say it, but we shall have to make the Germans suffer before we can make peace possible.

But what, I wonder, does he suppose is happening at sea? We forget, seated comfortably at home wondering why 'nothing happens' because there are no air raids over us, this war at sea which, J. A. Spender [a leading journalist of the day] last Sunday suggested, the Germans may have substituted for the blitzkrieg we all expected. Mr Churchill has stated that two to four U-boats are destroyed each week. The *Doric Star* on her way home from New Zealand and Australia has been attacked by the *Admiral Scheer* and reported missing. The destroyer *Jersey* has been attacked and damaged. We have attacked and damaged the *Admiral Graf Spee*.[8] (O glorious feat! Thirty-six Germans dead and sixty seriously wounded.) Magnetic mines cause losses daily – the week before last our merchant losses totalled over 33,000 tons. Daily, men drown and die of exhaustion in a winter sea while we sit at home wondering why nothing happens.

Doris Melling   *Saturday, 16th*. Walked through the fields to Little Crosby. News about the *Graf Spee* in Montevideo harbour. Stayed up till 12 for the news – that she had scuttled herself, or rather the crew had scuttled her. So that the people who were reported to have chartered aeroplanes in order to see what they thought was going to be a great sea battle had wasted their money. The captain went down with the ship.

Nella Last   *Tuesday, 19th*. There was very little bacon in town today and women were anxiously asking each other if they knew of a shop which 'had any in'. We eat so little bacon and cheese, but I'll get my ration and start using it in place of other things – meat and fish – in my cooking. Fish is very dear and, in my budget, not worth the price for the nourishment. I've always been used to making 'hotel' meals, as the boys call them – soup, a savoury and a sweet. If one is a good cook and manager, it's the cheapest way in the long run – cheaper than getting a big roast and chops and steaks for frying. In the last war, we were living tolerably well when many were complaining of dullness and shortness of food. Now, when I'm out two days and have to come in and make a hot lunch, my soup-casserole/omelette lunch is a real boon, for I can prepare it beforehand and it's no trouble to serve – a few minutes to set on the table.

Friday, 22nd. Now one cannot obtain either torches or batteries   Doris Melling
– at one time could get the complete article but no refills, with the result that one was accumulating large numbers of torches, for which it was impossible to obtain a battery.

Listened to grand wireless programme about Poland. Very, very impressive. Certainly the Polish view of the German mentality is different from ours – they say that we do not know what the German can be like, he is ruthless in victory and cowardly in defeat. I bet very few people would listen to a programme like this – they are all too busy waiting for Tommy Handley [star of the radio programme *ITMA*], and such people. I am convinced that people in England do not realise what we are up against. They think that what has happened in Poland could never happen here, but I sometimes wonder. Have just asked one man did he hear this programme, and he replied, 'No, we turned off.'

Streets absolutely thronged with people. Crowds of soldiers, sailors and RAF men. Hope everything is being looked after properly while they're away. It would be just like little old Hitler to have a slap-up 'do' at Christmas time, seeing that Sunday is a favourite day with him.

Saturday, 23rd. Hustle and bustle everywhere. Lots of men on leave. Helped Mum with the shopping, which seemed to be proceeding apace. Evidently no shortage of money. Heard lady in grocers asking if she could have extra butter for her son, who was waiting outside, and who was in the RAF. No mistletoe to be had, but plenty of holly with lots of berries. Shortage of bread – tried three shops without success.

Muriel Green *Monday, 25th.* Morning received a pair of gloves from a lady friend also a box of 'Black Magic' from another. Jenny bought me a Penguin book and bar of chocolate; could not afford any more. We had a good laugh because I received a letter from a girl whose father has an antique business which has flopped. The mother has got a job in a petrol rationing department and the father is in a pantomime as the front legs of a horse. Jenny had a letter from a lady in Surrey who said she has one girl evacuee. She had three, but she sent one girl away as she broke out with impetigo and one little boy nearly frightened her to death, as he strayed down to the station (half mile away) and watched a porter cross the line and followed him and fell over the live rail and was nearly electrocuted. The station-master brought him home burnt on the legs and arms. So he had to go as well.

Doris Melling *Wednesday, 27th.* Everyone very jaded. There is no getting away from the fact that Xmas has not been a *real* Xmas this year. There is one big fact which takes a lot of getting over. Most people stayed at home. Kay rang up. Said it had just been like another weekend to her. Vincent and Winnie away, and Wilfred in France – not like the old reunions in the previous Christmases.

Saw a WAT [ATS member] on the platform at Waterloo. She looked terrible. All the men round about looked as if they were frightened of her. Have not seen one WAT or Air Force girl who looked decent – all of them are fat and bespectacled, or else very severe and gaunt.

Wednesday, 27th. Jenny and I were cooking mince pies when we   Muriel Green
heard a very loud aeroplane and saw through the window a very
peculiar looking plane. We both said at once, 'I am sure that's
a Nasty.' But we both stood and watched making no attempt
to take any precautions.

About five minutes later we heard more aeroplanes and
Jenny rushed out and said she saw three Spitfires chasing over
after the other aeroplane going very fast. A few minutes later
the first plane went dashing back and the three others went
over again, and Mother and Jenny rushed out in the garden and
then rushed back declaring they could hear gunfire. The dog
barked and jumped about and I was still eating my dinner and
refused to get up and Mother announced that if there was anything to be seen she wasn't going to miss it. She said we might
as well be killed while we were excited as anytime.

Friday, 29th. Rationing to be introduced Jan. 8th. Butter,   Doris Melling
bacon, sugar. Views: Chief clerk in office, 63: 'I thought the
Germans were supposed to be starving. What about us? Look
at the coal, electricity and gas rationing – all a waste of time.
And then all these notices in the train about not talking about
the war – anyone would think we were surrounded by enemies
in a beleaguered city. The thing I object to is the upset which
is caused by it all – rationing, I mean.'

Elderly man in shop: 'Don't believe it's necessary. It's only to
find work for some of these people up in London. It's the same
with evacuation – don't believe in it.'

Saturday, 30th. Roads terribly slippery. Went long walk with
K plus dog. Saw battle cruiser in the river – presumably the
one damaged by torpedo. Policeman standing on guard at Hall
Road and Blundellsands stations. Talked to one of them about
the gunfire we could hear. Said we were fighting with money
as well as men. Was quite talkative.

1940   ALONE

After a bitterly cold winter the Germans turned their attention to western Europe. In April, Denmark and Norway were rapidly overrun; British and French counter-attacks in Norway failed to dislodge the invaders. In May, Belgium and the Netherlands were invaded, and German forces pushed through the supposedly impregnable Maginot Line in eastern France. With the Allied troops diverted to the north, another German army group swept through the Ardennes, then swung south into France. The British Expeditionary Force, which had landed in France in October 1939, was trapped in a narrow pocket near the Channel coast. Under heavy bombardment, a flotilla of ships and small boats evacuated over 333,000 men from the beaches of Dunkirk, 100,000 of them French.

In Britain, morale was low. His position increasingly untenable, Chamberlain resigned in May. Winston Churchill, after his 'years in the wilderness' back in government as First Lord of the Admiralty, succeeded him as prime minister, after the Foreign Secretary Lord Halifax withdrew when Labour leaders indicated that they would not support him. Churchill formed a coalition government, and on 4 June delivered a rousing speech to the House of Commons, broadcast that evening to the nation:

> We shall go on to the end, we shall fight in France, we shall fight on the seas and oceans, we shall fight with growing confidence and growing strength in the air, we shall defend our Island, whatever the cost may be, we shall fight on the beaches, we shall fight on the landing grounds, we shall fight in the fields and in the streets, we shall fight in the hills; we shall never surrender.

Churchill had no illusions about the gravity of Britain's situation, but in the national consciousness the humiliating retreat from Dunkirk somehow became a 'miracle'.

By June the Allies had withdrawn from Norway, leaving the Norwegians to surrender unconditionally, while the Germans had also occupied Paris. An invasion of Britain seemed imminent: on a clear day German troops on the French coast could see the white cliffs of Dover. At the end of July, the Luftwaffe began an intensive assault on coastal defences and Royal Air Force bases in southern England. On the ground, people watched as the Battle of Britain was fought in the skies, Hurricanes and Spitfires engaged German bombers and their fighter escorts, and 'dogfights' raged over the cornfields. Then, with the RAF stretched to the limit, the Germans abruptly changed their strategy – German bomber losses had been unacceptably heavy – and began bombing urban areas at night. London was attacked on 7 September, with many civilian casualties. Other cities – Birmingham, Liverpool, Coventry among them – were bombed. The 'blitz' had begun. But the German objective of obliterating Britain's air force had failed. Given a chance to regroup, RAF Fighter Command decisively intercepted a massive bomber attack on 15 September. Hitler decreed that the invasion of Britain was postponed indefinitely.

Meanwhile there was more food rationing: bacon and butter were restricted to four ounces per person per week, sugar to twelve ounces. The Ministry of Food, under Lord Woolton, distributed pamphlets advising on cooking with limited ingredients, and a 'Dig for Victory' campaign encouraged civilians to turn their gardens over to growing vegetables. (An unforeseen effect of rationing was an improvement in the nation's diet.) By mid-1940 the conscription age had risen to twenty-eight. Since single men were called up first, there was a rush of marriages.

JANUARY 1940

Monday, 1st. I started the New Year well by making a start on a hated job that has been on my mind to do as soon as I got a bit of time. My brother gets a lot of good clothes which are   Nella Last

only half worn when he has finished with them and with a few
hours spent in slight alterations they make good working suits
for my husband – or Cliff when he was home. I don't know why
I so dislike the job for it is not noticeable when finished and I
would tackle anything in the sewing line but the fact remains
that I groan to myself when I see them arrive!

I was cold in the warm house while my cold has been on
me and wondered about the poor wretches in Turkey in their
20-foot snow drifts and blizzards.[9] I picked up a paper in which
an astrologer said 'a new world is being born' – it certainly
looks as if this one is dying …

Christopher Tomlin, 28-year-old paper salesman, Fulwood, Preston

Tuesday, 2nd. I doubt if it could be colder than it is today, for
a week it has been impossible for me to make diary notes outdoors. It is difficult enough to write my orders with fingers
heavy and numb. Thanks to my insurance agent who advised
me to buy quinine and phosphorus pills, I can stick it better
this year.

I got another torch battery from a customer who manages
a big cycle store in town. I asked for him and was invited into
the office – he doesn't want his assistants to know. He tells me
I need never be without a battery if I will ask for him.

It strikes me those who sacrifice most in wartime are
mothers like mine who aren't strictly entitled to dependants'
allowances. My mother loses £5 because Dick is in France. The
government takes such deprivations for granted. I chatted to a
customer about the new age groups – 20 to 28 – to be called
up this year and said 'Thank goodness I have at least a year left
in civil life!' Her nephew purposely volunteered for service in
the job he wanted just before his group was called: it's common
practice. I want to be anything other than an infantryman –
cannon fodder – but don't know what to join. I'm not a trades-
man. I know much about printing but I can't print. So what
the deuce will they pop me in? I'm very short-sighted and have
that distressing complaint – itching piles. So sincerely trust I

stay a civilian. My brother laughs at his friends who laughed because he joined up in September. Now they are pathetically eager to choose a position instead of being shoved into an unpleasant one.

Tuesday, 2nd. Classes 23 to 28 definitely to be called for registration soon. This will pretty well include all my friends. I am afraid the 28s thought they were quite safe for a bit, but this will be a shock to them, although of course they will not be called for actual service at present.

Met I for lunch. Says L is sick and tired of the army, and would be jolly glad to get back to civilian life. Café crowded with shoppers who had come in for the January sales, presumably. Still plenty of khaki about. Noticed how inferior everything seemed to taste in the café – smaller portions too. Lots of people are saying how used we will get to margarine in time.

Monday, 8th. First day of rationing. Was served with about a spoonful of sugar in the café. Butter hardly noticeable on roll. Last night heard one of the German radio stations giving news in English. I've never heard such rubbish in my life. Of course, the Hore-Belisha business was a good target.[10] Also heard programme in English purporting to come from a nightclub in Berlin. The object of this was to show that the German people were in fine spirits. Broadcaster said he had had to reserve table two days ahead. All the latest dance tunes were being played – except British and Jewish ones. He also had with him an Italian, who said he was very much impressed by the way the German people could think for themselves, and how they were enjoying themselves in spite of the war. He said this was good propaganda – the other agreed with him, but the next minute he said they did not mean the programme as propaganda. I don't think they really knew what they were trying to do.

Doris Melling

FEBRUARY 1940

Muriel Green   *Saturday, 10th. Mon anniversaire et j'ai dix-neuf ans!* I received
War Begins at Home [Mass Observation publication]. We are
very pleased with it and are especially gratified because we have
four observations printed in it. I have one on evacuation and
Jenny two, and one we both claim because we both put it. The
only snag about it is we daren't lend the book to anybody in
the village now because we are afraid it would 'get round' who
we had written about and it is not very complimentary to the
village behaviour. Also had a new hot-water bottle and fancy
coat-hangers. Three ladies came to tea with mother.

Christopher   *Friday, 16th.* A miserable east wind sent the dust swirling into
Tomlin   nose and eyes. I walked three miles to deliver stationery. Dick
went back tonight and left depression behind him; we miss him
so. He is the life and soul of the house. He left me 7/- worth
of cigarettes from France which were presents to him. He also
bought Benedictine, Cointreau, Cognac, eau de Cologne and
a beautiful silk scarf for mum. Though Dick is away and out
of work, I am determined to make a staunch fight to keep us
going. But this vile weather! It is snowing now.

Jenny Green,   *Thursday, 22nd.* Snow disappeared very quickly last night. A
26-year-old   nice fine day, quite busy in garage. Three coupon swindlers
garage   dealt with. They mostly have 90 miles to go, ill wife, etc. Our
assistant,   mechanic announced his intention of sending a pork pie to
Snettisham,   his brother in the BEF; I tried to warn him of the danger of
Norfolk   poisoning. 'But there's nothing else would give him so much
pleasure and I know they keep three days in the winter,' he said.
I gave it up and hoped for the best.

Friday, 23rd. I was minding the garage alone this afternoon
and went out into the garden a minute, heard an aeroplane and
realised a German plane was above me, flying very low and

quite slowly. A very big variety. I felt quite pleased with myself
to think that I had definitely seen another. It appeared to have
come from the sea over the marshes, turned over our lawn and
circled back towards the North Sea. I watched to see if it was
pursued but saw no more aeroplanes. I saw two women with
shopping baskets and the postman and another shopkeeper had
recognised it but stood out in the road too, to see if there was
any further fun. Everyone I told wished they could see it and
started looking up as well. The butcher said he would give
any money to see one and our mechanic was very disappointed
when he returned, said he would not have taken on a job for the
afternoon if he had known.

The wireless says reports of enemy aircraft over the Norfolk
coast are unfounded. I felt quite annoyed and switched over
to Bremen [German radio station]. Mr Smith in the dialogue
talks just like a customer of ours, which always amuses us.

MARCH 1940

Monday, 4th. A distant relation came to see Mother and told
her how his brother died last Sept. 'The shock of the war upset
him so that his stomach turned over so that he could not pass
anything,' so he said. He rushed from London to his mother's
in the country, and said he dare not go back. After a week and
nothing had happened he decided it was his duty to stick to
his job (postal worker) and went back, but after a week they
wired for his brother to fetch him as he was dangerously ill.
The brother did, and said he would not have known him: in
this week his hair had gone white and he looked a physical
wreck. They took him to hospital and an immediate operation
was ordered, but he was too weak to live through it. He was 50
and had a terrible time in the last war, and now his only son
was about the age to go.

Muriel Green

Wednesday, 6th. At 8.30 Jenny called up the staircase, 'Did you hear a noise last night?' 'No.' 'An aeroplane crashed and burnt out on the common.' 'No!' 'Yes, Mr K just told me, he was coming home from the parochial meeting and they all saw it fall, and followed to see. Burnt right out. About 8.30 p.m.' He told her how they had dashed to the place, and all stood round and watched it burn. Then someone stirred the fire and the guns began to go off. The crowd ran away as fast as they could, while the bullets whizzed by them. I wonder some of them did not get shot.

After lunch George turned up. He has had tonsillitis and had a week's leave since last Wed. He suggested we should go for a cycle ride, so we decided to go and look for the smashed aeroplane. We did and found it in a field. There was only burnt twisted metalwork and bits of it were all over the field. I picked up a bolt and put it in my pocket. Lots more people were looking. All of a sudden two aircraftmen ran along. They said they weren't supposed to let anyone come close, and if their corporal came back he would be furious. They imparted to G that under a parachute lying there was the pilot's foot they had just found. They said they had run away to watch another plane which had just landed about a quarter of a mile away, but as there are so many dykes on the marsh they could not get over to it, and they seemed to have landed safely so they thought they had better continue to guard the old wreck. We could see the other plane in the distance and they asked if we knew the best way to get to it.

G picked up a live bullet and put it in his pocket much to my annoyance. I am terrified of cartridges and guns and always suspect they will explode, and he always has the gun and shooting mania. We got away and cycled down the lane to the nearest point to the other plane, and walked ever so far across marshland and it still seemed in the distance. An army officer and a private were following behind, and caught us up and asked if they were going the right way to the aeroplane.

We said we thought so and walked the rest of the way across planks over creeks and bogs to the plane.

Two airmen were sitting on the wings and two women were just arriving with a pot of tea, cups and saucers, a tin of milk, sandwiches and cakes and giving them to the airmen. About six soldiers came up and saluted the officer and talked with them and they went off back again. Five grammar school boys and about seven other small boys and girls were rushing round the plane climbing on the wings and peeping inside. Two young men stood watching and a girl wearing trousers was trying to attract the attention of the same, who were talking to the airmen. We all stood and watched them eat and drink the tea the women had set out for them. The propeller of the plane was smashed and a pool of oil was running out of the body somewhere. The children were swarming all over it and running round and saying what certain parts of it were. The two women kept telling the two airmen, who were not hurt but rather shaken, about the poor young pilot killed the night before last and telling them how lucky they were to be all right. One of them said, 'We should never have landed her in the dark, as it was we only just missed that ditch.'

Wednesday, 20th. A golden letter day. A letter from Dick says he is now a 1st-class wireless operator having passed a very stiff examination. It is almost unknown in the RAF for an aircraftman to jump from AC2 to AC1 in seven months: it takes most aircraftmen two years. We are delighted with the news. A few days ago Nazi airmen killed a civilian and wounded others in Scapa Flow, so now we pop across to Sylt to give Hitler hell. An eight-hour raid in which we made a damned mess of the island. About time we moved! Perhaps the war will not now be a let's pretend one.

Christopher
Tomlin

APRIL 1940

Doris Melling   *Sunday, 7th.* Went a walk with K. Was telling me all the news.
Everyone is getting married and engaged, or else having babies.
Made me feel rather stale and out of things. Lord Castlerosse
in the *Sunday Express* today says that if any girl ends up in this
war not married, then she is simply not trying. Most of my
friends have made such messes of their married life – no proper
homes, keeping in their jobs, and such. Joan is going to have
another baby in September. Says this is definitely the last, and
if we want to knit anything, now is the chance! She expects Bob
will be called up soon, and will only be a private. I don't know
how they will live.

Jenny Green   *Tuesday, 9th.* W arrived to work in quite a panic about Germany
invading Denmark.[11] Had I heard? No, I had not. Waited to
see if anyone else mentioned it. They did not. Later W returned
from Lynn and said he saw it on a hoarding that they had
invaded Norway as well, so we put on the one o'clock news to
find out. Went to see a neighbour who is spring-cleaning. She
had a very old mac on the linen line which she said she was
airing in case she had to flee. She thought if you were a refugee
you wanted to look as scruffy as possible and then they would
get up a fund for you.

Muriel Green   *Tuesday, 9th.* I was astounded to hear via Jenny and W of the
invasion of Norway this morning. It seemed such an extraordinary thing for Hitler to do. I suppose he had to do something quick, but I did not realise he was getting so desperate. It
worries me as to what he will do next. He seems to get nearer.
Jenny thought of packing a bag, also W, but he can't see why
it would be any safer the other side of England. Not another
person who came to the shop mentioned the invasion all day,
but in the evening I went to see my great-aunt. She said she
was astonished by the news.

Tuesday, 16th. At last there are air-raid shelters in Fulwood,   Christopher
two in the next street to where I live. There is one between   Tomlin
Fulwood maternity hospital and Fulwood garrison. There are
many noticeboards directing people to them.

An old client – an Irish woman – is suspected by her neighbours of being a member of the IRA.[12] They follow her in town,
ask the postman if she gets letters from Eire and are within
hearing distance whenever there is a caller at her door. My customer is a Catholic, her husband fought in the last war. And
both her father's and mother's people were British Army folk.

Friday, 19th. Afternoon Jenny and I went to Lynn. Did some   Muriel Green
shopping and walked round all Lynn, and picked up some
leaflets for MO. We went to W. H. Smith and Sons' best and
biggest bookshop in Lynn to buy a Penguin book, and asked
if they had got *War Begins at Home* just to see if they had. I did
not expect they had as I have never seen it there, and if the girl
had produced it I was preparing to say it was too expensive.
Anyway, she had not got it, nor *Britain*. I felt very insulted and
offended with the shop. She did not even seem to have heard of
them either which was all the more annoying. I also asked for
Oxford pamphlet by a WEA tutor we had. This they hadn't
got either. Nor any of his other books.

Before we caught the bus home we went in the town library
to ask if they had got 'our' book (we always call it 'ours': hope
MO doesn't mind, but you see we've never had anything we've
written in print before and claiming 14 lines and Jenny 25
lines we felt a proprietary interest in the publication, and that
everybody ought to see and read it) and were delighted to see
that the paper cover was pinned up inside the main entrance
with other new books they had bought this month for the
library.

Monday, 22nd. Only one post a day 9.30 a.m. after today and   Jenny Green
collections at 10.30 a.m. and 4.30 p.m. Postman has to push

the mail in a barrow one and a half miles to station now and this is just amusing the village because they have never seen it done before.

Two evacuee mothers walked from the beach to catch a bus to Lynn to the Jewish Festival. They told me that the woman whose bungalows they live in is trying to get rid of them for the summer: 'Yesterday she took all the blankets, said the government said she was not to supply bedding or cooking utensils any more. Gave us two ragged old brown blankets. The kettle holds just five cups of water. It's a job bathing the kids with it. You have to fill it up quick and keep the bath hot until you get enough to put them in. She was all right with us until now and we put up with things like that to keep the children safe.'

MAY 1940

Christopher Tomlin

Friday, 3rd. I am stunned, very disillusioned and afraid of our retreat from Norway. Because I understood Mr Chamberlain was 'ten times more confident of victory' and he made me believe we would drive the Germans out of Scandinavia. Now the wind is out of my sails; I feel subdued and expect to hear more bad news. I am afraid because I know the wrong men are at the helm. Haven't we, can't we, find more men of Churchill's breed? Considering the millions there are in Britain surely there's one man among them who can outwit Hitler?

Doris Melling

Saturday, 11th. Mr Chamberlain has resigned and Winston is to be PM. I think this arrangement is more satisfactory to all concerned. Dutch lines are holding well. The Allies have announced that they will take such steps as they consider necessary if open towns are bombed. At least, if the British don't the French will. Did some gardening this afternoon. News of terrific fighting in Belgium and Holland.[13] Two hundred

German planes reckoned to be shot down. Anthony Eden new
War Minister.

Tuesday, 14th. Woke up at five. Laid in bed and heard the men   Muriel Green
go to work at the shingle quarry. I was not listening but overheard the word 'parachutes' by two workmen. The next two
a few minutes later were also talking of invasion of England.
Everybody round here has it in their minds about what we shall
do if invaded. Most people seem to expect it. Most have very
wild ideas about what we ought to do.

Why have we not had instructions? Why not a Public Information leaflet on the subject along with other wartime instructions we have had? After all we had plenty of pre-war on ARP
and ever since the war not a word to the civil population on
what to do on enemy invasion. I wonder if the government has
any plans. Everyone here is wondering if we stay put or hop
it if they land. Some think both ways. We keep debating the
subject of fleeing or remaining, and do not know whether to
pack a case as some people have or not. We have had our hand-
bags ready with bank books in since the day war was declared.

Sunday, 19th. Walked over the marsh and back by road. Mrs F   Jenny Green
called out to a man digging in his garden and asked the latest
news. He began to curse about the Belgians, 'They ought to
be chopped right up and blown to pieces. I was there in the
last war and three of my pals were shot in the back in bed.
I'd never trust a Belgian. They're worse than them Germans.'
Came home to lunch and minded the shop the rest of day.
Several people about. The Dutch and Belgian invasions have
had hardly any effect on our trade, much less than the Norwe-
gian. I suppose like the crises they're getting so frequent that
nobody takes any notice.

Wednesday, 29th. The *Daily Mail* tells how and why the BEF   Christopher
is hemmed in. I want to do something – I am ready to face the   Tomlin

bloody Hun. I register on the 15th of June and now await it with cold fury, sadness and determination. We will beat back the bloody swine or die. We will never surrender. Maybe the incompetent leaders in France have gone.

The Empress cinema was quarter-full. *Frontier Marshal*, an excellent film. At 'God Save the King' we all stood still – not a movement until the last bar.

JUNE 1940

Nella Last *Tuesday, 4th.* We all listened to the news and the account of the Prime Minister's speech and all felt grave and rather sad about things unsaid rather than said. Sometimes I get caught up in a kind of puzzled wonder at things and think of all the work and effort and unlimited money that is used today to 'destroy' and not so long ago there was no money or work and it seems so *wrong* somehow … feeling there was a twist to life when money and effort could always be found to pull down and destroy rather than build up.

Doris Melling *Tuesday, 4th.* News this evening of Mr Churchill's speech in the Commons. He said he had thought it would have been his duty to disclose to the public the biggest military defeat we had ever suffered. Instead, 335,000 men had been saved, and 50,000 lost, besides a lot of lost equipment. Although it had been a wonderful thing, we were not to look upon it as a victory – wars were not won by evacuations. It was indeed a wonderful speech, and even the BBC announcer got all het up about it.

Wednesday, 5th. Slowly but surely the British public is realising the predicament we are in. I mentioned in the office that I had heard we were to work another hour per day; one clerk replied: 'After that speech of Churchill's last night we can expect anything.' The general opinion about the speech is that it was a good one, a fighting one. The ending, where he said we would fight to the last, and never surrender, seems to have made the biggest impression.

Saturday, 22nd. Letter from Dick arrives. Tells us to watch the Mediterranean: 'The war will be won or lost there.' Spain and Italy with Germany will try to seize Gibraltar and block the Suez Canal, thus cutting our sea communications and bottling the fleet. Egypt and Turkey, who are now wavering, will then go over to the Axis powers.

Christopher Tomlin

Notification from the local council – evacuees are coming from Manchester. It wishes to know those willing to take children and threatens forcible reception if the response is not satisfactory. If they force children on us I will be roarin' – we've done more than enough for Britain with Dick and I in the forces. I refuse to have my home ruined.

Monday, 24th. Details of the humiliating armistice terms for the French[14] – they have got to hand over everything, including the navy. Everyone very downcast. In the office they all look terribly worried. Some French sailors in Liverpool today. Are we to treat them as friends? The whole thing has proved that no one can be trusted – we have been let down everywhere. One woman this morning: 'Well, at least we know where we are now. We are not helping anyone but ourselves.'

Doris Melling

Peace terms confirmed this evening. Listened to a major from the BEF on the wireless, telling how to overcome fear and take best possible cover from dive bombers. We need more of this. If the public, and particularly the women, can stand up to air raids, it will be half the battle.

Tuesday, 25th. Things started early today for at two minutes past one this morning I was awakened by the loud wailing of the air-aid sirens. I slipped out of bed, put on a pair of trousers

Frank Edwards

over my pyjamas, and then donned a mackintosh, and went downstairs. Whilst partly dressing I heard a British machine, or it may have been two, flying at a good rate over the house.

On arrival downstairs, my people and I joined the young couple who live in the flat below and went into their sitting room – we have no Anderson shelter. We lit cigarettes and the time was spent talking about different things – the war least of all. During this time there was not a sound to be heard from outside. The first hour went pretty quickly, after which we began to feel a bit sleepy, but continued talking. The second hour seemed a bit longer than the first, or so we thought as the clock struck three.

We did not have anything to drink, but the people downstairs went and got some biscuits and cheese of which we partook. About 3.15 we thought we heard gunfire but were not sure, but a few minutes later we certainly did hear a report from guns. Time went on and at 3.40 we began to wonder if the 'All Clear' had sounded and we hadn't heard it, particularly as we could hear the trains running again now.

At 3.45 we went into their front lounge and found it was quite light in the street and a man living opposite was standing at his front door and appeared to be fully dressed. We had only been looking out of the window about two or three minutes when the 'All Clear' sounded. The fellow opposite vanished indoors, as if by magic, closed the windows of his lounge, and I expect, like us, made straight off to bed. It was just 3.50 when I went upstairs.

When I called in for my *Telegraph* at 7.50 this morning I found that my newsagent had not received any papers – printing evidently held up during the alarm. Was surprised to find quite 50 per cent of people I questioned went out of doors (apart from going to shelters) at some time or other during the period of the alarm.

Muriel Green   *Thursday, 27th.* We ran out of petrol today and had not yet heard the truth about petrol scheme. We had our cheque with order for a load returned but they didn't say why. All customers know why and are furious about going to somewhere else.

About a month ago our neighbours stuck paper in strips on all their windows to stop glass flying. After a fortnight another house was done, and in a few days about six houses had followed suit. It then spread rapidly and on Sunday we counted 135 houses in the village (all working-class) and 36 of them had pasted paper on the windows. Patterns are mainly lattice diamonds and squares. A few like sunrays and some Union Jack pattern. Mostly have used white paper but a few brown. Most of the houses have done every window even over the front doors but a few have just done the bedrooms. Some houses have the windows done all one pattern, and others have mixed them and those done quite glare and show up where they are not done even. Some look very funny and are so stripy it must be difficult to see out at all.

This evening we thought we would do some of the shop windows and decided to strike an original note and do pictures instead of patterns. We did one side office window with fir trees, rabbits and birds, and the other side we started being topical and putting aeroplanes, and then I thought of putting straight pieces for searchlight beams. During supper I suggested putting a parachutist in the space below the plane which we did and Jenny cut out a man with a gun and tin hat shooting at him in one corner. Then I filled in the space with bombs falling. It really looks quite good. All the kids are very pleased by it and nearly everyone that goes by remarks and laughs.

JULY 1940

Tuesday, 9th. This morning's newspapers gave a prominent place to the announcement about tea rationing which comes into force today. Most of us of course heard Lord Woolton's

Frank Edwards

statement about this on the wireless last night. But it was interesting to notice this morning that in three independent newspapers I saw, each gave a different figure for the number of cups of tea which could be made from the ration of 2 oz. Taking the best grade of tea one paper gave 25 cups, another 24, and a third 20 cups. Most of the people I spoke to on the subject used ½ lb. per week and did not know how they were going to make do on the 2 oz. ration, but all said they supposed they would get used to it. One or two people described the ration as 'a bit of a blow' but nobody grumbled about it.

Today's Funny Story. A quick-fire comedian at a south London music hall, speaking of Hitler and invasion, says, 'Well, you know what to expect, Herr today and gone tomorrow.'

Muriel Green   *Thursday, 11th*. We heard today they are only having Cambridge University Summer School for one week instead of two separate ones, and as Jenny had arranged to go one week and me the second (Aug. 3–10) we are in a bit of a muddle about it. We are both very keen to go and we don't see why we cannot go together as there is no trade now, but Mother is annoyed about stopping here alone. We have had a terrible row about it, but anyway we wrote saying we will go the same week. Mother will either have to have someone to sleep here or go out for week.

Jenny Green   *Wednesday, 24th*. Had a dreadful shock this morning, an essay must be written before I can go to the Summer School. Decided to start at once to get it over, so at 2 p.m. began 'Hitler aims at conquest, Stalin at security. Do you agree?' Muriel simultaneously began 'Why the League of Nations failed' which I considered the easiest, but her being the youngest, I had to give way and between us we got very muddled. Got out all the books we could find. As I had never tried to write an essay for ten yrs, I could not even remember how, without Hitler and Stalin to confuse me.

AUGUST 1940

Friday, 9th. Well, today started off in good style for on arrival at   Frank Edwards
the office we all found on our tables a sheet of paper folded into
three, bearing on the outside the words, *Important to every worker.*
On the inside was an announcement that our company was going
to present a Spitfire to the Air Ministry and that £5,000 was
needed. Subscriptions were to be made during the four pay days
of this month – the fund closing on the last pay day. Everyone
seemed to be very enthusiastic about the idea and in the course
of the day, in every office and throughout the factory, a poster
showing a Spitfire with suitable wording was displayed.

Then, again we had another surprise, for ENSA displayed a
notice that another concert was to be given in the canteen from
12.45 to 1.45, during the course of which Basil Dean [theatre
and film producer, and director of ENSA], another gentleman
and J. B. Priestley would pay us a visit. Now, Mr Priestley, in
addition to being a favourite of mine, also seems to be everybody else's favourite, and we all hoped and rather thought he
would speak, but no, we were wrong. He just strolled about
amongst the workers and listened to the concert, and at the
end it was given out that we were to listen to his Postscript on
Sunday night when we should hear about ourselves. So until
Sunday we must wait.

Friday, 16th. Diary commences from the time when the sirens   George
sounded at 7.20 p.m. Mr and Mrs Robinson were out together   Springett,
– without their gas masks. I was about to go out. Miss Rob-   30-year-old
inson was at home washing up the teacups. The siren wailed.   writer and
She left the scullery and came in to me in the kitchen. Miss   gardener,
Robinson said, 'Oo, Mum and Dad are out and they haven't   Bromley and
got their masks.' I tried to comfort her by saying that there was   Sidcup, Kent
very little chance of gas.

'I wish they were home,' she said.

'They won't be long.'

I shut the scullery window and fetched my mask. She wanted to look out of the parlour window to see the AFS men at their stations opposite; but I wouldn't let her. I thought the kitchen was safer. She seemed worried about her father and mother. I put my arm around her. At that moment the front door bell rang violently. Mrs Robinson was on the step.

'Let me in! Let me in! Quick!' She banged on the glass panel. I walked (unhurriedly) to the door and opened it. She – pop-eyed with fright – rushed in, grabbed up her mask and Mr R's mask. Taking no notice of the daughter, she prepared to rush out again. I was amazed.

'Where are you going? Where's Mr Robinson?' I said.

'Oh, 'im. 'e's miles behind. I'm going down the shelter under ——s (a nearby store).' (Mrs Robinson has made no ARP whatever on the grounds that 'Hitler wouldn't dare to come and I'm not messing up my house and windows and things for a chance bomb, which won't come, anyway.') She rushed off with two gas masks.

'Do you think I ought to go too?' said the girl.

'Think for yourself,' I said. 'You're old enough.'

'I think I'll stop with you. Fancy her going off like that!' Her voice was faltering.

I put my arm round her again and we went into the kitchen. She was silent and on the verge of tears. 'Fancy Mum going off like that. All self! Don't worry, I shan't get hysterical. I say my prayers every night.'

I felt her pulse. It was rather rapid. So was my own. Then I turned on the radio, but the music was very 'highbrow', so I switched off. I sat on the edge of the table and presently she took hold of my hands and I cuddled her up against myself. (This display of affection or the desire for protection seemed suddenly to come to the surface. I had not noticed it to any extent before this air raid. She was not with me during any past warnings.) We remained silent for at least ten minutes. Listening. Then she said, 'My tummy aches.'

'That's excitement.'

'And yours?'

'No, but it feels taut,' I replied.

A few minutes' silence while we cuddled against one another. Then the siren wailed 'All Clear'. She patted my face and pulling away rushed out into the garden. I followed. Within two minutes Mrs Robinson returned from the shelter.

'What are you two doing out in the garden?'

No answer.

'Haven't you finished washing out those stockings *yet* – or the tea things? Leave it all for me, I suppose. Me, with all the shopping to do!' She departed, angry. I was left alone with Miss R, who hinted that she wanted more 'comforting', but I said that sometimes people behaved differently during an air raid to what they did in normal times. I felt an ass.

Saturday, 17th. Warm. Sunny. In the afternoon when in a local park, I saw a blind man with his Alsatian guide-dog. Another man, standing near by, told some children that Alsatian dogs were German dogs. Whereupon the children ran across to the blind man and asked him if it was a German dog. He replied, 'Yes, I suppose she is – strictly speaking.'

'Then I shall shoot it,' said one little girl of five years.

'If anyone shot my dog,' said the blind man, 'I should shoot them!'

An old lady (working-class), overhearing the conversation, remarked, 'Fancy 'im sayin' that loverly dog's a German!'

Thursday, 22nd. About 8 p.m. I went along to the Thompsons. We spent half an hour telling jokes and schoolboy howlers. Then Miss Thompson (16, schoolgirl and young Communist) said, 'Trotsky's gone. Why they wanted to bump him off I don't know!'

'Rather pointless,' I remarked.

'Absolutely, much better have bumped off someone who was

more modern – I mean modern in the way of this war. Of course
it's no good killing Hitler – that won't stop the war now.'

Beyond that remark I've heard no more war talk today.
Everyone has lost interest in the whole business, it seems. I feel
that way too: have done for weeks, months. I am a Conscientious Objector: I expect I shall have to suffer for this pretty
soon, because I refuse to compromise to the state even to the
extent of registering. I should have registered with the 29s but
didn't. I shall stand by my convictions and am prepared to go
to prison for I will do nothing to assist any government either
directly or indirectly in any way. I heard recently that there
are over 100,000 men who have not registered in the National
Registration and therefore have no ration cards. They are determined to avoid war service at all events.

Doris Melling   *Wednesday, 28th.* We are becoming so war-minded. For
example, when one hears of a person out in a car, one auto-
matically thinks, 'Wonder where he got the petrol from?'
Then the line in a popular song of the moment, something
about, 'When I dream of home', there is a line about a lighted
window, and every time I hear it I think to myself 'bad blacking-out'! We won't know where we are when this business
is over and done with, and we can have all our lights on. I
should imagine this will be the only difference it will make,
because we shall all be so poor that we won't be able to afford
petrol and other luxuries, which in pre-war days were almost
considered necessities.

10.30 p.m. Just going to bed when the blue-pencil sirens
went off. Went into the shelter, but nothing happened and we
came out again. About 12 o'clock the All Clear went. About
1.30 I heard planes coming over. Didn't feel inclined to get up
though. Then the guns started to go off. No warning at all. It
seems as if when we get the warning, nothing happens.

Friday, 30th. Well, well, well. We had the Biggest and Best air

raid ever last night. It was amazing. I have never heard such a
row going on in my life.

10.20. Warning. Immediately could hear planes and firing,
guns and bombs. Simply terrific. Felt very calm and not the
least frightened. Every time I heard a 'crump' I wondered where
it had landed. As each plane came over and dropped its bombs,
another one appeared. There must have been a good many.
Some of the very heavy guns went into action. The wash-house
shook like the devil. I thought the Gladstone Dock was getting
a pasting. Heard a screaming bomb, but didn't hear it explode.
This went on till 2.30 without a break. Just as we thought
everything was all clear, they would start up again. Smoked
innumerable cigarettes, and felt hungry. Pa kept wanting to
have a look out and see if there were any fires. I wouldn't let
him. Kept getting annoyed by a few flies which persisted in
whizzing round our heads all the time in the shelter. Tried to
make out the different noises – which were bombs and which
were guns, and where our planes were – if any. I don't think
any went up at all. Got to feel cold. Kept wondering when
and where it would all end. Every time I heard a fresh plane I
wondered where it would drop its load.

About 2.30 a lull set in. One of our planes went over. We
returned to the house, and had something to eat, feeling, to
say the least, very shaken up, but smiling. We decided we
would risk going to bed. I felt very tired. About 3 o'clock the
All Clear went. I think they must have waited till they were
really satisfied that everything was OK. Could hear people
getting home from the pictures. It really is no joke. I shan't
go out to the second-house pictures any more. Fell sound
asleep.

On the way down to the office this morning everyone was
looking out for damage. I never expected anywhere to be standing up, but couldn't see anything much knocked down. There
was nothing to do but stare out of the window, because there
were no morning newspapers. Felt rather excited, personally. I

think that was a proper raid. I detest sitting in a shelter with nothing happening.

George
Springett

Saturday, 31st. 12.45. Have been reading for 20 minutes. Distant bombs and occasional gunfire. Vibration. Planes seem to be operating singly. Another is overhead.

1 p.m. Nazi planes over. Just about to begin lunch. Distant bombing. Mrs Robinson leaves for public shelter. Out of curiosity and thinking I might pick up a bit for MO I go too: my first visit to a public shelter. This place is under a local furniture depository. Holds 60 to 70 people. Forty-four here at present. About 12 have come out of houses – rest from street. Mostly women and children – about 75 per cent working-class. One woman out of house has brought a basin of beans to skin and cut up. Another knitting. A pedestrian (upper-class woman, middle-aged) is doing a crossword. After a bit, she chats with a middle-aged man (independent class by the look of him). They chat about castles. My landlady and a few of her local cronies chat about food. Food seems a great topic at the moment. Presently my landlady starts telling people I am on MO. Some of the women are interested. I explain a bit between intervals of writing this. None of them have ever heard of MO (all working-class).

SEPTEMBER 1940

Doris Melling

Wednesday, 4th. Everyone getting very mad about these raids. Apparently we are just here to be hit at. It said in one of the papers that it was a fine sight to see the Spitfires taking off after the Germans. I dare say it is. I would like to see it around here. I feel strongly that there is too much fuss being made about London. Liverpool is a very important place, and I don't think it is being defended as well as it might be, and the civilian is taking the brunt of it all. How long we can go on like this I don't know. So far as military damage is concerned, little has been done, but it's the little man in the suburbs who is getting it.

Went to bed at 9.15 but it was no use. Ten o'clock heard the sirens going. No sooner had they sounded than things began to drop. Pa stood at the door, and I shrieked at him to come in. He said he was waiting for me. I crouched down where I was. The raid lasted from 10 o'clock to 4.30. At 3 o'clock I went in to bed, I couldn't stand up any longer. Then another plane came over, and Pa got up and told me to do likewise, but I was too tired, and couldn't raise myself. I didn't hear the All Clear siren at all.

Thursday, 5th. We had a fine display in the sky last night between 9 p.m. and midnight. The Germans dropped flares all over the place, looking for their targets, I presume.

In several places over London a hundred searchlights or more formed cones of light, in the apex of which there was a German plane and then the guns began to send shells; some shells went a little wide, but many seemed to burst right in the apex of light, which shifted about like a moving pyramid, from the north across to the north-east and east of London. As the pyramids (there were two or three of them in different localities) shifted, some lights went out and other searchlights took their places, concentrating on one spot, following the dodging planes in the sky.

They were too far away from Sydenham for me to actually see the planes, though once or twice I thought that I caught a glimpse of the planes as they dived and circled trying to escape from the lights and the bursting shells, which must have given the pilots and crews a hell of a time. I have not heard where bombs were dropped and it was impossible to say whether the flashes were from big guns or bombs. Some parts of London must have been well peppered with bits of falling shells, but I heard nothing here, but wore a steel helmet in case a bit should choose the spot on which I stood near the house.

Herbert Brush, 71-year-old retired electricity board inspector, Forest Hill, London

Frank Edwards   *Wednesday, 25th.* What a night, what a life! At 8.10 the sirens
sounded heralding the nightly blitz. Guns started banging
away and we went down our cellar. After about half an hour
a bomb dropped uncomfortably close and the whole house
seemed to shake. Fifteen minutes later there was the most terrific explosion I have yet heard, and the whole house felt as
though it lifted right up. Dust blew all over the place and a
little later we could smell burning. We went upstairs and had
a careful look round everywhere in case there might be any
incendiaries but such was not the case. However, we found that
the blast had blown several panes of glass out of the front of the
house and one or two out of the back.

AA guns were banging away, one moment sounding as
though they were outside the front door, and a few seconds later
a bit further away. Then very close again, and so on. And so it
went on all through the night until six o'clock this morning
when the sirens sounded the welcome 'All Clear'.

Thursday, 26th. At six o'clock this morning it was sufficiently
light to see that most of the other houses in our end of the road
had also lost their windows, but the houses on the opposite side
were OK. It later transpired that these houses had lost their
back windows whilst we had lost the front ones.

We had to walk down the road, but despite the terrific
explosion we could not see any property missing, but we knew
something must have gone not far away. When I set off, two
hours later, to catch the bus for the office, I turned into the
main road which runs at the end of our road, and what a sight
met my eyes. Most of the houses had lost all the glass out of
their windows and all the shops were in a like condition. Piles
of glass lay in the front gardens of the houses, but in the case
of the shops, mostly it had been swept into piles in the gutter
by the ARP services.

Outside a confectioners' and tobacconists' lock-up shop on
the pavement were showcards, boxes of cigarettes, packets of

sweets, packets of chocolate, etc. Next to that everything from a chemist's window had been blown out, including the shelves. An off-licence was in a similar state, and so on. The district looked properly devastated. Little groups of people stood about talking of the damage, etc.

When I returned home in the evening this looked like a town of wooden windows and doors although wood wasn't the only material used for repairs, for from what I could see of it every possible substance available had been pressed into service. This damage had all been caused by the blast from a land-mine which had been dropped on houses in a road a good half-mile from this house, and it was around there that much structural damage was caused.

Friday, 27th. Warm. Sunny.

George Springett

9.20. This afternoon dozens of enemy planes came over the town. The local sirens did not sound at all. It's fast becoming a scandal. Planes overhead in the barrage and the streets crowded. People scuttled for shelter. I watched the fights from a doorway. A piece of shrapnel fell within a couple of feet of me. Young George Thompson, who was with me at the time, kept it. We were fascinated at the sight of the planes and the puffs of smoke from the shells. We were torn between the desire to watch and the desire to take cover below ground.

As I read these lines, the nightly siren has just sounded – 12 minutes *after* the gunfire began. It has been suggested that the police are so interested in watching the fights that they forget to sound the sirens!

Friday, 27th. P on the phone tonight. Says he will not be required to join up after all. Doesn't affect him. I am very glad. Says that he is living in his digs although nearly all the windows are blown out. All doors blown off, no electricity or water at first. Says they are about the only people living in the road. Mrs and Mr C go to the public shelter. They, too, were

Doris Melling

away at the time – the first time they have slept away from home since the war. That is Providence, if you like. Spoke to J on the phone, when the warning went at 7.30 p.m. Raids till twelve o'clock. Not too bad though. Could see a big fire.

OCTOBER 1940

Herbert Brush   *Saturday, 5th.* I have filled in a form offering my services as an air-raid warden between 8 a.m. and midnight. I never could stand the small hours in the morning out of bed; especially the hour before sunrise; that always got me down when I was on shift in the works, and would probably be worse now. I feel I must do something even if I only patrol a street in readiness to do what is necessary when the time comes.

Monday, 7th. I went by bus as far as Westminster to have a look at the damage done by a bomb to the Houses of Parliament. When I arrived at Westminster I walked round to the place where stands the statue of King Richard I. The bomb had dropped in the road not far from the tail of his horse, but I noticed only one hole in the horse and that Richard's sword was bent with the blast. It must have been a louder noise than Richard ever heard in his life. It has destroyed a part of the large window behind Richard and smashed every piece of glass on that side of the building.

But it made me angry to see the damage done to Westminster Abbey: all the glass gone from the east end of Henry VIIth Chapel and there may be damage inside but that I could not see. Lumps are chipped out of the stonework of the chapel in dozens of places, and the marks will always remain to show the skill of the German airmen.

I walked along Whitehall and Charing Cross Road and turned up Great Russell St. At the end of Great Russell Street in Tottenham Court Rd there is an awful mess; one of the worst

I have seen. I walked along Tottenham Court Rd, picking my way between the heaps of rubble and rubbish of all kinds and looked for the shop where I had my hair cut by a lady hairdresser about ten days ago. That shop now forms part of a huge heap of building material, shop furniture and all kinds of things smashed to pulp. I can only hope that the lady hairdresser was not there at the time when the bomb, or bombs, fell.

An artist was sitting in the midst of the ruin painting a picture. He and I were the only ones in the street as far as I could see: a raid was on and all the shops were closed.

That is a good time for anyone afflicted with bookitis to walk along Charing Cross Road, because as soon as the siren sounds a man rushes out and puts up the shutters and clears the books away. The shops must employ full-time workers on that job now; no sooner are the shutters up than they have to be taken down, and as soon as they are down they have to be put up again. There was a raid on while I was in Charing Cross Road so I did not buy a book, nor even stop to look at one.

Wednesday, 9th. I went with W to her doctor's as evidently her nerves have gone wrong with the strain of driving a car under war conditions. On her way to Cambridge she came under machine-gun fire from the air and had to hide in a hedge near an aerodrome while an attack was in progress. Then at Norwich there were several bombs dropped in the vicinity during the night. The doctor says she has shell-shock and has made her up a strong tonic and recommended complete rest for a fortnight or so.

Wednesday, 9th. I went to a local chemist to get myself a bottle of medicine (a rare thing for me these days). Think a few doses of 'Liver and Stomach mixture' might help to cure my infernal backache – might be due to constipation. Anyway, I said to the manager, 'How's trade these days?'

'Oh, fair, but people aren't taking anywhere near the amount

George
Springett

of medicine they did before the war – especially nerve tonics and the like. Now there are customers of mine who in peacetime had a bottle of tonic every few weeks. Now you'd think in these strained times they would want three times the amount of nerve mixtures. Never believe it, they don't. These nervous people positively revel in raids. It seems to me the jittery ones now are those who were calm in peacetime. It's odd.' I took a lot of tonics and Sanatogen for six weeks before war was declared and the first six weeks after. Since last April, I've had no tonics of any kind. Odd as it may seem, until the spell of backache, I've had really first-class health since the blitz started!

Herbert Brush *Sunday, 13th.* The early part of last night was noisy, but later it became quiet, and when I looked out about 10 p.m. no one could have guessed that there was a war on. The moon made it nearly as light as day and the air was absolutely still, and the least sound could be heard half a mile away, and yet within ten minutes there was the sound of a plane overhead and the screaming of a whole stick of bombs coming down somewhere in the vicinity. After that I went to sleep and did not wake up until 5.30 a.m., when I left the dugout and went to bed, in my clothes. I have not worn any pyjamas now for more than a month and I only undress completely to have a bath. There are many more like me.

I was told by a lady that she had been to a cemetery near by to visit a grave, but a large bomb had fallen on some of the graves with the inevitable result that several dead bodies were scattered about. Men were putting down lime and she was not allowed to go near the place, but the stench was terrible.

George Springett *Friday, 18th.* Fog at first, then dull. At 2.30 a.m., approx., I was awakened by a terrific explosion. The house rocked, but none of the windows were smashed. Had a sensation like a mild electric shock in my hands and head. It seemed that the explosion was very near. I went into the front room where Violet was sleeping.

'You all right?'

'Yes, the floor shook.' She seizes hold of my hand. I pull away and go out to the back garden, but can see no damage. Felt rather shaky. Ate some biscuits and drank some water.

Later in the morning I went out to view the damage (which proved to be over half a mile away). One big house was completely demolished. What seemed so amusing was the contrast of grim-faced men digging for bodies when, over their heads in the branches of a tall tree, hung four women's coats, a shirt and some curtains. The sight of the dangling clothing seemed funny. Wasn't, of course – just tragic.

Saturday, 26th. The worst night yet. After a day of continual **Herbert Brush** alarms I had just gone to sleep when about 10.30 p.m. the dugout rocked all ways at once and I thought that our last hours had come this time. I came out of the dugout expecting I don't know what, but the house still stood. There was a bright light in the road and I soon found out that it was an incendiary burning near the fence next door, so I took a bucket of water which was standing ready and my home-made stirrup pump and hurried to the fire, which was caused by one of those beastly oil-bombs. I and a warden soon put out the blaze with the spray and then there was time to look round.

A fire at the bottom end of Kirkdale had started and was gradually getting brighter until the flames lit up the whole district and we expected that Jerry would soon be back with a fresh supply of bombs. The shaking of the dugout was accounted for by a bomb which had fallen in Thorpewood Avenue about 200 yards away. This bomb had made a huge hole in the road and cut one house clean in two, and seriously damaged several others. We were lucky to escape with no damage as far as I can see. The shaking stopped all the clocks in the house, one an electric clock which has run off a battery for months without attention. Sticky oil is all over the road this morning and if it gets on one's shoes it takes a long time to get off. If that bomb had fallen on the house nothing could have saved the place, with all that oil on the rafters and furniture. Luckily for us it fell in the road about forty yards away from the house in a straight line, and sprayed the oil all over the fences and footway and across the road. The PO pillar-box where we generally post our letters is now black instead of red; it was within ten yards of the oil-bomb. I noticed when the postman was clearing the letters that none of the stuff had gone through the slot. It took me a long time to clean the oil off the rubber hose and pump and off the soles of my shoes, but I have still got the smell of the stuff in my nose.

3 p.m. W and I went round to look at the allotment, but it was a case of looking *for* the allotment. Four perches out of the five are one enormous hole and all my potatoes and cabbages have vanished. Apparently the bomb fell on the footpath between two allotments and when it exploded had preference for mine, although I must say that there is not much left of Hardy's, and the plot on the other side of mine has a huge pile of my earth on it. The result is that all my work there has been wasted, absolutely wasted, and the potatoes at Christmas certainly will not come off my allotment, though if I have sufficient energy for some deep excavations I may find a potato or two somewhere in the mountain on each side of the ten-foot hole. When I went there the other day I noticed that there were several nice cabbages nearly ready to eat, and I meant to dig potatoes this weekend. Now I should have some difficulty in finding the place where they stood.

Doris Melling   *Sunday, 27th.* Got into bed, and saw a bright light shining through the window. Thought to myself that the stars were very bright tonight. Sat up in bed, and could see three very bright, still, lights in the sky. Just for the moment I thought it was the end of the world. Then they started to drop, slowly, with smoke pouring down. Then they would stop, and then fall again. I had heard machine-gunning going on before, and concluded that some Jerry had shot a balloon down, and what I could see was the cable ablaze. The lights weren't flares, because I have seen them before. Got back into bed feeling very excited. I wouldn't have missed that for anything. Guns still popping, sometimes very close, but I slept the sleep of the just.

Thursday, 31st. As usual we spent 12 hours in the dugout last night. We have got used to the hard lying now and go to sleep as easily there as in bed, though I must own to a stiffness in the morning, when I am glad to double up on my bed for an hour or so. I can't double up much on two 11-inch boards; that, with the cushions, makes my bed less than two feet in width. I can't lie with my face to the wall, because if I double up at all my posterior overhangs the bed and that is not a comfortable position; the other way round my knees sometimes overhang, but that is not such an uncomfortable position.

Herbert Brush

As usual we are in the Andy [Anderson shelter] for the night, and as I have fixed up an electric light for each, it is easy to read while in residence. I keep half a dozen books on various subjects on a small shelf I have put up, and I read until I get sleepy enough to rest on the hard bunk. Tonight I have been reading *The Streets of London* by J. H. Smith, published in 1861, and very interesting for that reason, as it describes the streets as they were then (1861) as well as giving a little history of each street. I imagine that an exact description of some of them today would be interesting for future readers who see them in maybe 100 years and are able to realise what the bombs have done to them during the last two months.

NOVEMBER 1940

Monday, 4th. Yes, we awoke this morning to find that no alert had sounded all night and this is the first bombless night for fifty-seven nights, which, I think, is an occasion to be chalked up.

Frank Edwards

Travelling to the office on the bus I was turning over in my mind some of the events for this coming week, amongst them being tomorrow's presidential election[15] in the States. Just at that moment my eye caught a rather unusual headline in a newspaper being read by a young man sitting two seats in front of me: this read, 'Only God and Hitler know what will happen in the USA.' Whether this had reference to tomorrow's election, or to the part played by America in the war, I didn't know.

On the second half of my journey home tonight my bus had a 'clippie' – woman conductor. I boarded this bus – a No. 9 – at Hyde Park Corner. Shortly afterwards this young woman conductor, neatly attired in grey and with a peaked cap, came upstairs saying in approved style, 'Fares, please.' She was supervised by a male conductor as this is of course the first day on which 'clippies' have made their appearance on the Central buses. She didn't seem to be experiencing much difficulty in learning the job and the fellow conductor told her, when in doubt, at which stage to punch long-distance tickets.

Herbert Brush *Tuesday, 5th.* Guy Fawkes' day. The fireworks we have nowadays are a little more noisy than those we let off in the vicarage garden about sixty years ago. It was not possible then for the most vivid imagination to picture England as it is today, and I wonder what it will be like in the year 2000 AD. More comfortable to live in then than it is now, I hope. Probably, by then, everyone will have nice comfortable underground dwellings to live in and surface houses to visit on fine days in the summer to get a little sunburn on their sallow skins.

I hope that Roosevelt will win the election in America, because we know that he is on our side: the other man has only said that he is, and Hitler might prove to be too clever for him, a beginner in the game of playing with other people's lives.

Frank Edwards *Wednesday, 6th.* When I got home tonight I found a letter awaiting me which contained news which put me right off my stroke. It contained the news that the house (digs) at which I lived in Birmingham – and from which I had sent many reports to MO – had been demolished through enemy action and the people who lived there: husband, wife and their daughter were all killed. They were, of course, personal friends of mine, and the whole affair is a shocking tragedy.

Whilst reading this letter the sirens went – time 6.15 p.m. More planes than ever seemed to come in and AA fire was terrific and we took cover in the cellar soon after the guns had opened fire. We had not been down there long when we heard a bomb come hurtling down and it sounded so close that we thought it must be coming on us. It struck the ground and the house shook violently and there was the noise of falling glass and what sounded like bricks. We quickly turned off the electric light and gas at the meters and then went upstairs to investigate.

The damage caused was the result of blast, and resulted in glass blown out of some windows; the french windows which were locked and bolted had been wrenched open and some of the glass had gone; a lot of whitening had come down from the ceilings, especially in the lounge, and more cracks in the ceilings – they already had quite a number. We learned many of our neighbours had similar damage. The bomb itself fell on the bank of the river which runs past the end of the road. The actual spot where it fell is about two minutes' walk from this house. There were no casualties.

Thursday, 14th. I arrived in Leeds at 8 p.m. The station was dark and almost empty. A few soldiers were walking up and down. No one knew where No. 11 RAMC depot was, but one referred me to the military police, and through them found where I had to go, and what tram to catch. It took fifteen minutes – a 2d ride – to get there, and I followed a group of soldiers in the barracks. We talked of the buildings, about six large blocks with lawn quadrangles between them. One man said, 'It's a good place, mate,

Henry Novy,
21-year-old
clerk, Royal
Army Medical
Corps, Leeds

but they're bloody strict – you'll find out.' A new recruit joined
us, and both of us enquired about the life very eagerly. We arrived
at the main block, the cookhouse, called Macaulay. The corporals took our names and particulars, gave us an army number, a
marking out number, the number of our squads and rooms.

They gave me my kit, a palliasse, a mug, fork, knife and
spoon. Then I asked about some food, and they led me in the
kitchen, three huge rooms, very hot. I was given plenty of cocoa
and a meat pie. I chatted with the cooks on duty and the sergeants who were taking me round. My first impression was
one of great relief. I thought the place beyond all expectations,
good buildings, central-heated, good NCOs. I had a game of
table tennis on a small table in the dining hall, and then I went
to bed at about half-past nine.

In my room the three other fellows were working-class. I
didn't know their names. We introduced ourselves as we were
lying on the palliasses, but I forgot. One queer-looking little
man, dropping all his h's and most pronouns, came from the
coal pit. In the far corner I saw the man with a torch, a tall
hefty man with a pointed nose and very shining popping-out
eyes. He was employed at Boots. The other hardly spoke. After
a few minutes on the palliasse I heard complaints from all sides.
My own was terribly hard, and I had no pillow; my teeth were
aching and soon I had a headache. I felt depressed and tired
out. I tried to sleep, but I kept thinking of home, and all I had
left went round and round in my head, ceaselessly, persistently,
and I tried and tried to sleep but couldn't. At times I felt so
depressed that I wanted to cry, but I couldn't. The first night
was hell, and all I had seen that day, the people I had met, the
people I had left, and it all went round and round all night.

Muriel Green   *Friday, 15th.* Planes began going over ours about nine last
evening, and they were going all night. Distant gunfire and
the noise of the planes all sounding Nazis kept me awake practically all night. Hundreds of planes must have gone through

and afterwards as I write I think they were on their way to Coventry. In the country here as they go over I lie in bed and feel snug. I keep thinking it would be more sensible to be downstairs in case on their way to more important targets the raiders should drop bombs or be shot down. But the bed is more enjoyable than the chance in a million of my life being saved in case – I also feel that the chances are fair in favour of being ill through being without sleep and in the cold than being hit by bombs. I wonder, as I lie and hear the hum and the wallops in the distance, where they are going for; somewhere is going to get a trouncing. I also wonder what the pilots feel. After all somebody loves them even if they are Nazis, and they are risking their life and fighting for their country the same as our men that go bombing. Poor Coventry people. How bitter and hopeless they must feel today. How long can it go on? How many years must all live in fear of the unknown horrors that so many of us have not yet experienced?

Friday, 15th. I was having lunch today, with a friend, when Frank Edwards during the one o'clock news a communiqué was read regarding last night's air raid over Coventry. When the casualties were mentioned as being in the neighbourhood of 1,000, I found myself saying, 'Oh!' I must confess that I felt somewhat worried at this news, and profoundly sorry for the people of this city. I was born in Coventry and lived there 13 years. Also my first job was in Coventry, at which job I worked for eight years. In addition I have relatives and friends living there and so of course the place is really my hometown. From what I have read in this evening's papers the city received a most vicious and unwarranted onslaught.

Saturday, 16th. All morning we struggled with our kit. I sorted Henry Novy everything out, we cleaned our buttons, and spent all morning getting ready. After lunch we went to march out. I passed, but my three roommates were sent back. They cursed and cursed, but cleaned them. Twice they were sent back. Eventually we walked out, but only to be stopped at the gate and sent back because we wore no gaiters. We had to go back for a sergeant, one came over and at last we got out of grounds. We had to go to buy brushes, button sticks, dubbin, all sorts of things we were supposed to have in our kit but didn't get. We also bought a bulb for our room. Leeds was crowded out. The greatcoat and boots were dreadfully heavy and stiff. Only half an hour after coming out my feet began to burn and blisters started to come up.

Eventually I lost my mates and dropped in a chair at Lewis's. I had an ice-cream and a cigarette. I was pleased to be alone. My feet were so tired. I felt wretched. All these things rushed in the first few days of this new life can make you feel really sore – physically and mentally. In common with most of the recruits it's what I left behind. It has really made me miserable. There is so little that can be done about it, it's so hopeless. I can't help admiring how they get things done, how in little over two days 400 men act like one, accept a new and completely uncongenial routine, get used to what you've never done. I hate it all, especially because I feel there's nothing that can be done. A man said to me today, 'How do you feel about army life?' 'I don't like it much,' I answered. 'I hate it,' he said. 'HATE it. I hate the principle, the whole bloody thing. But you'd be surprised, some fellows revel in it – some across your room, they love it, getting away from home, escaping their dreary life. But I loathe it.'

Wednesday, 27th. Again today I heard little war talk or none. All there is, is limited to, 'What's the news today?' (when the paper man comes); 'Oh, the Greeks *are* doing well,[16] Christ, they're tough.' And then, 'Oh, Coventry (or Liverpool, or wherever they live and know people) got it again.' There are always a few people worried about their homes, although letters are coming now in great numbers. When a man hasn't heard for two days he begins to worry, after three he is worried to death, after that he wants to go. Today was really the day with grumbling at its height.

DECEMBER 1940

Wednesday, 4th. Last night when we were just in bed anyone   Muriel Green
listening would have heard this conversation between Jenny's
and my bedrooms.

Jenny: 'I did the most awful thing today, I can't think what
you will say when I tell you.' Me: 'What?' Jenny: 'It was the
most appalling mistake, I hardly dare tell you, you'll be so
terribly upset.' Me: 'What ever did you do?' Jenny: 'The most
awful terrible thing, simply atrocious, I can't think why I did
it, my dear.' 'Go on, tell me the worst quick.' 'It's been on
my mind all day since I did it, and I simply daren't tell you
before, it is so awful.' By this time I was getting desperate
about what she had done, and was expecting to hear she had
broken something very precious or something more tragic still
and she said at last after a lot more suspense, 'It's really terrible
but what do you think I did? When I made that cake I made
a mistake and made it with the butter ration instead of the
margarine!' All I could say was 'You fool!' It took me some time
to hear how much of it she had used and she said three whole
ounces. Being Tuesday it is particularly annoying as she only
left about enough for today. I certainly expected to hear she had
done something far more irreparable than that, though. I was
getting quite frightened about it until she told me.

Thursday, 5th. Before I start today I must mention two sides   Henry Novy
of the life here – dirty jobs and dirty talk. Filth and swearing.
It's funny how men react to it when they get together. Smutty
stories go round quite a lot, often pure dirt and without much
point – a whole lot of fellows shrink from them, and despise
the tellers. Swearing is terrific. Everyone swears, from the CSM
to the scruffiest private, or most babyish face. Dozens have told
me they never swore in civil life, but that it just caught on here.
In many rooms swearing has been forbidden by the roommates,
many make a real effort to get out of it, or check the coming

habit – in spite of this I still hear everyone swear, including myself, without knowing I do it.

Herbert Brush *Thursday, 12th.* I see by the papers this morning that the main blitz was in the Midlands, but I should not have guessed that after the time we had last night. No sooner had one plane been driven off than another could be heard approaching, and they kept this up most of the night. A lot of heavy stuff was dropped somewhere but most of it was several miles away in the direction of London.

I did not get properly to sleep until the early hours of this morning, being continually shaken up by the bangs from the big guns and earth tremors which I took to be bombs. I am glad to notice that we are giving the Italians gip in Egypt now,[17] and I am wondering whether L, my son-in-law, is in the thick of the fighting there. If so, I imagine that M is much worried as the mechanised forces have to be in the van of every fight.

It was very cold last night, but with hot-water bottles in the dugout we do not notice it much down there. The place is warmed up with a paraffin stove for an hour or so before we go in, and with the curtain drawn across the entrance to the leading-in passage it keeps warm enough all night. Curiously enough there is good ventilation, as the cold air seems to spill over the edge of the entrance and fall to the bottom of the dugout, forcing the warm air out of the top. This makes a draught near the entrance so I have fitted shields to keep the draught off the bunks on each side of the dugout. It is quite a comfortable place now, when one gets used to the cramped space and the inability to turn over without falling off the bunk, for folk of my size.

Henry Novy *Friday, 13th.* We were married today. By 11 it was all finished. It was a lovely day for us. We got up late, and hurried to the registrar. There we found a soldier pacing up and down the street, a lance-corporal of the Green Howards, Dunkirk, long and pale face with almost violet circles round the eyes. He was quite willing and good-natured – he worried about not being a resident, being in Leeds to see his sweetheart. Then we found a round-faced little woman, with shining round eyes and quick little legs. She knew all about it, and had witnessed three other marriages. We had to wait a while, and then were ushered in (literally) a large rectangular room. I didn't quite see the walls, but they were big and bare – there was a big oak table with a big oak chair at the end. We all sat in a row on stiff chairs. The clerk came in and asked particulars – was puzzled by my row of Christian names. I produced my pay book and certificates and this satisfied him. He filled in a few forms, slowly, in a dignified way. Then the registrar came in and sat in the big sculptured chair. We all got up, and I repeated after him, 'I ... know not of any legal impediment' etc. ... Then we all signed. We were married. We all shook hands, and they muttered wishes. The little waitress disappeared, she was late. The soldier came with us, walked down Briggate, and the pubs were closed, so he left us, and we walked arm in arm, looking at the shops. It was grand, being married at last. We had lunch in a little Hungarian restaurant, in a cosy little alcove. Then we went shopping. The fog had gone by the afternoon. We bought some food in Lewis's and went to eat an ice-cream, and then back home to have some tea. I wrote to mother and tried to tell her why I should get married and how I did get married.

Monday, 16th. I spent the best part of today in and around the big stores in Kensington. There were plenty of shoppers amongst which many men were in evidence. Things are much more expensive than this time last year, but everyone seemed to be purchasing practical gifts; things to wear and use was the order of the day. Most of the stores have a toy fair for the children, but I saw very few children in the three stores I visited which is doubtless accounted for by evacuation. There were not

Frank Edwards

so many decorations about but there was plenty of colour about and all the departments looked bright and cheerful.

There is a very big run on biscuits these days – these seem to be the favourite shelter food, and there was a crowd of quite 50 people surging around two assistants in one of the stores, all wanting to buy biscuits.

Doris Melling *Tuesday, 24th.* Xmas Eve. Left MOI at 3.30 in order to get a bus. Everyone saying: Where will it all end? Poor old Liverpool.

Afraid we won't be able to get to Frodsham [to see her mother]. What a miserable Xmas. Haven't even got a pudding. P, my darling, rang up to wish me a 'Merry Xmas'. He is very depressed about the damage to the docks. Met Geoffrey W today on leave. Says he is going to Salisbury to train as an officer. Looks very well, but doesn't like the life much.

News says we are continuing the good work against the Italians.

Nella Last *Wednesday, 25th.* Everything was perfect – chicken stuffed with slightly flavoured 'sage and onion' with added sausage meat and browned sausage cooked with the potatoes in tin. I steamed sprouts and cooked creamed celery and there was a good if 'light' Xmas pudding with rum sauce. Celery, coffee and biscuits and cheese. The table was gay with my embroidered cloth and lovely chrysanthemums I had bought and there was port and nuts to end with. All is so quiet and still tonight – I pray it is so all over the country and that people can enjoy themselves a little and sleep serenely tonight.

Herbert Brush *Tuesday, 31st.* A very quiet night. Nothing happened worth recording. 9 a.m. It is still so dark that a light is necessary to see to write this. The last day of a year which will be remembered by everyone as long as they live, unless 1941 has even more unpleasantness in store for us.

Tuesday, 31st. Here I am once again trying to put something on to   Doris Melling
paper. Really, I never get a minute these days to do anything.

Well, this is the last day of the year, and what a year. Still,
if next year is no worse, we shall manage. Personally I think it
will be a darned sight worse, with a great deal of personal sacrifice all round. One can't even get a spot of powder nowadays to
put on one's nose. Went away for the weekend, and enjoyed it,
although the conversation ran on bombs the whole time. Spent
Saturday afternoon playing a glorious game of tennis with P. It
really was marvellous. The weather is grand, and we had four
sets. I caught the 6.30 out of town and was terrified of being
caught in Liverpool in a raid, and being there all night.

I have not mentioned the terrific raids we had a bit back,
one Friday and Saturday. Simply awful. Destruction all round.
It does depress me. H came home for the holiday, and believe
me was scared stiff. He heard a bomb drop about two miles
away and threw himself on the floor. I had to laugh, and I
think he felt a little bit shame-faced at what he did. Traffic all
disorganised, but it is amazing how soon things recover. Land-
mines and time bombs all over the place. Real damage at the
docks, for the first time.

Talking about the invasion. It makes me feel ill. I think it
will be attempted, in the midst of terrible air bombardment,
gas and Hell let loose. P says what are the Home Guard for?
But are there enough? In country districts I am sure quite a big
force could land, and if they weren't stopped might do damage.
It doesn't do to think too much about it. I am sure they will
never make the attempt on the coast; they know what is in
store for them already.

Announced this evening that steps must be taken to provide
fire-watchers everywhere, after the dreadful raid on London.
I hear many of the fires started here on the docks could have
been put out if there had been sufficient men. Posters seen in
bombed shops: 'Bombs or no bombs, business as usual.' 'Open,
but please use the door.'

1941 A BLEAK PROSPECT

Throughout 1941 the news from abroad was largely depressing. In North Africa, the desert war continued. Despite some successes, the Allied forces there were hard-pressed after the arrival of the German Afrika Korps to bolster the Italian forces. In eastern Europe, Hungary, Rumania and Bulgaria were now effectively Nazi puppet states. In the Balkans, Yugoslavia and Greece fell and in May the Germans took Crete, and with it control of the eastern Mediterranean. At sea, capital ships were lost and in the battle of the Atlantic, U-boats and the Luftwaffe inflicted heavy damage on the merchant ship convoys which were vital to keeping Britain supplied with fuel, food and raw materials. Then, in June, Germany invaded Russia, diverting troops and military equipment from other fronts. Would this, people wondered, overstretch German resources? It did not seem so as the Germans swept through Ukraine. On 7 December, the war suddenly became a world war when Japanese planes attacked the US naval base at Pearl Harbor in Hawaii. America immediately declared war on Japan and Germany. Britain was no longer alone.

On the home front there was more rationing and more conscription. Women were increasingly drafted into the armed forces – the army (ATS), the navy (WRNS) or the air force (WAAFs); many more were now working in factories or, as 'land girls', in agriculture. Clothes rationing came into force in June as more factories were taken over for munitions production. 'Make do and mend' – recycle and repair clothes – was the government message; quality clothing at reasonable prices was in short supply. In December a 'points' scheme for buying food was introduced.

Meanwhile there was the daily threat of air raids as the blitz continued. In one night in May 1,400 Londoners were killed, 5,000 homes were reduced to rubble, and the chamber of the House of Commons was destroyed. Throughout Britain cities and towns endured many nights of bombardment. Plymouth was attacked five times in a week at the end of April, Liverpool endured seven successive nights of raids at the beginning of May. 'Britain can take it', said the propaganda posters; and mostly the population was stoical. Morale, however, was not quite as high as the government suggested. As some of the Mass Observation diarists in 1941 reveal, there were rumblings of discontent. People wanted to know when there would be a chance to fight back.

JANUARY 1941

Thursday, 16th. Called up. The last week before going, many people wishing me goodbye – all sorts of odd people, some I very rarely see, casual acquaintances, and so on. The usual greeting is 'I hope it won't be too bad' or 'Well, the war may be over very soon.' Only a very small number indeed said that the army was good fun or hoped I'd enjoy myself. Nearly all of them shook me by the hand, a very rare sort of greeting. At one of my best friends', a sort of farewell toast is given in coffee and cakes. Mother says, 'I don't think it's as bad for you as for me. I'll be left with nothing to do, and you'll have plenty to occupy your mind.' My personal reaction to calling up is to a great extent relief. The period of waiting is over, and I know exactly where I stand.

Len England, Royal Army Ordnance Corps, Hinckley, Leicestershire

At the station, there are vast numbers of conscripts of all ages. Nearly all of them brought friends and relations. Much more emotion than usual is shown. Many women are crying, making no attempt to hide it, here and there men are embracing their wives and sweethearts, and showing no self-consciousness about it. As the train leaves, one woman runs right up to the end of the platform, and waves a handkerchief till the train is out of sight.

Thursday, 16th. I have never felt so buggered in all my life as I do

Henry Novy

now. I remember a few days when I first came to the depot when things did get me down, but the 23 miles we did today, almost without breaks, just make everything else seem trivial. It was so hard going on frozen roads, tremendously steep hills, that eight people collapsed and two of them were ambulance cases. Old regular sergeants were limping. When we came in our room I sank on to my bed and couldn't get up. I couldn't even keep my back straight or my head up. Arthur came in and crashed on the floor. George staggered in, helping himself with the walls. And then the captain congratulated us on our wonderful marching! Naturally the march was so strenuous that today there is nothing else but a march to report. No one read a paper, no one heard the news, no one talked about the war or anything else except the march, and how bloody it was. Of course they took some pride in it, were quite pleased to have done 23 miles, but they were, like me, quite buggered at the end of it.

George Springett

Tuesday, 21st. Rain. *It's come!* The worthy gentlemen of the tribunal sent me this morning a form stating that *my name will, without qualification, be removed from the register of COs.* In other words these old blighters have dismissed my objection. Strike me pink! I *didn't* expect unconditional exemption, but to be struck off the register! Words fail me! I shall appeal; the form states that I may do so within 21 days. I've got a damned headache as a result of this news. In order to appeal I have got to send to the HQ for *another* form: more delay. Oh, well, the longer the delay the nearer the end of the war!

Len England

Wednesday, 22nd. In afternoon CSM gave a lecture. Began by warning us against venereal disease, and describing exactly the symptoms of syphilis and gonorrhoea. Added that a professor had said that if anybody felt that they must get sexual relief, it was better to have another man than a prostitute. Made various other points, obedience, loyalty, etc., in all of which he pointed out quite clearly that we didn't join the army because we wanted to, that we were having to sacrifice a lot, and so on, and we'd just have to make the best of a very bad job. This attitude of rather exceptional frankness pleased everybody immensely, not bullying, but not wishy-washy.

Evening to the pictures. Afterwards to the YMCA for food where John made a stream of wisecracks to the girl behind the counter. Says afterwards, rather apologetically, 'I've never flirted before in my life. I've only been in the army five days, and now look what I'm doing.' Adds to what I feel to be true, that he feels different as a soldier, he can do things he wouldn't have thought of in civilian life, and it was perfectly natural. I also feel more authoritative and self-assertive in uniform.

FEBRUARY 1941

Friday, 7th. I went to the YMCA for a cup of tea. The fall of Benghazi[18] is talked about the hell of a lot. When they announced it on the wireless several corporals cheered. For the first time there is war talk, and almost universal admiration of Wavell's troops [General Archibald Wavell was commander-in-chief of British forces in the Middle East and North Africa]. The general trend of the talk is, 'Oh boy, can't they make it! One hundred and sixty miles in two days.' 'They were 60 miles off yesterday.' 'That's the British for you.' A lot were persuaded it will decide the war for us.

After duties I went out as soon as I could. We went to see the much discussed *The Great Dictator*. I thought it was good, with Chaplin really brilliant. One can feel he compromises even now with the capital viewpoint, but he is effective. It's the first effective mouthpiece of sense and decency I have seen, not full of the bloody Union Jack. It was very moving, and at the end the full house clapped its appreciation. I asked a porter, 'Do you get many coming to see it?' 'Many?' he answered. 'It's

Henry Novy

been full since it came: queues all over the place.' The appeal
to the soldiers, the speech of the terrified man in front of other
men, the Churchillian exile wanting to buy his life with that of
one of his five hosts and protectors, the brutality of the regime,
and the threats that the system could spread if the people didn't
stop it, its appeal to the people – all this must have terrific
effect. In the barracks I heard it discussed again. One man said,
'Well, I didn't like it. The speech at the end was tripe. What
was it for anyway? The film was all right. But I can't see why
they say it's so marvellous – and believe it or not, it's the bloody
speech they talked about! I'd rather go to the Empire and have
some fun.' It definitely was the speech they talked about, and
as more see it, more talk about it.

Nella Last   *Sunday, 9th.* When I listened to news I said to my husband,
'Does the war news seem real to you – do you worry or rejoice
much?' and he said after consideration, 'Not really – war seems
to have receded since we had few air raids over England.'

It's really astounding to me sometimes how little I *do* think
of war! I'm terribly single-minded I know and think of what
I'm doing to the exclusion of most things but when I consider
how much of my life now is centred on 'war things' – bandages, comforts and money-raising for same – and yet how little
I think of 'big things' I'm often amazed at my 'limited vision'
and wonder if others have it too.

Monday, 10th. I put a piece of butter the size of a nut in my pan
and put chopped leek, carrot, cabbage and turnip and a little
celery and closed lid tightly while vegetables steamed together.
Then I added water and a few butter beans and a little barley
and when it came to boil two Oxo [stock] cubes and a little
vermicelli and it was very good and will do for two days and
then perhaps I'll be lucky enough to get a bone. No one used
to bother with jelly bones or sheep heads or bacon bones from
grocer and I used to feel like orphan Annie sometimes when I

asked for them! Now I think the *Kitchen Front* talks are making people 'soup-conscious'.

Wednesday, 12th. Whatever happens now I seem to be fed up. Henry Novy
I learnt that only ten failed the clerk's exam. I passed. Such a
terrible trial! If only we could get posted quickly, and know
where we stand. That's the wish of everyone. News of the war
isn't too bright, fear of invasion as usual, Willkie not sure of
a British victory unless America helps immediately, Roosevelt
cannot promise American help will not draw her into the war,
but it might not, whilst a German victory would inevitably
mean war for America, and a lousy war! Now they're just being
hard-faced. The Senate has still not passed the Lease and Lend
Bill.[19] What a mess! Bulgaria is infiltrated, Rumania an enemy
state, Russia a comfort. Where are we going?

Thursday, 13th. New NCOs have been made, me among them. Len England
I can sense very little resentment as yet against these sudden
promotions, but there is a feeling that they cannot have been
judged entirely on merit in only four weeks of squad drill.
There is also a certain amount of worry among the privates
who are my close friends as to whether this will alter our relationship at all.

Friday, 14th. There is a great deal of anti-Semitism in the army:
there are no Jews in our battalion, and the feeling is not so
much directed at individuals as at the race. It is not confined to
the 'rank and file', two of the most intelligent people I have yet
met are confirmed Jew-baiters. The argument usually runs like
this: where are the Jews in the army? There are none because
they all have managed to get the soft jobs and have wangled out
of conscription. In just the same way, the Jews were always the
first to leave danger areas. The Jews hold the purse-strings, the
country has been taken over by them. Individual Jews may be
pleasant enough, but as a race they are the root of all evil.

Henry Novy,
Catterick
military
hospital,
Yorkshire

Thursday, 27th. It was a rotten dismal day today, a steady rain came down all day long, and later a wind got up, now it whistles around our barrack room. There was nothing exciting or new in the routines and nothing outside it either. I had a letter from my Darling which cheered me up a lot, as now we can see much more clearly how the next few weeks are going to turn out. It's always such a nuisance when the letters take days to come, and when things happen quickly and everything gets mixed up. It makes me so impatient and nervous. I listened to the air-raid news carefully tonight. They said the raids were intensive everywhere, especially London and South. It worries me not to be there, and have to wait for days for letters. Especially now, if they start their real air and sea offensive, coupled with an intensified submarine campaign, God only knows what we shall do.

MARCH 1941

Len England

Monday, 3rd. Am writing this while waiting to be marched off to Donnington. [When Len was transferred to Donnington he was promoted to Non-commissioned Officer of the Royal Army Ordnance Corps.] Half our lot have already gone, some to Didcot, some to Branston, all a good way away. A lot of handshakings and good lucks as each detachment marches away. Not a great deal of over-sentimentality, or 'Hope to meet you again': I think everybody realises how unlikely such events are. The feeling is identical to last day of term or the end of a holiday. Everybody packing, standing around talking, laughing and cracking jokes as each lot disappears, and then – this is important – forgetting all about the others as soon as they go.

Friday, 7th. One point about our departure from Hinckley that I had forgotten to mention. Marching down to the station,

there was exactly the air that is supposed to typify the British
army. Everybody in Hinckley knew that we were leaving, and
they were waving to us, calling out 'Are we downhearted?',
winking. We were doing the same, cheering, singing, waving.
We pass a nurse: corporal yells, 'What about a cheer for the
nurse, lads?' An enormous cheer. The spirit is very infectious,
I'm cheering and waving as much as the rest though usually I
feel rather superior to this. This is the first and only time I have
noted this feeling, which seems mainly pride at being part of
such a great and important organisation.

Wednesday, 12th. I took a bus from King's Cross to Charing
Cross Road, and had a hunt around the several bookshops to
find something I could take home for my Darling. I found
something very nice by Steinbeck, only just published: *The
Grapes of Wrath*, and I bought it.

Henry Novy,
London, on
leave

It was queer coming to London again after so long in the
bloody army. Things didn't seem quite real, and there were so
few soldiers about that I could hardly believe my eyes. I did
see a lot of Red Caps in Charing Cross Road, and instinctively
crossed to the other side. I don't like these people now, and
somehow they frighten me. Anything looking like authorities
frightens me now, and I keep clear of it if I can.

My mother was glad to see me, and said I looked well, and
strong, broader perhaps than before. I was glad to get home,
and had plenty to talk about, but I kept the army out of it as
far as possible, because mothers aren't the kind of people to tell
about army routine.

Wednesday, 19th. Milder. 9 p.m. Writing until teatime, then
over to Yvonne's house to enquire if she was free on Sat. A most
rum situation has arisen and I'm hanged if I can understand
it. It's like this: I knocked at Y's front door and she opened it.
On every other occasion she has more or less seized hold of me
with both hands and pulled me inside. This evening she stood

George
Springett

holding the door open almost 18 inches. She seemed rather surprised to see me and said: 'Didn't you get a letter from me this afternoon?'

'No.'

'Well, you'll get it in the morning and when you get it you'll want to phone me.'

'Why?'

'You'll see.'

'Well, are you free on Sat.?'

'Yes.'

'Well, coming out to play?'

'No.' (very softly)

'Well, Sunday, then?'

'No.' (still softer)

Then I realised that Yvonne was going to cry and before I could say any more she *very gently* shut the door in my face and murmured, 'Goodbye.' I stood there for a bit half-inclined to knock but on reflection decided not to, so cycled home. Very perplexed. Can't understand this at all. There has been no row, whatever. There must be *something* wrong! Well, I suppose I shall get this letter in the morning.

Thursday, 20th. Mild, heavy mist. 9.30 a.m. Yvonne's letter. Strike me pink! Here we go! I'll quote a chunk of the letter so you can see for yourself what has happened:

> I'm very sorry to have to say so, but my parents made it very obvious to me last night that they resented your presence in our house. They have fits of not taking a fancy to some fellow or other and that is that!
>
> The reason for their objection to you is that you are a 'Conchie'! I am afraid it will be impossible for me to see you here for knowing my parents' attitude if you did call. I beg you not to ... I am afraid that is the position and there is nothing I can do about it.

I will now await a rather angry letter from you.

Yvonne

P.S. If you *deliver* the answer, pop it through the letter-box. I advise you not to knock!

Fireworks! Well, I'm ——d! Of all the blinking hypocrisy! Pa and Ma Wynyard *invite* me to their place, apparently make me welcome (knowing all the time that I was a pacifist), then when it suits 'em they upset Yvonne and get her to tell me – they haven't got the moral courage to face me and tell me personally!

Monday, 31st. I haven't had much time to look around me today, but I couldn't fail to notice the tremendous outburst of war interest and discussion which followed the sinking of the five Italian battleships and cruisers.[20] Everyone talks about it, and applauds the feat of the British fleet. One man said at tea, 'It's the only bloody service that knows its job, with the RAF. There's no bloody red tape in the British navy.' Another chipped in, 'Every bloody service has done something, except the fucking army. The bloody thing's no fucking use at all.' Everybody thought it was a magnificent victory, greater than any we'd had, and they laughed all along as the announcer described the proceedings of the battle. At the mention of the *Warspite* hurrays went up, and one man shouted above the din, 'Christ, the bloody *Warspite* was there! Fucking good, eh!' and all the others cheered him. They talked about it all night, most of them taking the line that it was a marvellous show, 'showing the cunts what we're made of', smashing them to bits. But nearly every discussion brought the Germans in, and almost in the same words said it would have been a different story if the ships had been manned by Jerry.

Henry Novy

APRIL 1941

Henry Novy   *Sunday, 6th.* This morning we heard the declaration of war on
Yugoslavia and Greece[21] on the seven o'clock news. It came
as a shock and was so neatly announced that most of the lads
said, 'WHAT?', not quite believing it, being really surprised.
One lad sums up the attitude very well: 'It was the only thing
to be expected, but it was a surprise all the same.' Everyone
was surprised, very, but as soon as they knew they said anyone
who didn't expect it must have been mad. The way they have
reacted these last two days has been quite funny. They were all
hot and happy at the smashing of the Italian fleet. It carried
them off their feet, and they completely forgot that they were
in the dumps early in the week, when news was bad and things
going badly even on the wireless. When they heard of Benghazi
it was Wavell choosing his own battleground, but somehow it
destroyed all their enthusiasm, it shattered everything below
the surface and made them fed up once more. When they heard
about the new declaration of war they decided that on the whole
it was good for us, and that Hitler would have a job, but at the
same time they caught a glimpse of a terrific struggle, with a
lot of men sent East, and a long war. I expect that's why they
started to complain about the place again, and to say they were
fed up and browned off with 'this bloody war'. Maybe the short
bread rations had something to do with it, but I heard at least
twenty fellows say that in the afternoon, at tea table and in the
NAAFI, and once again, with an interval of a few days, they were
fed up with the place and fed up with the war.

Len England   *Thursday, 10th.* Introversion. I have mentioned before the
gradually increasing singularity of interest that is experienced
in the army. Nothing outside immediate existence begins to
matter very much. Lack of interest in the news I have frequently
commented, and even a complete and disastrous upheaval like
the present one in Greece and Yugoslavia is of little more

importance than the fact that the lance-corporal next door has lost his stripe for pissing outside his hut. Sex is one of the things that ceases to matter so very much. In a discussion the other night between all types in the hut it was agreed that this could not be entirely explained by bromide in the tea. To some extent, it was due to the utter change in living conditions. I personally find it the same with religion. I am becoming less strongly God-conscious, though I still am able to get furious and dismayed at there being no Communion Service on Good Friday, and though I miss my – at all times rare – Bible-reading very much. My faith isn't becoming less uncertain, it is only fading more into the background.

Easter Monday, 14th. Great preparations for latest adventure tomorrow. I shall be glad to get away from our business as it is so depressing seeing it so unlike our beloved business of the piping days of peace. Feel full of anticipation and excitement of going and wonder what my fate will bring. I have never been so far from Norfolk before. Everyone here keeps saying they will miss me. This depresses me more than leaving as they all seem so sad about it. I tell them I shall probably be back in a month sick of the soil and gardening. I am looking forward to getting there and finding out what it is like. I have not seen London in wartime and hardly know what changes to expect. Lots of bombs dropped near here this morning. We heard them shake the house.

Muriel Green

Tuesday, 15th. Rose at 6 a.m. and caught 7 a.m. train to set out on great adventure to Dorset as a garden apprentice. Jenny upset me crying a little when she saw me off, but I soon got over it. Crowded train and elderly female relation as travelling companion. Arrived in London 10.30 a.m. Disappointed in balloon barrage: I was expecting to see something much bigger. Saw lots of bomb damage, but on the whole London looks much the same to me as before the war; the people do anyway. Taxied to

Waterloo with luggage and then walked around ending up at Lyons' in Regent Street for some lunch before catching 12.50 train, which I nearly missed. Arrived Salisbury 2.30 and found bus after some difficulty and parked luggage. Spent 1½ hours until bus went, looking for Food Office for emergency ration book and Labour Exchange for insurance card. Very rural bus and market-day crowd.

There are five girls here and head lady gardener, quite young. All girls very nice: from Kent, Yorkshire, Letchworth and all over between us. We live in a charming 'ideal home' old cottage and have a sweet bedroom each, bathroom, kitchen and lounge common-room. All delightful. I can see I shall be quite happy for a month here. Food is sent in ready-cooked from manor house and is plentiful. We had high tea when we arrived. 6.30–7.30 the lady gardener who lives with us gave a lecture on pests and spraying. After that, light supper and I had a bath and bed at 10 p.m. I am quite satisfied so far with my 'war work'. Wish I was here for longer than a month. I haven't done any gardening yet, though! Tomorrow I start.

Len England   *Friday, 18th.* Leave rota up, I'm down for Thursday week, May 1st. My first reaction was one of pure, blithe joy, but already, after five hours, I've settled into the rut again. Main reason is that the news is so bad that I reckon leave is almost sure to be cancelled. But I feel that another point is that the break with civilian life has been so complete that the thought of going back to it if only for a week seems quite unbelievable. Air raid on London causes worry for Londoners. I myself am very relieved to have a note from mother to hear that all's well.

Muriel Green   *Saturday, 19th.* Spent morning sweeping paths ready for weekend visitors and return of the colonel, the master of the manor. Then we pollinated the peach trees by tickling them with rabbits' tails on canes. We finish at 12 on Saturdays. I caught the 1.10 bus in to Salisbury to shop. After shopping and trying about three shops for nearly everything I inspected the cathedral and close and several of the ancient streets. I thought the close lovely and the cathedral. A very quaint old town and quite decent shops.

I went to the Labour Exchange to find out if I had to register. I did not think I had to, but did not want to be fined £50. An elderly gentleman met me at the door and said, 'Have you come to register, miss?' I said I did not know, and he patted me fatherly-like and said, 'If you go upstairs my dear, the young lady will tell you.' I did, and met another girl coming down. She smirked at me and giggled as though it was terribly funny and she was nervous: as though she had signed her death warrant. The girl at the desk said not this week and I retreated hurriedly in case she changed her mind. I met several more girls on the way out who all smiled nervously. The elderly man was fatherly ushering them all in and he asked the verdict and was very sweet about it. I always thought one was bullied at Labour Exchanges, but today and last week I was treated with absolute kindness and almost love! I had never been inside one before. All the girls here are like me avoiding factories etc. One is a Conscientious Objector and the others just taking care of themselves like me. I returned from Salisbury by 5.30 p.m.

Evening: sitting by fire, talking and reading. Miss C the organiser returned today and brought her radio, so I heard the news tonight for the first time since I left home. We have *The Times* every day brought for us, but no one seems to read it. Miss C does but the others don't seem interested in the international situation and are very vague about the war. Here we should certainly not know there was a war on if it was not for the fact that we have our butter on separate dishes with our names stuck on with stamp paper and our jam in jars likewise. I have never heard less aeroplanes and not one at night since I came. It is 2½ miles from the nearest village and all fields for miles so it is just too safe and remote.

Maggie Joy   *Monday, 21st.* Are we really going to lose this war? The Nazis
Blunt   sweep from triumph to triumph making no mistakes while we
              make all the mistakes. Have been trying to find a reference in
              Barbellion's Journal to quote here. It was something like this –
              viewed in historical perspective would it really matter so very
              much if the Germans had control of the Continent for the next
              100 years? What is a 100 years in the thousands that have gone
              and are to come? He was wondering this in the last war, one
              wonders it again now. Or was it the despair of a sick man?

              God alone knows what we shall be called upon to endure
              these next few years but as others wiser than I have said, it
              is not what one endures but how one endures it that counts.
              There were bad raids again on London last week. Planes over-
              head again tonight. The horror of that sound has become dulled
              by familiarity and resignation.

Len England   *Tuesday, 22nd.* Rang up mother yesterday. She is taking the
              sensible attitude of our leave and not believing it until I actu-
              ally put in an appearance. I too can't believe it will materialise
              somehow. One of the things that worries me about a return to
              London is reaction to the blitz. I was no more frightened of it
              than most when I was in it, yet being away from danger for
              three months has softened me and already there is quite a real
              fear in my mind of being blown up.

Maggie Joy   *Monday, 28th.* Our troops are evacuating Greece. We still hold
Blunt   Tobruk.[22] Churchill's speech last night – well, everyone at the
              canteen this morning pronounced it excellent so I suppose it
              was. But the division of aims among our own people and our
              maddening inefficiency threaten, I think, to lose us the war.
              There are people who want a new social order, but not Hitler's.
              There are people, belonging to the Old School, who are terri-
              fied at socialism and Hitler. There are the powerful sets, appar-
              ently in control of the war and trying to preserve 'democracy'
              for their own ends. The confusion is terrible. Germany solves

it at the moment by liquidating all opposition to its one ideal, ruthlessly. It is not the right way, but it is the ... or appears to be, the quickest ... We shall discover in time, including Germany ... but how long, O Lord, how long?

Tuesday, 29th. I think we could live in Shotley completely away from the war. For a minute one can, sometimes for several hours. But then the spell is broken. And so it goes on. It isn't easy to go out in the country and think of nothing but the spring and the bursting buds. The river's very nice, and fresh, and we love to sit near the waterfalls, but we can't help thinking about ourselves, the friends we have, where we shall have our baby. All the time the war comes up, we talk about it, think about it, worry about what it might bring to us. We don't bother about an invasion. Most people think there never will be one. Some think Hitler never intended to come. But there's the food, and the army, all the shifting about, going abroad, the heavy raids, the rotten news on the wireless. You can't escape it, and I think it's worse when the country is beautiful and when there is peace all around you. It is then that it seems most futile, and the bigger shame. To me it seems heavy and tiresome, something that's got to be got over, a unification of fascism in slaughter. The more struggles, a harder fight. In spells of passion one forgets, whether it's in bed, when two warm bodies take each other, or in the sunshine and the spring, when the roaring water drowns all thought. It's nice to be a clerk in the RAMC, it's nice to live in a place like Shotley Bridge. But wherever you go, it's always war, war, war, and I hate it because it makes me weary, and worried.

Henry Novy, Shotley Bridge, County Durham

MAY 1941

Friday, 2nd. I was admitted to hospital today, and didn't go home after my morning's duty. They put me straight to bed

Henry Novy

and I was only coming round about six at night. They cut through my gum, and extracted some roots. The ether they shoved down my throat made me awfully ill, and I didn't know much of what was happening to me all day. In the morning the whole office was talking about the war, as they now do every day. They were quite excited about Irak [an anti-British revolt posed a threat to oil supplies from the area], and thought Germany would march into Turkey. The feeling that something big is going to happen makes them so excited that they talk and talk all day about it. They don't seem to remember Greece as a disaster. All they said about it was about the wonderful evacuation.

Later on in the evening I was sick, painfully sick because I hadn't eaten anything since the morning breakfast. I felt better, though the foul taste and smell of ether filled my bed. The night staff came in at eight o'clock, and I was able to sit up in bed. I had a look round the ward. Most of the beds were full, and in the one next to me was an old man with terrible wounds. His face and scalp were all bandaged, also his arms, which he rested on two pads placed on the bed. Out of the bandage his hands stuck out, just two lumps of red shapeless flesh, with thick stumps, about half the length of ordinary fingers, going off in all directions. I saw the nurse pull out a pillow from under his knees, that too was full of blood, and I saw huge red scars on his thighs. On the same side in the corner there was another old man, with a head full of bandages. When I was half awake I had been wondering why I could see light when I looked at his nose. The nostril was like a window with light showing through. At one time he turned round, and I saw he only had one wall of the nose: all the rest was gone.

A young fellow from the other side came and sat on my bed. He was one of the three who were brought in on Friday. He talked to me a long time. He was terribly fed up being in hospital, and was worrying about all the pay he might lose. He was

trying to put an incendiary bomb out when it happened. He
had no sand, just the top of a dustbin. He was putting that over
the bomb when it exploded. It blew back in his face, and threw
his fists back in his eyes. All he had was two ugly black eyes,
one of which he couldn't open. The other two were the same,
only they got it worse. There were four of them at the start, but
a bomb exploded in a fellow's belly when he tried to put it out,
and blew all his guts out. He was dead. A miner saw it explode
and turned away, but he was too late, and it took all the side of
his face off, blowing his teeth out of position. He was out on
strike then, about some of their men being paid only 4/11d a
shift. The other one was a very bad case, on the Dangerously Ill
list. He was bending over the bomb to put sand on it when it
went off. Everything blew in his face. One of his eyes was gone,
a cheek was torn almost off. Eight bones were broken inside
and he had a punctured jaw. They were going to operate on
him tomorrow, and try to save him. The young lad told me all
that, and had a lot to say about incendiary bombs and air raids.
'They'll never catch me getting down to another one,' he said.
'What will you do, Jim?' he asked the minder. 'Get out of the
bloody way, they ain't things to be trusted, ye know. They can
kill you without you knowing.'

Friday, 2nd. Leave has begun. Just as until the very last moment
at Donnington the thought of home seemed impossible, now
the army seems just as ridiculous. For just a short period, three
or four hours, after I returned I was bewildered and couldn't get
used to my new surroundings: the rooms seemed too large and
too light, I vacated the lavatory quickly thinking that somebody was bound to be waiting. Then I had a bath, changed into
civvies. As soon as the strange, rather naked, feeling of these
wore off, the past three months just vanished. All the friends
I've met seem to have been seen only yesterday, the things that I
do I just carry straight on with. There is no connection between
military and civilian life, as I keep on emphasising: switch your

Len England,
London, on
leave

surroundings and Hyde forgets Jekyll, or Jekyll Hyde. Some people, however – perhaps 50 per cent of first leavers and 20 per cent of others – like to wear uniform on leave, wear it all the time. I think the feeling inspiring this is pride, pride in being a soldier in doing your bit. I personally have no pride at all in being a soldier: only a dull longing to be a civilian again.

Henry Novy *Sunday, 4th.* In the ward this morning there was a great deal of discussion about the fighting in Irak, but it soon developed into a technical discussion between several gunners as to the efficiency of aerial machine-gunning. They thought the casualties from that kind of attack were very heavy, and terribly dangerous. A cannon shot from a German fighter had blown the left side of a young Scotsman's face away, machine-gun fire had mutilated two others. They thought things would go a lot easier if America came in, and gave us some arms. It was stuff we wanted, without stuff we were done, and the men couldn't do anything. When the news was given about Merseyside several patients shouted, 'Why don't they give it them back?' There was a wave of indignation, but also of discouragement amongst the young soldiers. They, far more than the civilians, seem to hate aerial bombing, and to be afraid of it most acutely. They have all been at Dunkirk, and their eternal complaint is about the Jerries having all the stuff.

Muriel Green *Friday, 9th.* Last day in the manor garden. Onion setting most of day. I have to make up the greenhouse store no more. It was the only thing at W. Manor I shall not be sorry to leave. Evening I had exam before leaving: ten questions on gardening. I passed and qualified in the first round as a gardener. Tomorrow I bid farewell to the girls and Miss D and C. I am sorry. I hate saying goodbye to people you know you will only by chance see again. I feel it is the end of another chapter. Tomorrow I begin a new one. I have been very happy here. The month has flown. I am now used to working in the garden all day and must say I love

it. I adore the sun and the fresh air. It has been a rest cure. That
is a rest from the war. I have worked harder than ever before in
a month. If I had been at home the days would have dragged;
especially as the war news has been so depressing. Nothing
but setbacks. I cannot see the war ending with us winning
for years yet. Two years at least even with American help. It is
getting harder every day to get at Germany. We seem to get
just pushed back and back with less foothold in Europe. I have
not had time to worry or peruse over the situation since I came
here. I am right behind and in fact only know the vague outline
of the events of the past month. Perhaps I shall catch up if there
is a radio at the next place, and I should have longer to read
the paper perhaps if there are no other girls to chat to in the
evenings. I do wonder what it is going to be like. I look forward
to finding out tomorrow night and next week.

Saturday, 10th. I have arrived at Empingham. I arose and had
special separate breakfast and said my farewells, sad to leave,
but anxious to get here. Miss C took me in car to bus-stop with
luggage. I had till 4 p.m. in London before my train left for
Oakham. I took a bus to Oxford Street and wandered along a
bit looking at shops and air-raid damage and then had lunch
at ABC restaurant. I had promised myself since I first began
Mass-Observing that the next time I had any time to spare in
London I would go to MO's office and see what I could see. I
easily arrived by Underground at Holland Park and found Lad-
broke Road. I was at number 82 straight away and then wondered should I walk by, or had I the cheek to go and ring the
bell. I looked at the place a few minutes and decided that after
all MO ask awfully cheeky questions and I had written tripe
for them that I would not tell a living soul and they deserved
inquisitive people going to look at them! I felt I was getting
my own back if I did waste their precious time and bore them,
as I find they waste lots of mine and some of the questions bore
me and annoy me awfully, but I always answer them.

I rang the bell and then felt daft because I had not any real reason for calling. The door was opened straightaway by a middle-aged servant. She asked me in and asked me my name and never asked me what I wanted. I felt sillier still when I got inside and was not quite sure how to explain my mission (my sister had written persistent letters telling me to go and find out what the MO place was like when I came through London – if it had not been for her I should have not felt so inquisitive) or what I had really come for or expected to see. It was semi-dark inside as the windows were boarded up and after a few seconds standing in the hall feeling sillier every second a young man, with hair cut long standing out at all angles as if he was frantically busy, came out and asked me who I wanted to see. I asked if Mr Willcock was in, not expecting he was and he was all I could think of as he always answers our letters, and we already feel quite familiar with him especially as he reads the bilge in my diary! The young man (who I suspected was Tom Harrisson because I had heard his voice on the radio) said that Mr W was at Letchworth and asked what I wanted to see him about. I said nothing really only as I was passing through London and had written so many times to him I called out of pure curiosity. He laughed and said he was sorry he was not there and said he was desperately busy writing a report and could not spare the time just then to talk to me. He asked if I was one of the voluntary observers and I asked if he was Mr Harrisson and said I was pleased to meet him.

I said I would depart as I could see he was busy and he explained again just how busy and how sorry he was he had not known I was coming. He asked me to come again and when would I be in London again. I said not for years probably and he said again, how sorry he was and how busy etc., etc. Mr Willcock was often there and would have talked to me and shown me things, only everything had been evacuated. By this time I had got as far as the door and when Mr H had opened it I had a good look at him. I said, 'Good Afternoon,' and he again said

how busy and sorry etc., etc. and if I came again let him know
personally and go and have a meal with him or something. I
was quite thrilled being asked to go again, but did not think I
should have the cheek to go and waste his valuable time again,
only I did not say so! I said 'Good afternoon' again and he said,
'Good Afternoon,' and shut the door.

I came away and for the next half-hour could do nothing but
laugh to myself about it. I wondered what TH really thought
and how he probably was cursing inwardly all the time he was
being nice and polite. I expect he was terribly annoyed but
I was triumphant that I had actually been and not quite got
kicked out. He also had thanked me so much for doing the MO
directives, etc. I thought him very charming and did not mind
at all being got rid of, as I expected it. I was very glad I went,
however annoyed he and the MO in general would be about it.
I knew how Jenny would laugh and it really was funny.

I came back to Oxford Circus by Underground and it was
2 p.m. I walked along viewing the damage and ruins and
up Tottenham Court Road. I thought I would walk back to
St Pancras as I had loads of time and I like walking in London
as it gives you more time to look round and see things and
people. It was about 3 p.m. when I got back at St Pancras. I
had some tea and after getting case and ticket, train was in, so
at twenty to four got in for a good seat.

The Colonel, an elderly military-looking man, came to meet
me and introduced himself. Got in his car and he drove me five
miles to Empingham, talking all the way and telling me about
the garden. He seemed very pleasant with me and I think he
will be all right to work for. He told me how I was to live with
Marples the gardener and his wife and they would look after
me. He deposited me at the Ms'.

The gardener is about 65 and very nice-looking with white
hair. He has been very ill and is still rather slow and feeble in
his walk. He is awfully nice and amusing to talk to and I think
I shall like working with him. His wife seems a very homely

kind old party at 65 with white hair. Their cottage is very clean and neat, not exactly modern, no electric light and some of the pictures do not bear looking at. My bedroom has fairly plain wooden bed, dressing-table and wash-stand and rather quiet pink and green china on it. There are four pictures (Tintern Abbey in a gilt frame, a music exam certificate and two photographs: one a group at a dance and the other a group at a garden party some years back). None of these are very big so will not offend the eye too deeply. The mantelpiece has several ornaments including a white shepherd and shepherdess, all quite bearable. I had a poached egg for tea and ham for supper. Bread and butter and jam, cake and biscuits all home-made thrown in at each meal.

Maggie Joy Blunt *Tuesday, 13th.* Rudolf Hess, Nazi Party leader and Hitler's deputy, has flown in an Me.110 from Augsburg and landed by parachute on farmland in Scotland, without arms or ammunition, and is now somewhere in Great Britain recovering from a broken ankle.[23] If this is true, if the man is sane, if it is not part of some deep-laid Nazi plot, the implications are tremendous … and the romance of it! It is the best piece of news we have been given for months.

Muriel Green *Tuesday, 27th.* Showery all day again. Morning spent at market garden picking rhubarb for contact of local Women's Institute who is coming up this week. Waste of sugar I call it. Of all the foul acid stuff! Afternoon spent weeding the paving-stones again. Several interludes of talking to the staff. All assured me the said paving-stones had not been done since the war. I heartened and thought that the war might be over before they want doing again and the gardener's boy demobilised. Evening went for a walk with E. At lunchtime Mr M who has been in house kitchen and heard news said the *Bismarck* was sunk. We heard it on news at six and after hearing we had also lost four destroyers and two cruisers it does not sound a great deal to make a fuss about as we lost the *Hood*[24] on Sat. A neighbour told us again in the evening. Everyone seemed very bucked.

Thursday, 29th. A fit of depression with regard to the news, **Len England** worse than I've ever seen before, is spreading over the troops. Crete started it, and the *Hood* finished it off. In the middle of last week over 50 per cent considered Crete already lost, and derision reached a new height this morning when we announced a new strategic withdrawal. There are, of course, still a few non-thinking optimists who say we'll win the war before Christmas, but, I think generally speaking, the masses have *for the first time* considered the possibility of defeat. A general trend is this: 'Every time we meet the Germans we get driven back. We're even losing on the sea, and we're supposed to have command of that.' The infallibility of the Germans is an idea that is rapidly gaining ground.

Friday, 30th. We heard the evening news, and the Haw-Haw **Henry Novy** stuff, about Crete being done for,[25] and all the ships going down. I got Moscow news at 10, but was a bit late, and missed all the important part. All we heard were a few things about the condition of people in occupied territory, how much meat they ate, 1½ pounds a month in Finland, how much bread, etc. Then she started a talk on the advantages of a socialist economy, but we cut her off. It isn't a talk on economy we want, but news. I have never felt so eager to get news, hear something of what is happening or what is going to happen. But everywhere there is silence, concealed facts, understatement, over- or under-emphasis. It makes me feel fed up, and all of us listen each time, to hear nothing, and we get fed up and feel tired. It's the same as when the spring offensives were about to start. One feels there is something in the air, but we don't quite know what, and aren't able to guess. It's just fear, hanging, waiting for something. I thought Roosevelt's speech would lift the veil, but it did nothing of the kind. It was just a mild, moderate statement, saying nothing new, nothing we didn't know or expect. I feel that there too is something hidden. Then suddenly, following hard on FDR, comes Eden [Foreign Secretary] with a half-baked statement of war aims. I wonder if Franklin Delano is getting scared of a failure to bring the States in it? It may be that, it may be something else, hidden, but there is something, I can feel it, and I can see that people around me are feeling it too. We just wait, and nothing happens.

JUNE 1941

Muriel Green *Thursday, 12th.* Digging up tulips all day. Weather glorious. I thoroughly enjoy working on days like this and yesterday. Mrs M amused me at lunchtime. She hardly reads the newspaper. She said, 'Have we still got that little place we took the other day?' (Syria,[26] she meant) 'It's about time we gave it up and evacuated it, isn't it? We always run away when we have these advances.' She laughed as she said it.

I am having great trouble with the milkman these days. He long ago altered the times of milk delivery to coincide with the times I go to work! I nearly always manage to meet him and he is most persistent about stopping me and asking me to go for a walk. I always have some excuse and these wet nights have been a help as several of them he had arranged a date, I said it had been too wet and did not go out. Last time it was fine, but I still did not go but he is *not* offended. He arranged again tomorrow night. There don't seem to be any young men except farm workers left here.

Tuesday, 17th. Working all day. Last two days a heat wave and too hot to move. Trying to keep in shady part of garden. I am sunburnt tonight. I am also almost in love! Or is it in love with love? Ye Gods, what fools men do make of themselves! I went out with my French Canadian soldier again tonight.

He is sweet. What it is to be young and foolish! It certainly is good for morale in wartime to be made love to! I am not quite sure if I am happy about it or not. It is pleasant. It is fun. He is nice and a gentleman. I would not go out with him if I did not feel safe and trust him. He is lonely and so am I. We are both away from home and friends. How silly life is! I am meeting him Thursday. I am not quite sure whether I promised to go back to Canada with him or not! I will be his friend anyway. I blame the war for this!

Thursday, 19th. The cigarette problem is acute. Have failed to get any in Slough these last three weeks. The village tobacconist had yesterday a few Woodbines. In London last week I managed to get a hundred and Verrey had collected some tens and twenties for me which I am trying to make last but with the greatest difficulty. I cannot do without them. It shocks me to find that they have such a hold on me. Verrey tells me it indicates a craving for sex but frankly at the moment I would rather have the cigarettes …

Maggie Joy
Blunt

Sunday, 22nd. When we came back from the park, the news was on and the little boy, K (aged 12), dashed out and told us Germany had invaded Russia.[27] R was excited as he thought the Russians would put up a good fight and we should soon now win. Mr G came in at lunch and said he thought the Russians would soon collapse or make terms for giving Hitler the Ukraine and it would then be worse than ever for us as he would have the wheat and oil. R's friend (26), engineer, was wearing a red tie he said in honour to the Soviets and was very optimistic over situation. In the cool of the evening we talked to neighbours over garden fence. They too felt optimistic and thought with Russian help we could now whack the Germans quicker. Mr G persists they could hardly beat the Finns.

Muriel Green

It will certainly be the test of Russian military machine and Red air force. I am hoping they can put up a good show. If they collapse or compromise it will make it a terrific job for us and I should doubt our final victory. I would never trust Stalin not to give in yet. I only hope he doesn't. It seems grand if they will fight with us. We listened to Churchill's speech. The Gs say they get sick of his rambling descriptions. They have been excited last night and today because we shot down a fair number of German fighters today and yesterday.

Maggie Joy Blunt *Sunday, 22nd.* On the hottest day of the year we hear at 9 a.m. that Germany has invaded Russia and at 9 p.m. that the declared policy of the British government is to aid all nations who are victims of Nazi aggression. (Accurately, Churchill said: 'Any man or state who fights against Nazism will have our aid. Any man or state who marches with Hitler is our foe.')

WE ARE GOING TO HELP RUSSIA! Churchill made one of the cleverest speeches of his career; bolstered the Conservative heavyweights most wonderfully for the shock. I smoke my last cigarette to him: think this is the most important day of the century. We ally ourselves with the USSR at last! Cripps [British ambassador in Moscow] must have been doing excellent work.

JULY 1941

Muriel Green *Tuesday, 1st.* Evening I cycled to village four miles away to meet my second airman I arranged on Saturday night. Said I would meet him again Friday night. I am meeting the other one Thurs. night. I am going to be in a mess soon. Oh dear! I should never be doing this if I was at home. It's because there's nothing else to do, I think. It is rather amusing to see how daft chaps will make themselves. They are all looking for a permanent girl to go out with. All say it's so different from the camp and being with other fellows, being shouted at and ordered about. All want sympathy bad. After we had walked one mile this one began some rather amateurish love-making (he is only 20). I can't say I really enjoy it, but it is amusing to see how soon they start! This one began talking of marrying me after an hour. He is a very nice fellow, but I don't believe in quick war weddings. I think I shall soon be sick of being common and getting off with soldiers, etc. My excuse is I am mass-observing the forces' love affairs!

Sunday, 20th. The Russian–German war is regarded very favourably by most people here. It is definitely thought that the Russians are winning and that resultantly the war must be considerably shortened, probably ending this year. Here the argument is constantly, 'It can't go on at this pace for much longer.' The ideologies of the two countries are hardly ever mentioned, and the political possibilities of the Anglo-Soviet pact are not considered. But the refusal to play the 'Internationale' did definitely cause hostile comment.

Len England

V for Victory is also the subject of discussion, though a majority opinion holds it to be a publicity stunt that has misfired. But Vs have been chalked up in huts, in lavatories, and a popular joke has arisen from the fact that the two fingers up sign looks like a V.

Wednesday, 23rd. Warm. What ho! My first set of 'medical' papers have arrived. I am required to 'submit' myself, etc. Submit, indeed! I won't submit – so what? Read one of the papers to Mr and Mrs Robinson. The old man was silent at first – at length he said, 'Are you going?'

George Springett

'No!'

'Coo!' He clicked his tongue and stared into the empty fireplace. 'Don't talk to me about all this objection, I don't believe in it!' (No doubt he was thinking of his three years (1914–17) at the front and felt that if I refused to go, he had, in a way, fought to no purpose – that he wanted to see me go through all he had experienced just because *he* had been through it!) Mrs

R looked rather glum and remarked, 'If you don't obey them I suppose you get about 15 years.'

I laughed. 'Not quite so long – about 12 months, I expect!'

Met Mrs Thompson (47, middle-class). I showed her the papers I had received. She read them and sighing handed them back making no remark whatever. Later on, however, she said, 'I suppose it will be an interesting experience if you go to prison.' I agreed. 'It isn't so much that I object to having my liberty taken away,' I explained. 'It's the rotten food that I shall detest – I get indigestion as it is. I've heard that the grub in gaol is vile muck!'

Doris Melling *Wednesday, 23rd.* Last night, before going to bed, looked at the sky and discussed possibility of a raid. The sky was clear so I decided they wouldn't risk it. Thought how awful it is to be coldly weighing up the likelihood of a raid. P made me laugh about the raid the other night. He and his fellow lodger and the landlady all got under the table in the kitchen, there wasn't room for the landlord, so he had to stay out. They must have looked awfully funny. He said he is not going to get up any more, and was disappointed there weren't more bangs.

Then heard a plane, then gunfire, then the warning. Got up. Felt mad. Heard the woman next door shrieking, 'Come on, Gerald.' Silly woman. 'All clear' after about 20 minutes. Went back to bed – then a terrific explosion. Got up again. Then gunfire. Police whistles. Didn't go out. Made some tea and had something to eat. Returned to bed at 3.45. Couldn't get to sleep. Bed cold.

Talking about it this morning, people can't understand:

a) Why, if there is a plane, more gunfire is not heard.

b) What our planes are doing.

c) Why sirens are sounded for one plane – not apparently a bomber.

d) Why the ridiculous censorship prevails. Surely the

Germans know they are over Liverpool, and yet they put one line in the *Liverpool Echo*, saying 'AA guns have been in action in a NW town', when the whole population has been dragged out of bed! It seems that we are all children!

Thursday, 31st. Listening to the messages across the sea from separated families made me realise that if only heartache in every land could be piled into a visible heap, war would stop at once. The real havoc of war goes on unseen, inside folk. Though all that one sees is bad enough.

Edie Rutherford, 39-year-old housewife, Sheffield, Yorkshire

The general attitude to USA at this date seems to be hostile. The feeling is that with all they are doing, they are helping themselves as much as us, and are content for us to do the dying. Frankly it is a point of view I myself am in agreement with. If we could fight this war with factories (as USA seems set on doing) we would not mind. It is our life-blood which pours and that is the real worry.

AUGUST 1941

Tuesday, 12th. I hear planes in the night outside. Though we have had no enemy activity over this area for many months, that sound still spells a dread – I wait half-consciously for the siren and the noise of gunfire. The clocks went back an hour this weekend. We have enjoyed two hours of extra daylight for three of the summer months. During June it was not dark until after 11.30 and has saved me all the bother of blacking-out. My home-made blackout frames are falling to pieces. I want to find a handyman to make me new ones and mean to ask at the canteen.

Maggie Joy Blunt

Talking of milk. In October we are to be rationed to ½ pint per adult per day. I can manage with this but with three cats it will be a watery ½ pint and there will be no milk puddings.

Mrs P at the canteen informed me that for herself and husband she has six pints a day! We look forward to a lean winter – more and more food rationed, fuel rationed, clothes rationed. Oil for lamps is difficult to get now and has been for some time.

Len England *Sunday, 24th.* Now that the incident is fading, one is hearing more of the emotional impact of Dunkirk on this country. Recently I have heard of two very interesting cases. One, a Marks and Spencer manager, was in a town where the exhausted men passed through. The hotel where he was staying refused them food. Straightaway he went to the store, took nearly all the eatables from it, gave them away all along the train. He admits tears streamed down his face as he saw men too exhausted to peel an orange. Though reserved, he volunteered a week later, he could not stand the thought of doing nothing. Another, a special constable, at the time admits that it nearly drove him mad. For weeks he spent day and night helping them, rarely going home, completely ignoring family and fiancée, doing nothing else, thinking of nothing else but of these wretched men. In my own case from a firm pacifist position routed within a week, vowing, though a natural coward, never to cease fighting while the Nazis were winning. There are large numbers of volunteers here – many in reserved occupations – and nearly all seem to have joined up in the period of last June.

SEPTEMBER 1941

Maggie Joy   *Wednesday, 3rd.* Two years ago, we are reminded by press and
Blunt   BBC, war was declared. For two years I have been lucky, living so happily here. But the time is coming when I shall have to make sacrifices, like everyone else. There seems no hope of the war ending for years. The future appears dreary and incalculable. I cannot expect anyone to understand what it will mean to me to give up my indolent cottage life. The problem of what

to do with the cats, for instance, seems appalling. They have become individuals whom I love, who love and trust me. If the worst happens and I am pushed into uniform (don't WANT to be pushed into uniform), no one will want to feed and care for three cats for me. Stella might be persuaded to have Dinah or the Kittyhawk, or perhaps M, or perhaps they would take one each. But that leaves Ginger. It seems inevitable that Ginger would have to go ... But here I go, worrying about things before they happen.

Sunday, 7th. Every Wednesday afternoon we have regimental   Len England
training and go into a field and march up and down, or put gas masks on. We man defence positions and are not told where or how to expect the enemy. We have not been shown a grenade, or a tank gun, there is no sign of a tank trap round about, the whole thing is run on 1914 lines. I was reading Tom Wintringham's article on invasion in an old *Picture Post* yesterday, and I was appalled by the little I knew about the tactics of invasion. Since joining the army I have only had one lesson on tactics, and this told us how scouts worked when infantry were advancing in column across open country on foot. This is the honest truth. All I know about parachute troops is gained from the MOI 'Miss Grant Goes to the Door', all I know about invasion is from *Picture Post* and various articles in the evening papers.

I am not the only one to be exasperated by this. Nine-tenths of the depot says exactly the same, that regimental training is a fine idea, but the stuff that we do on it is quite useless. Given the interest, they'll do the work. This was clearly revealed last weekend when a big rush job kept most of the depot working right over the weekend, many doing 24 hours non-stop. Normally at this there would have been an enormous uproar. But the rumour had been widely circulated that the stores were for Russia and there was hardly a murmur. Constantly I heard people express opinions like this.

'We know what we are doing now, we feel that the stores we are sending out are going to do some good. It's not just aimless like it usually is. The Russians are doing their bit, and it's up to us to help them as much as we can. I don't mind working any hours in a case like this.'

Henry Novy,
RAMC,
Woolwich,
London

Wednesday, 17th. I heard a newspaper vendor shouting, 'Russian respite near the end', and when I bought a *Standard* I found that Fadden, the Australian prime minister, had made quite an alarming speech, saying that no one could really predict the outcome of the Russian struggle, but that it was very grave indeed, and that, amongst other things, he was by no means satisfied with the part played by Australia in the struggle. I feel rather oppressed and worried about the fight for Leningrad, and the German push across the mouth of the Dnieper. I wonder whether they are really advancing successfully all along their line. At times I cheer up and feel confident, at other times I feel most black. It is difficult to say what the lads are thinking here at the moment. They talk quite a lot about the fact that we are doing nothing, shout at the government, and grumble a great deal. But on the whole they don't openly worry about the Russian fight. They seem to have great confidence in Russian staying power, and I heard several people back them to win in any case, even if we didn't help. I feel they are still rather apathetic, and tend to look on the papers with the end of the war in view, and not so much the things we should do immediately to relieve the pressure on the Russian front. The attack on Leningrad is getting more comments than most features of the fighting, and the broadcast by Frank Owen [journalist on the London *Evening Standard*] was heard by some, and given great prominence in their talks and arguments. I feel that slowly the enthusiasm about the Russian struggle is mounting, and the admiration, the pro-Russianism is increasing very quickly.

Saturday, 20th. Kiev, capital of the Ukraine, has fallen. The

Germans claim it in their communiqués, and the Russians only claim that they will kill as many of the attackers as possible. The general reaction was much more marked than anything else since I came here. Literally I heard no one talk about anything else all day. Their mood was one of seriousness. They thought it was dreadful, that the war was beginning to go wrong, that Jerry could never be stopped. A few thought it wouldn't affect things, others said that after all it was only a German claim, and that Kiev had not fallen yet, they'd only believe it when the Russians admitted it. I had no illusions, but the feeling of the lads ran so high, they talked so much about it, that I began to feel like them, depressed in turn, and elated, varying with the people I heard or talked with.

Moreover it was the people not usually talking politics who criticised most. On the whole it can be said that the fall of Kiev had a great effect, it stamped on everyone the idea that the war in the East was very serious indeed, and that we must do something about it. Some were panicky, and thought Hitler couldn't be stopped, but even those thought we must do something. Pro-Russian feeling is certainly at a peak.

Saturday, 20th. I HAVE GOT A JOB. Don't believe it, but there it is, beginning on Oct. 2nd on an architectural paper in London. So much to do now in preparation and tidying up don't know where to begin. Saw T yesterday too (another architect editor) and he thinks also that there will be a boom in architectural journalism after the war. Germany claims to have taken Kiev but Russian communiqués do not confirm this. The fighting on Russian soil is terrible, *terrible*. We feel that our aid is tardy, we fear the weight of anti-Russian influence in power.

Maggie Joy
Blunt

OCTOBER 1941

Wednesday, 1st. Churchill made a speech, very long, and on the

Henry Novy

whole very good. He said a lot about the war, how it was going, the losses German shipping was suffering, much more than our own, which were definitely down. He talked about the strength of Germany, the only real shortage being in planes. He talked about the fight in Russia, and again promised that the Russians would have all the help we could give them in the shortest possible time. Beaverbrook [Minister of Supply, 1941–2] and Harriman [American ambassador in Moscow from 1943] were in Moscow doing their work, and so everything would be complete and ready.

The whole speech was very subdued, especially in tone. There was nothing so terrible as, 'We shall fight in the hills, etc.,' but what he said was more becoming to a nation in the position of England. It dealt with practical issues, such as production, though of course it never touched real issues. It only talked about them, never dealt with them. Somehow I feel that he has taken to heart just a little bit of what [prominent Labour politician Emmanuel] Shinwell and so many others told him. He is being more conscious of rising public opinion, and the Russian Tank Week must have opened his eyes a little about real feeling in the factories.

Muriel Green, under-gardener, Woodbridge, Suffolk

Tuesday, 7th. Working all day. Evening went to library and my Scotch soldier walked half back with me and said goodbye as they were probably leaving any day and I shan't see him again. He is sweet and I just had to let him kiss me for our final parting. I did not want to really as I have not known him a very long time (two weeks) but they were going away and probably overseas and I may be the last girl he will kiss before he goes, maybe the last girl he will ever kiss. Bless him. He is too nice to be killed ...

Henry Novy

Saturday, 11th. This is the happiest day I've ever known. Today I had the telegram that told me that a boy was born to us, yesterday afternoon. For a few minutes I was tremendously happy, as though we had won something we'd been fighting for for years. Then I thought of Pris, and all she had had to go through. It seemed dreadfully unreal to be here, isolated, not being able to do anything to get near her, to comfort her. Now I know that the leave we have been putting off for nearly three months will be here in a fortnight. I know that our plans can go ahead, and that there is more urgency than ever to get in a better position, to be able to feed them, and get them over to London, to find a flat, to get out of the RAMC, and try to use my brains a little more actively. I hate to think of myself as an opportunist, but I must be one, or otherwise I'll be the mug, and we won't be able to be happy together. When we are together again, then we will be able to work out our plans, and think of the future, and be happy again in the London we love.

It was with my mind off most things I did, or tried to do, that I got through a hard day's work. I made mistakes all over the place, caused the QM to say, 'Do you want me to get promoted to corporal or something?' but he was quite happy and cheerful when the others told him I had become a father. Everybody in the office was excited about it, and crowded round to see the telegram.

Wednesday, 15th. The belief that one gets in the army is that hubris is followed by nemesis. Recently I have had a run of little points of good luck, culminating in leave being up earlier than I expected. I began to get worried and unconsciously began to wait for, and expect, bad news to balance it. I got it – leave put back – and after I had recovered from the shock I was glad, I felt that things would now straighten out. Then two more strokes of good luck came, and reached a culmination in my leave being put *forward* before the other date. I am now living in hourly anxiety waiting for the bombshell to drop. It seems little short of absurd that a reasonably intelligent bloke like myself should believe in this sort of direct balance of Good and Evil, but I am convinced I am only one of a large majority.

Len England

It is presumably a sort of defence mechanism provided by the mind to counteract the army's habit of changing its mind at the last minute.

The news from Russia gets steadily worse, and while all faith in our allies seems to have vanished few people seem to realise the importance of this step. We all say glibly, 'Moscow is as good as lost, and with Moscow Russia,' but hardly any of us realise the enormous importance of this single German victory. We still tend to say, 'They've still got us to deal with, and they won't find us as easy.' Complacency is our middle name.

Henry Novy   *Friday, 24th.* Moscow is terribly strong in the desperate defence they're undertaking. Lozowski said that Moscow would never fall. The threat to the Don basin is increasing rapidly. On the whole the war is still going very much in Germany's favour, and I can't see it change until we do something in the battle. Again in the press there are statements that invasion is mere folly, with Lord Gort's [Commander-in-chief of the British Expeditionary Force in 1940] despatches as proof of the terrible fate awaiting the unprepared expedition that tries to affront the mighty foe. I still don't think all these excuses cut much ice with anyone, certainly not with the majority of us. The lads are strangely apathetic about war news, but about the conduct of the war they are bitterly critical. I suppose at least 80 per cent would favour a Western front, and would support the idea by going as far as volunteering as field ambulance workers, right in the front line.

I notice I hear far more criticism of Churchill now than I have ever heard. I think that the enforced inactivity, the strangeness of the place, the softness of this faraway life, all combine to make the lads wish for action, and at the moment, with Russia in the middle of a terrible struggle, the Western front is their pet alternative to boredom and useless inactivity.

Muriel Green   *Wednesday, 29th.* I must say it is pretty great being a land girl

here. Everyone treats us as heroines especially the soldiers.
Nothing but admiration is forthcoming from them and the
villagers, especially during this cold weather. Many of the soldiers say they feel ashamed as they sit by and watch us work, for
we do far more than they. They are going for their breakfast as
we go to work at 7. At dances T and I are immensely popular
and I am sure it is because of our work as words of admiration
about it come from all our partners. (It certainly is not our
looks as I now weigh ten stone and T does too.) Tonight T's
soldier boyfriend and all his pals took us to an ENSA concert
in the village hall. It was very good fun as there seemed to be
hardly any other civilians there and all but us were boys. One
of the boys paid for me and I sat with another who took me
home. The concert, a variety, was really pretty good. Better
than many varieties I have seen and not particularly dirty jokes
as I expected. Community singing, conjuring, dancing, singing
and jokes and it all seemed to go down well with the troops. I
enjoyed it very much though I had expected to be bored stiff
for two hours.

NOVEMBER 1941

Saturday, 15th. Morning at work. General lament about the   Muriel Green
Ark Royal.[28] Afternoon G and I went to Ipswich on shopping
expedition. We went primarily to buy breeches to work in for
the winter. Ridiculous giggling situation in the tailor's shop
over trying them on. Instinct had told us to go in jumpers
and skirts and if we had worn frocks under our coats I don't
know what we should have done. We were served by an attractive young man of about 18 and we *had* to try them on. It
was terribly embarrassing, especially as I now have a 30-inch
waist! The young man conducted us to a cubicle, left us with
a mountain of breeches and jodhpurs and sat outside until we
wriggled into them. All the time he was asking when he could

come in and see if they fitted. We both giggled a lot, thanked our stars we had not gone alone and had jumpers on top instead of brassières! Other shopping, tea, followed by a visit to the library and supper before catching the 8.30 bus back.

Friday, 21st. Work all day and lunch at British Restaurant. Lunch there is always amusing especially as us three 'land girls' get so much credit and undeserved praise. We are taken for Land army and hence all kinds of questions are asked. Yesterday Lady Somebody suddenly yelped out from the other end of the table, 'Do you girls have to milk?'

Today they gave us all an extra applejack because we were land girls and doing such marvellous work: 'I think you're wonderful, especially in this weather.' Similar admiration is cooed from all quarters. We don't know whether to be embarrassed or feel smug. We all feel frauds anyway as none of us would be doing it if it was not a case of conscription being in the air!

Henry Novy *Saturday, 22nd.* News from Russia is bad. Rostov is claimed by the Nazis. Moscow is severely threatened. Our offensive in Africa is going well, and German tanks are being destroyed, but they are making the hell of a lot of it, and whatever way I look at it, it is still NOT a second front. It can't be, unless it affects the main front.

Wednesday, 26th. I don't feel so depressed at all tonight. Nothing has happened to make me particularly cheerful. The fight for Moscow is rapidly growing more acute, and even the fight in Libya isn't so cheerful. Then there is the menace of reaction hidden in every corner. Sir Roger Keyes, ex-Commando chief, told the House that it was the 'brass hats' who threw spokes in his wheels, and those of the premier Churchill.[29] In other words, even Conservative efficiency is attacked if anything but horses and age-old political balance of power is mentioned. God only knows what will happen if the Russians aren't strong

enough to win on their own. I suppose they must, if they are
to survive.

The business of the hospital goes on as before, with slightly
more work every day, more admissions and more discharges.
The volume of business is growing! Most of them are neurotics
and a mixture of gonorrhoea and syphilis, just to keep the ball
rolling. I don't think I've ever felt so useless than now, or in
the last two months. Even doing fatigues, cleaning out lavatories seemed to serve a better purpose than discharging patients
from the army!

Thursday, 27th. In just over a month, three good friends of   Len England
mine have joined the WAAFs; in each case their calling up
was reasonably imminent, and in each case they have will-
ingly admitted that they joined up in the WAAFs so as to
avoid being forcibly called up into the ATS. In all their minds,
there seems no doubt at all that the worst of horrors is the
ATS. As one says, 'If I register in the WAAFs as a shorthand
typist, I might get a job as a shorthand typist; but in the ATS
such qualifications make me first-class for scrubbing dishes or
driving lorries.'

I fail completely to understand why the authorities don't
do something other than postal propaganda to get women to
join the ATS. The adverts themselves seem to me superb, but
everybody knows that the conditions are not so good. And to
support this, the *Daily Mirror* splashes a picture of two ATS
drinking pints of beer ('I could never mix with that type') and
the evening papers run a line on women military police (even
more discipline). It just won't wash.

DECEMBER 1941

Sunday, 7th. Mild. The Japs attack American bases.[30] Personal   George
outlook on this fresh phase of war: the Jap leaders must be   Springett

mad! And I'm rather inclined to think the subordinates must be even more insane to be so willing and so weak as to obey their leaders. I feel that this new theatre of war will prolong the European activity, since USA will not be able to supply Britain and Russia with so many – or any – arms to be used against Germany. Mrs Robinson (aged 48) remarked, 'Huh! Can't believe all that paper talk! Any'ow we shall soon polish them off!'

Mr Robinson (65) said, 'They're all mad. Well, let USA 'ave a taste of what we've 'ad – see 'ow they like it! They ain't 'ad nothing to put up with.'

Violet Robinson (21), 'Coo! That will make the Americans sit up. Now what will Russia do?'

Stella Thompson (middle-class, 15½), 'I'm glad. It will make it improbable that the Japs will be able to attack Russia.'

George Thompson (13), 'Don't care! Anyhow, it won't affect us, so what?'

Edie Rutherford   *Monday, 8th.* Oh, so the impudent little yellow men declare war on Britain AND USA! Just like their sauce. AND begin the real stuff even before they let their declaration be known. Oh well, I hope USA won't use our kid glove methods but will go for JAPAN quick and hot. Now it is a world war. Such a shame and yet it seemed inevitable. Looks as if mankind has got to go to his lowest before he wakens to the perfectibility of the spiritual, real man.

Henry Novy   *Monday, 8th.* I had a letter and a parcel from my Darling today. It was nice to hear from her, after the long weekend silence. Back to work early, and with little to do. I took it easy all morning. The lads were all talking about the new war and Japan. There wasn't much sympathy with US. 'It'll do the bloody Americans good,' and not much respect for the Japanese: 'The bloody little yellow monkeys,' 'Bloody cheek, isn't it?' They were all quite excited about it, a kind of excitement well expressed by one of the lads in the office: 'Christ, you can't go on a weekend without a new bloody war starting.'

There was a scare about cancellation of Xmas leave, and much cursing was done by those who were due on the 23rd. I don't think many tried to think the event out very deeply, or its real implications. They didn't take the threat seriously. Just another bloody mess, new names, the whole world's in a bloody mess, there's no end to it. It wasn't even worth thinking about it, or trying to make it out. Just a maze, and trying to understand it wasn't much use. A few thought the Russians would burn out the Japs from Vladivostock, but I think more thought nothing of anything else but what was in the headlines, and probably didn't know that Russia is the nearest base to the main Japanese islands. Asked what they thought of it all, they generally shook their heads and answered, 'Oh, the whole bloody world's gone mad ...'

Monday, 8th. Work amid Monday depression and pondering over latest war situation. I had been watching the Far East for several days so I was not surprised though I thought Japan was bluffing. I am not sure whether new situation is hopeful of quicker victory or terrifying because it means Japan would not have launched the attack unless she thought now was the time for a fruitful plunge. I fear the latter as I always expect the worst, then I am near overwhelmed with despair if it happens and am often flooded with joy at it not happening. I fear for Russia if she had to fight on two fronts. It is certainly heartening to know America is at last united and in it with us.

Muriel Green

Tuesday, 9th. A light fall of snow and Japan's declaration of war surprised us on Sunday night. Now the Pacific is in the news and America is in the war. The whole world involved (except Ireland as neighbour Mr C remarked this evening ... Mrs C asks – Shall we ever see peace again?)

The whole world at war ... It is almost too gigantic a

Maggie Joy Blunt

thought for human intelligence. The German campaign in Russia has come to a halt.[31] (Those marvellous Russians!) But German power is not broken. During the winter one supposes they will now turn their attention to us and the Atlantic again. The NE coast was badly raided, we hear, last night.

Edie Rutherford *Wednesday, 10th.* It occurs to me our points scheme may not last long. USA will have so much to do now that maybe she won't be able to can food for us as well as her own people, her army, navy and air force. I can't see our extra sugar and fat going on much after Xmas. Already Lord Woolton has stated no extras at Xmas. Well, we can do without a lot yet and still be well off. Waste still goes on, not only in food but also in other goods. People like myself who deplore waste and try to check it are still looked on as funny, queer, or officious. Why aren't children taught in school that when the Govt pays for things it is THEY themselves who pay? Until folk do understand where Govt money comes from, they will go on wasting and blissfully thinking that it is not their business. I am sure such lessons could be put in such simple and attractive form that the youngest could begin to cope with the subject. One feels all the time that one is a voice in the wilderness and yet, all good things start with a tiny cheep. It is the courage and persistence with which a few stick to what is essentially right which bring it about in the end. I am still a pacifist despite it all, and one day we shall return to sanity and preach sense again.

Henry Novy *Monday, 15th.* What a bloody day! Ernie is on leave, and it leaves just three of us in the office, with the two women. Gradually I feel that office routine is getting the best of me. I did the same about two months ago, and then I succeeded in shaking it off. Now I feel it's coming again, when there isn't a moment one can use for leisure or one's own work, or else when there isn't the energy to do anything. It's a bloody bad way to get in.

Then there is the news. Bad from the Far East. Japs almost in Hong Kong. Singapore threatened. A yellow blitz.

Christmas Day. Mild. Four p.m. A quiet day so far. As Mrs Robinson was unable to get a turkey, and some chickens which Alf (Violet's husband) promised to send didn't arrive, so we had half a shoulder of mutton. The Robinsons were very disappointed but I didn't care. I pointed out philosophically, 'Well, we shan't make pigs of ourselves at any rate.'

George Springett

As a 'special treat' Mrs Robinson condescended to light a fire in her Sanctum Sanctorum (THE FRONT PARLOUR). Believe it or not, she has had only *one* fire in this room since last Christmas – that fire was on Violet's wedding day (Nov. 10th last). Violet had a friend in during the afternoon and as I write they are doing their hair before the front parlour mirror. I am sitting on the settee.

Christmas Day. Up late to make up for working mornings. I had several presents: two serviette rings, writing paper, artificial flower spray, two lots of soap and separate pairs of hankies. (I'm surprised at anyone giving coupons away in hankies.) We only had about a quarter the pre-war quantity of Xmas cards, and most of these from the sort of brainless people you *would* expect to send them. I did not send any this year. Xmas dinner of chicken (old hen) and wartime plum pudding and mince pies. After fetching milk and walking dog and calling on great-aunt and friends went for tea to lady friends and stayed evening over cards.

Muriel Green

Sunday, 28th. Xmas has come and gone and hasn't been too bad. I spent it at home, although the family were away. Enquiring from various people I elicited the fact that everyone had had ample enough to eat – and all commented on the fact that it really was amazing what could be done, and considering this was the third Xmas of the war. There were quite a few

Doris Melling

turkeys and chickens – where people got them from I don't know, because the restriction on imports from Eire affected the market. The prevailing price – controlled – 3/-, and 4/2d lb. dressed. A butcher of my acquaintance said this was ridiculous, in the old days he had killed, dressed and cut up a pig for 1/6d.

Muriel Green   *New Year's Eve*. Last day of 1941 spent washing down greenhouse. The soldiers gave us some hot water and it was much better than icy cold.

I have had many happy hours in 1941 and I do not regret any experiences. It is a good thing another war year is over. I am where I never dreamt of being this time last year. Doing what I always never imagined. I am not sorry. The time passes so much quicker with something to do all day. Goodbye and good riddance to 1941! I shall not forget the year I became a land girl. I wonder where 1942 will find me.

1942 WAITING FOR GOOD NEWS

America's entry into the war had been cheering news, but the British people were still waiting for a victory to celebrate. For much of 1942 that seemed an unlikely prospect. In North Africa, Rommel's panzer divisions launched an offensive in January, recaptured Benghazi, and swept eastwards through Libya. By June, Tobruk had fallen and the British Eighth Army was forced to retreat into Egypt, where a defensive line held at El Alamein. In the Far East, Singapore fell to the Japanese in February and by May the American forces in the Philippines had surrendered and the British had been pushed out of Burma. In Europe, the German armies continued their relentless assault on Russia despite fierce resistance.

At home, Hugh Dalton, the new President of the Board of Trade, introduced 'austerity' measures designed to save materials. The resulting 'Utility' clothing proved very unpopular; some women compensated for the shortage of silk stockings by browning their legs and drawing an ink line to represent a seam. Though they were less frequent than in 1941, there were still air raids, notoriously the 'Baedeker' raids on the historic cities of Exeter, Bath, York, Norwich and Canterbury. Despite the restrictions on travel, however, people insisted on taking their holidays, watched cricket and football matches, and flocked to the cinema and the theatre. Those who stayed at home could listen to radio programmes, including the much discussed *Brains Trust* which began in September.

Towards the end of the year there was at last some better news from abroad. In the North African desert Montgomery, the new commander of the Eighth Army, masterminded a counterattack against the Germans at El Alamein. As the enemy retreated, church bells were rung in Britain for the first time since 1939.

In November, Allied troops landed in French North Africa and advanced into Libya. On the Russian front the German Sixth Army was pinned down at Stalingrad.

Perhaps the tide was turning. Churchill warned the nation that this was only 'the end of the beginning', but for the first time since 1939 people could begin to think about the future. The Beveridge report, outlining a system of welfare provision 'from the cradle to the grave', was widely welcomed.

JANUARY 1942

Edie Rutherford *Thursday, 1st.* Looks as if it will soon be goodbye Manila.[32] Well, anything we are obliged to relinquish now will be but temporary loss. I don't know how Hitler feels today, but were I in his shoes, I think I'd realise that I had not entirely got my own way, and feel mad that the English are still upright and their island uninvaded! Surely his mind must by now have just an inkling of the inescapable fact that he will lose this war? To me it seems impossible that he cannot begin to realise it even if he began with highest belief in his own power, which I feel sure he did. Russia continues to push 'em back. Good. Rommel not ours yet but we still seem to have the trump card.

Doris Melling *Friday, 2nd.* I was looking today at a recruiting poster for the ATS, which depicted a girl in ATS uniform, looking angelically up to heaven. I almost felt like writing to whoever was responsible for such an atrocity, to tell them that the only way to approach the women of this country is to say to them, 'You want your men back home; you want a normal existence, and the end of the war. Well then, get on with the job, and help to bring this about.' This is what the women want to know from their men: 'When are you coming home?' The only way to persuade them to do what perhaps they do not fancy doing, is to offer them something which they want, and show them how they can help to get things back to normal themselves. It is no earthly use exhibiting glamorous posters, or angelic ones, for that matter. Regarding the unpopularity of the ATS, I have made several enquiries; the women say the same: the uniform is responsible. I can't quite see the point of this: surely the uniform of the Wrens, for example, is hardly glamorous. Probably the WAAF is more popular because everyone is thrilled with the exploits of the airmen and navy and wants to be associated with these units. Show women how they can help to win the war, and by not joining up they are hindering the war effort.

Saturday, 3rd. I went home tonight. To my great surprise I   Henry Novy
came to a banquet. Mother had invited a doctor friend of theirs, and they had a pheasant cock sent by the director of Dad's firm. We had a huge meal, and in between the drinks I heard news of the Russian offensive. The Japs were making progress in Malaya, and they had captured Manila, fighting now for the fortresses in command of the bay, fighting in China, in Borneo. We talked about it all just a little, but more of our comments were reserved for the cider, and how nice the bird tasted.

Wednesday, 7th. I am in a new job from today, in the Reserve Medical Stores, where I type a few letters, and do a little indenting. There isn't much to do, and most of the time I went round looking at things, and trying to make the work out, or discover where the work was. It felt grand not to have to rush about cleaning the office in the morning, and lighting fires. I took things very easy, and for the first time since I came here I had time to think in peace, and do a little planning for our future London life. I had two letters this morning, but none from my Darling. I still felt a little worried about her, though when I planned for us I had more confidence, and felt a little more cheerful. I think we'll manage to get things done, though it may take some time to get a nursery. It is extraordinary how difficult it is to get the most essential things if you are a young married woman nowadays. There is nowhere to leave your baby, you can't get enough money to exist if you don't work, you have to go through a means test to get any extra, and the means test of the present won't mean a thing unless you can persuade the authorities that you used to live like a duchess, and that your husband was a stockbroker. Otherwise, little doing.

Muriel Green, under-gardener, Huntley Manor, Gloucester

Saturday, 10th. T and I went to nearest small town. I had to register. Fierce woman asked me dozens of questions about my job, age, etc. I was not expecting to be asked such a lot and thought at registration you were only asked your occupation, name, number and age. All about previous job, employer, insurance, nature of work, etc. I have a big form with more details still to send within seven days. Ever since I have been wondering if I am glad I am in a reserved occupation or not. I think I'm reserved anyway although the papers say agriculture and not horticulture.

After all here I'm happy enough, and though the work is miserable in this weather we get lots of fun out of it with the soldiers, get higher pay and better living accommodation than any ATS girl. It is true our working uniform is not shattering and we get no privileges (or not so many) as an ATS girl and have to face the elements more but I think we get more admiration and are just as useful to the war effort. The smug haughty looks of the forces women at us in towns when we bear no mark of our 'nobility' and 'heroism' but prefer civilised best clothes sometimes make us wish we had a smart provided uniform of the forces, entries to the canteens, travel warrants home and seven days (instead of once a year and every Sunday off) quarterly. Anyway, I have had nine months' experience I shall not forget or ever regret.

George Springett

Monday, 19th. Snow. Violet received her 'call-up' papers. She said, 'Coo! What *shall* I do? Alf says he doesn't want me to go into any of the uniformed services. I won't! I won't! *I won't!* I won't go!' she yelled.

'Well,' I said, 'what are you going to do?'

'I shall get Alf to write a letter and complain and say I can't go.'

'But you *can* go.'

'I know, but I don't want to!'

'Why?'

'I don't want to go into the uniformed services or go on the land. It would kill me. You have to have awful inoculations.'

'Perhaps Alf can't do anything. This is conscription. You were saying the other night that we all should do our bit and you were grousing because I am a pacifist. Now you are trying to dodge your obligations!'

'I shall be a Conscientious Objector!'

'You can't now. You should have registered as one – or refused to register.'

'Why can't I be a CO? I object to going!'

'That's not conscience!'

'What is it, then?'

'Just a private objection.'

'Well, I object, anyway!'

Tuesday, 20th. Snow. By the way, I must mention that I'm growing a beard! Chin and upper lip only. I'm shaving the sides of my face. It's very interesting from MO aspect to record the comments of my friends:

Mr Robinson (aged 66) – 'What's all that dirt on your chin?'

Mrs Robinson (48) – 'I think beards make men look old. My father had a beard.'

Violet – 'How silly! What do you want to grow a beard for?'

Stella Thompson (18½, Communist) – 'Gosh! I like it. It's coming through reddish, though – I hoped it would be black. I bet you shave it off if people remark!'

Max, friend aged 21 (middle-class) – 'It will look grand when it's grown. At present it looks bloody awful. Guess I'll grow a moustache, too.'

Many other comments were made. I observe that *working-class* people *object* but people of my own class (mid-class) are more tolerant. I have created a sensation among my Communist friends! I shall continue to allow it to grow. My friends seem more interested in commenting on my beard than talking about the war!

FEBRUARY 1942

Muriel Green   *Tuesday, 10th*. I'm 21 today! I shan't forget my 21st birthday. Apart from getting two greetings telegrams and achieving the first bath for nearly a month it has been the last word in flat. Totally depressing in fact. My oldest girlfriend sent me a wallet knowing the difficulties of wearing breeches, etc., when a handbag looks odd, and the next-door girls gave me a jar of raspberry jam. The staff at my former job and an old lady from home sent me the telegrams. Jenny gave me £1 and apart from that no one else hit the right day or else I'm forgotten. As for my birthday activities, it was spent in literally 'digging for victory'. Guillotining worms with a spade – uh! We gained an entrance into the manor house to bath and had a good soaking. We needed it. No birthday dinner or tea. Muddling scrap dinner and morbid tea as Mr and Mrs R arrived back from hospital in a fainting condition. She had her arm X-rayed, broken and reset and looked ghastly. I feel very melancholy about my birthday. I remember when Jenny was 21 how jolly it was, the large iced cake and presents and outing. I remember I thought what a lovely time I would have when I would be 21 and the things my poor father promised me. Perhaps tomorrow will be more pleasant but it won't be the same on a different day. I never thought there'd be a world war when I was 21. I certainly never thought I'd be a gardener.

Sunday, 15th. Breakfast at 8.45 a.m. and left after 10 and Henry Novy
walked into town. The food at the youth hostel was excellent
and rationed things not meanly distributed. The other young
people who included war workers and Conscientious Objectors
had come from varying directions of radius of 50 miles. Some
had cycled but most had hitchhiked there. They all were used
to hostelling and frequently spent their weekends there. Several
of them were from Coventry, Birmingham and Bristol and said
how lovely it had been during the period of the blitzes to go
out into the country for weekends. We had a packed lunch and
spent day in sightseeing in the town. After tea we returned
arriving 7.30 p.m. I had been expecting the fall of Singapore.[33]
I'm feeling very hopeless about the war situation. The Far East
is bad enough but when you hear the English Channel is a clear
passage to three German battleships[34] ... well!

Thursday, 19th. I went to the NAAFI tonight, and spent my
first soap coupon. I ran out of toothpaste, shaving cream, and
soap all at the same time. As I was also out of money it made
things very awkward, especially as I spend so much now going
home two or three times a week. My day was heavy again,
with much hard typing of lists with many copies all the time.
It doesn't tempt me to do very much at nights, and the main
thing I want is sleep, and get to bed, at whatever cost when
ten o'clock comes. Only a quarter of an hour now, and I'll get
into bed. I should have had a bath, but I had no soap. I still
have no razor-blades.

The war is now in the background just a little. Churchill and
the coming debate on production and the war will no doubt
provide excitement, and probably another vote of confidence.
The war in Russia has flared up again to a climax, with a heavy
Russian offensive in the Leningrad region, perhaps their first
decisive move to split the German ring. I was reading in *Soviet
War News* that the German defences there were excellent, and
therefore would be hard to beat down.

Port Darwin has been bombed twice, and now it looks that the Japs might make their defensive move towards Australia before their offensive moves towards Burma and India. This spring I imagine with some fear four big offensive moves by the partners, the Nazis pointing to Egypt and the Caucasus, meeting in Iran, the Japs to Burma, India and Mongolia. But only a few days ago my big fear was invasion of this country. Maybe it still is. That would terrify me, with the present state of our military preparedness and political wrangle. Christ knows what would happen. So many things seem to happen all at once. It makes me all dizzy and upset. Sometimes I forget that I must make a move pretty soon now myself, and try to improve my position. It seems far in the background with all the turmoil in front of us.

Monday, 23rd. It was Red Army day, the whole world celebrated it. Messages from Americans, British, French, messages from the reactionaries even, all took their hats off to the Red soldiers' effort. As Jack told me tonight: 'It hasn't half shown up Communism that has, no other country could have done it, only a Communist country, with the people really behind it.'

Pris rang me tonight, and we talked about the things we still have to do before the flat is finally settled. I had a short note from her tonight, she wrote as she was going to bed, and it made me happy to read it, and feel that we are so close and happy, with our home and our baby to work and fight for. It only makes me eager to do more, and want to take part in the war, I hear it everywhere around me. People want to take part in the war, and the hospital doesn't give them the ghost of a chance. Today they posted men of forty to field ambulances, one of them with five children, who can't hardly see, and doesn't go out at night for fear of getting run over! Civilian medical boards have classified these men A1, and that's apparently as far as the authorities will look. It makes one mad to think there are men here of 20 or 25, doing nothing, living near home, fit, and who would like nothing better than get out and do their bit for their country. The wasted skill, the wasted will to fight, and the terrible dreariness and dullness of life on their enthusiasm.

Thursday, 26th. After a year of furious argument against this **Len England** I have come to the conclusion that the army is dead right in keeping a soldier away from home. Not so much from home as from wife and sweetheart. If there is no reason why a soldier wants to get away from work or from camp, he won't mind the sudden imposition of an extra duty. If he knows that some-body is waiting for him, wondering what has happened to him, then any extra work, any overtime, puts him thoroughly out of sorts. The war becomes of secondary importance. I know this well enough simply by meeting Dorothy, and loathing the idea of overtime just because I know that it means not meeting Dorothy. And I know that the position is infinitely accentuated with men with sleeping-out passes who have the comforts of home as well as the comforts of a wife. Tucked away miles from either, there is a tendency to argue for total effort given only the time for the daily letter and the quarterly leave.

MARCH 1942

Tuesday, 3rd. Cool. Went to a local outfitter to get a pair of trou-   **George** sers. The manager produced a lot of 'Utility' trousers: shoddy   **Springett** stuff. I said, 'Haven't you got any pre-war trousers?'

'None at all, sir.' Then followed a long conversation about the war. He thought the war was a racket. Said that he thought it was due to the fact that the Church was corrupt. I told him that I was a CO. He nodded. After a bit more talk about paci-fism, he went to the back of the shop and produced a really fine pair of *pre-war* trousers.

'Didn't think I had 'em,' he remarked, and continued, 'I was

a CO in the last war. One of our assistants here is a CO too!' So
had I not mentioned that I was a CO I doubt if I should have
got those pre-war trousers ...

Very little war talk. Mr Thompson remarked, 'I expect the
Japs will get Rangoon.'

Monday, 9th. Milder. As I write, 9 p.m. news is being read.
Troops withdraw from Rangoon. How soon! Looks like a bit
of a wangle between the British and Japs. Doesn't seem as if
British have done much fighting for the city. Well, one can't
blame 'em! Mr and Mrs Robinson heard the news without
making a single comment – not even a grunt!

I forgot to mention that this morning I saw a friend who
refused to register for fire-watching (I've done the same).
They've just copped him for it. Like myself, he will do voluntary
fire-watching but won't be *compelled* to do it. He remarked, 'This
country is getting more and more Nazified every day.' I agreed.

Nella Last *Sunday, 22nd.* As we sat over lunch my husband said suddenly,
'Come on, let's go to Morecambe and not wait till Easter – who
knows what will happen by then.' I'm always game for a 'day
out' and we were off as soon as we were ready. Morecambe was
as busy as a 'season' day and we got out and looked at the shops
on the front. I'd heard of the 'luxury' at Morecambe but I gazed
in amazement in the chemists' shops. Displays of perfume, van-
ishing cream, cold cream, talc, face powder, lipsticks, combs
and nailbrushes – and good makes too. Yardleys, 4711, Ponds
– even Cotys! There was a shop full of toys and in one corner
of the window was a big box of packets of drawing pins – and
flints for lighters. The grocers had huge stacks of sardines and
salmon, even lobster.

We always do tea at the same place, Stocks, on the front.
It's a huge room with dozens of tables and wide windows over-
looking the sea. We did not feel very hungry and asked for
'afternoon tea' but were only brought bread and butter and

jam and the waitress apologised for not having cakes – she said there had been long queues yesterday when crowds flocked into Morecambe with it being so nice a day.

I looked round in shocked surprise at the *masses* of food served up. Most people were having a cooked tea, sausage, fish or chops with chips … People in restaurants should be made to give up coupons – it's a scandal in Barrow where men can get meat meals in the yard – and their wives boast that 'meat rationing is no trouble to them for they *always* get Dad's share divided at home'. Coupons had to be given up in the last war for meat meals – why not in this? With fish, cheese, egg or 'vegetable' dishes there was no hardship and no one grumbled then.

Friday, 27th. I *do* so love to do 'ordinary' things like jam- or cake-making and when I do nowadays I get more pleasure when to do so means thought and 'scrounging'. I came to bed to write and rest my aching back. I felt a great sympathy for many women who are working in industry and having to 'keep on' day after day and for all the tired ones who are doing harder work than they are used to doing and for the lonely ones who have not even the consolation of letters or doing their boys' washing and mending.

APRIL 1942

Wednesday, 8th. A nice morning, sun shining and not so much wind. Reading the war news each morning in the hope of finding something to cheer me up, is always disappointing nowadays. It seems to me that if India gets its Home Rule,[35] there is sure to be internal strife on account of religion. Cripps apparently thought that he could settle matters in a week or so, but no one seems to know for certain how to deal with such a mixture. It ought to have been settled in peacetime and not left to the hurry of the last moment.

Herbert Brush

I wonder what sort of mercy the Japs will expect from the Australians, after the way they murdered their captives in New Britain.[36] It makes one hot all over to think of our men being tied up and then deliberately bayoneted by the little grinning devils, and there seems to be no cause to doubt the accuracy of the story, though it is a little surprising that a single victim was allowed to live and get away to talk of what he had seen.

Muriel Green   *Saturday, 11th.* Morning at work and afternoon we went to Gloucester. Mock invasion on. We were going to a meeting of the WEA addressed by Sir Richard Acland [co-founder of the short-lived Common Wealth party], on reconstruction. From down the street we could see smoke outside the Shirehall and realised it was gas being let off. It was then 6.45 p.m., the time the meeting was due to start, so if we waited for the gas to clear we should have been late. We had taken our gas masks as instructed. By the time we got down the street to the Shirehall no gas was visible. We had not taken our gas masks out. Very few masks were visible except soldiers and an odd child. From across the street all *looked* OK, so we crossed.

A whiff of tear-gas, pleasant smelling, hit us in the nose as we were going into the building. A couple of soldiers wearing respirators were stuck outside on guard. We hurriedly turned and crossed the street, the whiffs we had inhaled having no effect. We saw a few people then enter the building so decided the meeting must be on inside. They appeared to go in without gas masks and with no ill effects. It was now 6.50 p.m. so we decided to risk it. We crossed the street again and arrived at the entrance at the same time as three men. They were not wearing gas masks and we asked the soldiers if the meeting was on. They had some difficulty in understanding the masked guards.

By this time we had had several whiffs of the invisible evil and so had they. They made a dash for the door and we followed, our eyes now smarting. We reached the inside and the inner room contained some gas but as it was obviously lesser it seemed no use producing our gas masks to wear *after* coming through the worst. Our eyes were running pretty badly by then. In a third room no gas had penetrated, and about a dozen people were standing laughing while they wiped their eyes. After wiping ours (we could only find one hanky between us) we went into the meeting which had already started.

Many other latecomers arrived with red eyes or looking dishevelled through wearing gas masks. Afterwards I wished I had put on my gas mask. If I had known it was so thick at the entrance I should have done. I suppose it was a case of feeling 'silly' to put one on when other people had not got theirs on. If everyone had been wearing theirs I should have put mine on. Everyone else was carrying theirs too. Talk about herd instinct! It was a case of rather having tears than looking a fright in a gas mask. The gas soon wore off and we enjoyed the meeting tremendously. Sir R. A. has wonderful principles and ideals in common ownership. If only human nature wasn't so abominable to make them seem too perfect to be accepted. The gas had gone when we came out.

Wednesday, 15th. A year ago today I began to train as a gardener and left home. I never regret leaving home but sometimes regret becoming a gardener. On fine days I don't; on wet days I do. I sometimes think it would be nicer in the services but doubt if you can join from a reserved occupation if you tried. Weekends I am quite satisfied but such long working hours seem tiring.

The war doesn't seem any 'wonner' after my year of effort. It is not particularly encouraging to think of scratching soil for several more years for 52 hours a week in summer and 48 in winter for the minimum agricultural wage, especially when you take pride in growing the vegetables and fruit to find so much wasted. Every garden is nearly as bad for that, but this is far the worst I have been in. I suppose in everything there is waste: that is what is the matter with the country. There seems so little full effort and so little result – so far. We may be tiring the Germans with air raids, blockades and Russian supremacy but what of the Japanese? I am not one of those people who think when we have cracked the Germans the Japs will go under. I suspect the white races will have to fight harder than that against the yellow and for a long time.

Herbert Brush *Sunday, 26th.* Have you noticed what a large number of people say 'I done it' instead of 'I did it'? I often hear it used by people who ought to be more careful. 'He done it' or 'They done it' is also frequently used. I don't think that I ever use these myself or I should not notice them in others.

For the last few days a couple of fast planes have flown close over the houses round here as though the pilots were trying how near to the chimney-pots they could go without touching. Just now I was in the garden and they went over about 100 feet up; one chasing the other as though they were having a game. Yesterday one of them came back three or four times. I suspect that the pilot has a girl in this neighbourhood and is showing her what he can do.

MAY 1942

Muriel Green *Friday, 1st.* We finished off the onion-planting at 15,000 plants. Heard a despicable tale today about the nursery garden where men are employed. A prejudice by the foreman against women and an order was given to the men that if they gave any assistance to any of the land girls, they lost money for the time. Two of our garden girls got hopelessly stuck one wet day in the clay on the hill with a full heavy cart. They asked the men in the nursery to give them a hand to shift it. The men refused, saying it was against orders. Both the girls were rather exhausted with the rain and the load and if the semi-crippled man employed in the garden had not been passing and helped they said they should have cried. I had not heard the tale until today. They said they were so disgusted, they would not tell anyone. If it had been me I should have raised hell over it, and told the squire who owns all the estate including our garden and the nursery. Talk about Nazis! There's lots of people as bad here.

Tuesday, 5th. The first few days of this month have passed quietly so far as I am concerned, and nothing untoward has happened around here. Today, however, it has been very good to hear that we have taken possession of Madagascar[37] – quite the brightest war news for a bit – and it is also pleasing to note that the Germans are losing quite a good percentage of their nightly bombers which they have been sending over for the last ten nights or so. But everyone I have spoken to thinks the enemy is quite mad to waste petrol and bombs, to say nothing of planes, on bombing such places as Exeter and Bath. They seem to have a most perverted idea of the morale of the English, if that's what they are trying to get at, and I suspect it is. **Frank Edwards**

Wednesday, 6th. A fine morning and no sign of the rain which is so badly needed on the plots. Watering with a can and cold water does not make seedlings grow, and I have begun to think that it is a waste of energy, though it keeps the plants alive. **Herbert Brush**

W told me that Norwich was hit very badly: 250 people were being buried in one grave the day she was there, and they say that nearly 10,000 are homeless. Jerry did not hit the castle or the town hall or the cathedral, mostly shops and small houses. The ugliest town hall in the kingdom: a bomb would have made it look more interesting.

Saturday, 16th. Queues for a few things seemed to have ceased, in particular for cigarettes. I don't think I have seen a queue for these since the higher prices came into force. On the other **Frank Edwards** hand the queues for animal foods seem to get longer than ever. Books still seem to be having a good sale though the new ones are an awful price – 8/- and 9/- for books which were 3/6d or 4/- before the war. But libraries have a great popularity these days as more people than ever are to be seen reading in buses and tubes. For thank goodness books are one of the few things one can get without coupons or the question of points.

When the conductor came upstairs to get his fares this afternoon he picked up a woman's glove evidently dropped by a passenger. When he got down the front of the bus he picked up the other glove and so found the pair. Holding up these he said, with a laugh, 'Two coupons, anybody?' which amused the passengers and as he came to go downstairs he said to me, 'No business anywhere, is there?'

Muriel Green *Monday, 18th.* General amusement among the garden staff today. A new girl was announced as coming to work. It was a pouring wet morning. A woman about 38 turned up in a man's suit. She told the disher-out-of-jobs she wanted to work outdoors. Everyone else had a cushy greenhouse job all day: B on the grapes and P and I staking carnations. The new dame hoed paths all day *without* a coat in her shirt-sleeves! She was wet through, but not damped in spirits, no! At five she came to Mr S and thanked him for having her, saying how she had enjoyed herself. All day she was absolutely full of enthusiasm. Everyone hurrying by in mackintoshes she told how she was enjoying working. She had walked four miles to work; she is evacuated from town with a husband and two children and is coming from 9 to 5 for five days a week. She hardly left off for meals and seems to think she is winning the war.

Herbert Brush *Tuesday, 19th.* A bright, warm morning and the barometer has risen a quarter of an inch during the night. It is pleasant to read about so many Nazis being slaughtered, but I wonder how many Russians are 'done in' at the same time. Moscow gives the number of German casualties and Berlin gives the number of Russian casualties. I wonder if either is anywhere near being accurate.

I tried in two places today to get razor-blades, without success. I have plenty of old blades but it does not seem possible to put an edge on these. If it was possible I expect that the makers would be asking for them to be returned, but I've seen no such request as yet.

Have you noticed how many different pronunciations there are of 'Nazi' by people who speak on the broadcasts. Churchill says 'Nazzi', others say 'Nartzi' or 'Nertzi' or 'Nassie'. I like Churchill's the best as he puts a snarl into the word.

JUNE 1942

Tuesday, 2nd. What a glorious summer day it has been. I haven't   Frank Edwards
seen the sky so blue or felt the sun so warm for a long time. It
must be summer really arrived.

Well, we certainly started something with Saturday's great raid,[38] for we now know that last night we made an encore of it, but on a different town. And neutral observers now put the estimated number of dead in the Cologne raid as 20,000. This may not be correct of course but what of the Germans' claim of 111 killed? It isn't as though the difference was but little. And it more than ever seems to prove that they dare not admit anything like the facts. German morale is very different to that of the British.

And I think the RAF must be going out there again tonight for as I write this I can hear planes passing over at intervals. It is well past midnight. I have not so very long come in, and it looks just the kind of night for a raid. The air is still very warm. The sky is beautifully clear and the barrage balloons are riding high. A true summer's night; it does not make one think of air raids with death and destruction raining down from the sky. It doesn't seem as though this summer's night can be turned into all the fury of Hell, but I think it's going to be – for the enemy.

Herbert Brush *Thursday, 11th.* My stiff neck is feeling better since I did a little gardening this morning. One of W's customers gave her about 50 spring onions yesterday and I have planted them, partly on the plot and partly in the garden. It seems quite impossible to grow onions, or lettuce, from seed on the allotment; no one has any luck with these; there must be something in the ground but so far we have not found out for certain what it is. It is not wireworm but some other enemy to the 'Diggers for Victory'.

9 p.m. I have been on the allotment most of the day, earth-ing up the late crop of potatoes. I was told that there was a slight frost this morning, but I have not noticed any ill effects on my plot. I put in some melon seeds a week or two back; they came through yesterday, and were eaten off this morning, in spite of soot around them.

Monday, 15th. I'm afraid that my letters recently have been dull reading, as I have had nothing to write about outside the common routine of daily life in a place where nothing seems to happen, and even the traffic along the road is growing less and less, and, at the moment, there is no sound to be heard except the song of a thrush or a blackbird and the occasional call of a cuckoo. If I went to the garden gate it would be ten to one against a single person being visible in the quarter-mile stretch of road.

I can't help thinking of Christine as I sit here, and wonder-ing whether she is a prisoner among the Japs, and obliged to live on one bowl of rice a day. If she escaped, surely some of us would have heard from her by now, though of course, a letter might easily take six months to come, or more.

I don't like the Libya news on the wireless this evening, but it is impossible to get a clear idea of the position from what is given on the wireless or in the newspapers. The Nazis must have managed to carry a lot of supplies and men over from Italy in spite of our navy, though a good percentage was lost on the way. But Hitler does not care how many men are killed if he can get his way; he has many more millions to draw on, and in a few years the wholesale manufacture of babies will give him a new army of fanatics, all of them even more like beasts than their parents. What will they be like after a second generation, if the war lasts so long? Inhuman bloodthirsty monsters, destroyers of everyone weaker than themselves, until the time comes when they will destroy each other.

Tuesday, 16th. My last day's leave. Tonight I cried bitterly. I had not cried for ages. It was not about going back. It was about the morbid depression settled on the East coast. It is pitiful. And this everlasting rain makes it seem doubly so. I cried because of the war. It has altered our life which can never be the same. To see the desolate emptiness of the seaside upsets me. When you are away and Mother writes to say the latest desecration, the latest boy missing, the latest family to sacrifice, it is just words. But in the home it is mortifying. Life will never be so sweet as before the war and the last two summers and early '39 were the most perfect years of my life when all seemed young and gay. I could have cried for hours had I not known it was upsetting Mother as she thought it was because I was unhappy in the West Country.

Muriel Green, Snettisham, Norfolk, on leave

Sunday, 21st. 6.30 p.m. I was tying up gooseberry jam in one pound pots when I heard the broadcast that Tobruk had been taken.[39] This gave me a considerable shock, as so much depends on that port. Now Rommel will have a try for Egypt without delay. This is the worst bit of news I have heard, and I can't help thinking that there is something wrong at the head of our army in Libya. There were only Italians in Tobruk the last time we took it, now there will be Germans to defend it.

Herbert Brush

Frank Edwards   *Monday, 22nd.* The news regarding the fall of Tobruk is most
disappointing and is rather disgusting, too; and to quote a
Kenway and Young expression, 'It makes you think.' Most
certainly there is something very radically wrong with the way
things are going and it is high time there was a proper clean up.
In any case we must be told the reasons for this sudden defeat;
for it is nothing else than a defeat.

JULY 1942

Frank Edwards   *Sunday, 5th.* The news from the East has been better the last
day or so, and today is not an exception. The battle for Egypt
is still a ding-dong affair and whilst I am not over-optimistic,
I certainly am not pessimistic at the moment, anyway. I have
just a feeling that now things are going a bit better they may
continue to do so. That's all, no more and no less.

A new series of programmes called *I am John Citizen* opened
on the wireless tonight. This was an honest-to-goodness he-man
programme and thank goodness did not include any crooners or
jazz, both of which I am heartily sick of. No, it was a programme
having plenty of guts and I felt was entirely representative of
John Citizen. Mr Charles Dorning who is the John Citizen in
this programme has entirely got the right idea of a new kind of
broadcast, and I shall look forward to the next of the series.

Herbert Brush   *Thursday, 16th.* My watch is still going, so evidently its bath in
methylated spirit cleared away a speck of dirt from somewhere
in the working parts. You can't get a watch cleaned or mended
in London under a month or six weeks.

There is not a square foot on my allotment now which has
not something or other planted on it; and I still have scores of
plants growing and just ready to plant out, with no space available. As it is, I have crowded things so that they will have scarce
room to grow. The borough council are actually repairing the

garden walls from which they tore down the iron railings a few weeks ago. Three men have been busy during the last few days; 'busy' is the wrong word to use when writing about corporation workmen working on a job. I ought to have said, 'Three men have been on the job.'

The war news seems to get worse and worse, and makes one wonder when the second front is to begin. This, to me, seems the right time to throw a big army into France, and to get them to re-enter the war, but of course there may be many things which are against this being done, the greatest of which may be Libya. I wonder whether the Germans know more about our intentions than we do at home here.

Sunday, 26th. A nice morning, but spoiled by the war news. I wonder when and where we shall start the second front which we have promised to do this year. An alert sounded at 6.30 a.m. and I got up, put on my trousers and shaved, then the 'All Clear' went and I got back into bed. Another alert at 7.15 a.m., so this time I got up, but by the time I had dressed the second 'All Clear' sounded. My giddy feelings returned yesterday and have not quite gone this morning, but the precautions I took last night have kept me busy this morning attending to nature, so maybe I shall be all right again soon.

The rain ceased and I went to the Museum this morning. I walked along Charing Cross Road without buying a book and went into the National Portrait Gallery which happened to be open and free between one and four o'clock. A stony-faced guardian sat on a chair near the door of the room in which the exhibits were hung, to see that I did not touch or mutilate the paintings. As I was the only one there he could keep his baleful eye on me. I looked at him as I came out of the door and was quite ready to say good morning or even smile, but his stony expression did not change so I said nothing and came out.

I went across the road past [the statue of] Nurse Cavell and had a look at the artist near the railings at St Martin-in-the-

Fields. He was trying to sell his picture of Stalin, painted from an illustration in some newspaper, and very good, as far as I can judge a painting, and I had just been looking at many which must be good or they would not be in the Nat. Gal. He was offering his painting, so he said, at the price of the canvas plus the paint, as he was hard up. He stopped when he saw me and asked how I was getting on. I asked him whether he was hungry and offered him some of my lunch which W had given me this morning, and this he accepted with thanks. He likes W's sausage rolls and this time I gave him a few cheese straws, nice peppery ones. The next time I see him I expect that he will have something to say about them, but I always feel a little doubtful whether a glass of beer might be more in his line, though I have no reason for thinking so.

Tuesday, 28th. 9 a.m. I woke up this morning at 3 a.m. to the sound of gunfire over London, and away to the north I could see the shells bursting and I thought I heard the bang of a bomb or two, but was not sure. That plane went away to the east and things were quiet for a few minutes and then began again near the same place, but this time more intense and I could hear the noise of several planes. There was a fine display of bursting shells and enough noise to wake the dead, but D did not wake, so I yelled to her to go downstairs in case the planes came this way. One patch of shells I noticed all burst together in a kind of pattern and I thought, by the direction, that the chessboard of guns on Blackheath had at last got a chance to do what could be done. I noticed what I thought were the big yellow-red flashes from several bombs, but could not be sure. The night was perfect and the full moon was shining in a cloudless sky, there was no wind and I could hear people talking a long way off, but as I had only my trousers and shirt on I did not stay in the garden for long. An old warden told me I should catch cold, so I went back to bed and at 4 a.m. the sirens woke me up again for 'All Clear'.

AUGUST 1942

Saturday, 1st. Judging from the weather today the holiday bids   Frank Edwards
fair to be very enjoyable, for it has been nearly cloudless all day
with an abundance of sunshine. Despite the government's appeal not to travel, a great many people in the buses and tubes
were obviously making for one or other of the London termi-
nus stations, as indeed from wireless and newspaper reports
tonight, it was an amazing struggle at Paddington, in particular, this morning and thousands of people seemed determined
to put up with every possible inconvenience in order to have a
few days at the sea.

My own feelings are that such an exodus in such times as
these is disgusting to say the least of it. I hope people enjoyed
those inconveniences, each and everyone. And just fancy some
of the servicemen couldn't get home for their leave because
trains were full. I should think this made the travelling public
feel ashamed, that is if they have any feelings, and it would
seem that many of them haven't.

Friday, 14th. I have been on the plot this afternoon and it was   Herbert Brush
so pleasantly warm that I could sit there without doing any
work. I meant to mark off the 4 p.m. line on my sundial, but
at five minutes to four a black cloud came up and hid the sun
until five minutes past the hour, so I left it for another day. An
old man, the father of one of the plot-holders, came and gave
me his life history as I sat there. Not a very exciting life as he
had been a milkman all the time, but he hinted that he had
seen all sides of life, especially in the early mornings.

Old Inge was as pessimistic as ever when I met him in the
street this morning. According to him the Germans will soon
beat Russia and then turn their attention to us and give us
'what for' with 1,000 bombers every night, with 2,000 of them
every now and then. He is quite a depressing man to talk to
about the war, and no one can keep off that subject for long.

Tomatoes and potatoes may be of interest for a minute or so, but after that it is: 'the life we shall be leading by the end of the year – that is, if we are still alive.' Very depressing, but if this weather keeps fine I shall not worry myself unduly, taking as my motto: 'Sufficient for the day is the evil thereof.'

Frank Edwards   *Thursday, 20th.* Today the newspapers have been full of reports of yesterday's big raid on France.[40] This morning I received, to my astonishment, a notice from Wembley ARP informing me that I had been enrolled for fire-watching in that borough. As a matter of fact I have not lived in Wembley since last January and when I left, or rather before I left, proper notice in writing was given to the appropriate authority at Wembley. So much, however, for that borough's records. I am returning the notice to them at the same time stating that I am an authorised fire guard in the borough of Barnes.

Herbert Brush   *Monday, 31st.* I wonder how the Russians manage to take their big bombers to Berlin, and back without loss. I'm glad that they have started on Berlin as they will not be so particular where they drop their bombs as we are, and those Berliners ought to have their houses wrecked after what they did in London.

Coming along the road just now I met a retired policeman who crossed the road to speak to me. I wondered why he did so, but it soon came out that one of his sons had just been reported missing in a bomber but he did not know where. He has four sons, one in the army, one in the RAF and one a sailor, the other is in the Home Guard and he thought that this was the most dangerous of the lot until now. It was natural for him to want to tell someone about it and he was on his way to the allotment to tell all his friends. His son is only reported missing so he may not be dead, only a prisoner.

SEPTEMBER 1942

Saturday, 5th. It was six o'clock before we had tea and I had a   Nella Last
plate of lovely sliced tomatoes – picked fresh off my own two
plants. I must try next year to have more for they have been
such a good thing. Ripening slowly I've picked one or two off
as they were ready and not had them all on the dish and had
to 'use up all at once' before they went bad. My husband had
a lovely big brown egg – I *do* feel so lucky when I have such
'dainties' without difficulty and blessing my hens and garden
many times a day when I've eggs in water glass to cook with,
one hen laying for the table, cockerels to think of for wonderful 'pre-war' lunches and my 11 strong vigorous little pullets
growing up rapidly and all being well to start laying by the end
of October. I'd be more 'self-supporting' if I'd more room – it's
grand to feel 'independent' of shops and rationing.

Tuesday, 15th. I changed my book at Boots this morning and   Herbert Brush
took out *Goering* by Kurt Singer. According to Singer a German
professor has published Goering's genealogy and traced his
descent from 1042, covering all the great names in France,
Germany, Aragon, Poland, Sicily, Sweden, etc., but Singer
gives his earliest ancestor as a soldier in the Thirty Years War
1659. But, according to Singer, Goering is Germany's most
dangerous man. The book was published in 1939, so there may
be some truth in what he says. Goering is the man to watch.

Friday, 18th. Today we had at the factory the visit of a tank   Frank Edwards
complete with crew. The tank was a Covenanter weighing 18
tonnes and was a most interesting piece of work and aroused
great enthusiasm amongst the workers. All the crew wore the
shoulder flash of a very famous Guards regiment. And the driver
told me in course of conversation, that they had been mechanised for about 12 months; and several other Guards regiments
were also mechanised now. This young man (the driver) was a

very nice fellow and explained to me all about the workings of the tank. I found the turret a most interesting part of it and inside it has to be seen to be believed.

Every opportunity was given to the employees to inspect the tank inside and outside, and the crew answered what must have amounted to hundreds of questions during the time they were with us – and they did not leave until 5 p.m. Before they went away they took a number of employees on board and took them for a ride just to finish up with. I understand that the visit paid to us is the fourth of a tour of war factories, in the London area, which started this week and will last three weeks.

Herbert Brush　*Tuesday, 22nd.* A dull morning and looks like more rain, but the barometer which was 29 in. last night has risen to 29.1 in. A man from the borough council came here yesterday to warn us to keep the dugout in good condition, as raids were expected to begin very soon: comforting, isn't it? As a matter of fact the 'Andy' has kept perfectly dry for several months now and I have not found a drop of water in the sump. Only cobwebs, but what can a spider expect to catch down there?

This evening I listened to the new *Brains Trust* with interest. One question was, 'How do spiders throw their strands of web across wide spaces?' Huxley gave what I thought was a very faulty, silly, answer. He suggested that the spider let itself down, walked across and climbed up to the selected spot, or words to that effect. Personally, I feel sure that the spider waits for a suitable gust of wind and then lets out silk until the end catches on something, then it climbs across, and if necessary strengthens the cable with a few more strands, as I have seen Matilda (the spider in the sun-house) doing, although I never saw her throwing the first strand, which she did at night.

OCTOBER 1942

Monday, 5th. I think that a dugout is fairly safe if the people   Herbert Brush
inside are a foot or two below the general surface of the ground.
A bomb would have to fall right on it to make sure of killing
the occupants. But so many of the Andersons I have seen in
London are practically on the surface with the soil piled round
them and very little on top: not enough to stop a bullet. Our
Andy is in a bank of clay and the top of it is several feet below
the high ground at the back. A good many of the sandbags are
rotting now in spite of the creosote I put on them before filling.
I shall have to put a few more bags on the roof if Jerry shows
signs of starting again.

The Morrison shelter is a good proposition, though you
might have to stay put for a time if the house fell on it. I don't
think that a Morrison would collapse in an ordinary house; they
are very strong in the right direction.

Second front. I wish that I could see a solution to that
problem. It is all very well saying that we ought to start a
second front now, but personally I can't see where it is going
to start with a good prospect of success; and it *must* succeed or
it *must* not start. I think that the Russians are getting anxious
because we have not made a start with the army as well as with
the RAF.

Friday, 9th. Such a wild wet day and beyond baking and   Nella Last
tidying round in general I did a little housework for outside
work was out of the question. I baked bread and scones and
such a nice apple pie sweetened with syrup and a custard with
eggs from my water-glass bucket. The wind loosened the catch
on the hen-house gate and I was horrified on looking through
the window to see them wandering round the garden and I'd a
real task to get them in the run again.

I felt a black sadness wrap me. I thought of all the winter
ahead – the winter that started on the heels of the flying

summer – the hideous second front bogey felt so close I could not escape. I looked at the lads' faces – the average age could not have been more than 24. Mrs Parkinson touched my arm and said, 'What are you thinking about?' I said, 'Oh, I don't know – always be glad your Ian is only seven.' She said simply, 'I *am*,' and seemed to understand what I meant.

Saturday, 10th. I got another half-dozen dollies finished, all 'lady' dollies ... I feel I want to get them finished. I hate 'mass production' and only the thought of the parcels for prisoners of war spurs me on.

We have felt so little effects of war as yet except a little bombing, little in comparison to 'three-quarters of Stalingrad being demolished during the first bombardment'. We have had food, shelter and warmth when millions have had none – what will be the price we will have to pay? – we cannot expect to go on 'escaping', there *is* no 'escape' for any of us. I saw a neighbour's baby today and I felt a sudden understanding for those who 'refuse to bring babies into the world now'. All this talk of 'new worlds' and 'after the war', no talk of the suffering, the anguish before all this is over.

Margaret said tonight, 'I love coming in here, you know, you always make me laugh.' It struck a chord; I often, so very often hear it: at centre, canteen, at the shop. A joke, a pert reply can make people laugh, but suddenly tonight I realised how seldom I felt like laughing myself. Am I losing my sense of humour, I wonder? I rarely laugh at the wireless jokes and *ITMA* and similar shows leave me *cold* – if not irritated. Perhaps it's because I'm so tired – but then I don't get much relaxation and have to make my work my 'fun'. Perhaps it's because every minute of my life has to be planned and worked to a timetable to get my housework and cooking done, to get out to centre and canteen. I've so little time to read and none to lose myself in a book ...

Monday, 19th. I'm not well perhaps, nervy probably, or it's the time of year, but the longing to talk and listen to 'intelligent' conversation sometimes *chokes* me. There's the wireless, but I don't always agree, or understand, and would like to answer back. I tell myself sternly that I should 'count my blessings', think of the problems and the heartbreaks of others, and not grizzle. I talk myself into a decent frame of mind, as my fingers fly over my endless sewing, and then look up and see my husband's vacant expression when I pass a remark about something that is being broadcast. He has not been listening. I say, 'Are you tired?' and he says 'Yes' – or 'No'. I say, 'Are you worried?' and he says, 'No.' He told a friend that his main thought and chief delight was his food, that he *liked* eating and, as soon as he had had one meal, started looking forward to the next! He added piously that he was always thankful I was such a marvellous cook and manager! Sometimes I could YELL. I feel I'd like to peel off the layers of 'patience', 'tact', 'cheerfulness', 'sweetness' that smother me like layers of unwanted clothes. What would I find under all the trappings I'm credited with? I might be surprised! I know how people feel who 'disappear'. They get up one morning and look out of the window – maybe just up a long road, maybe the sun is shining, or there's a bright poster on a wall, or a ship's siren is hoo-hooing its way out to sea – and they go and go and GO.

Monday, 26th. What an awful day. I haven't known a more   Frank Edwards
miserable or depressing [one] for a long time, for it has simply poured with heavy rain all day. This morning soon after 11.30 there was an alert and shortly afterwards we had the danger signal at the works and this lasted about ten minutes. Some of the girls sought shelter, though not many.

    This evening when I got to Home Guard I was given a notice by the o/c telling me that I was being transferred to another platoon in the same company. This will make it much better for me as this platoon works from this district, in actual fact quite close to my home, and so it will cut out travelling which I have had to do until now. My first parade in the new platoon will be on Friday evening next.

NOVEMBER 1942

Herbert Brush *Monday, 2nd.* The museum is closed for a fortnight, so I took the bus as far as Regent St and went to have a look at *The Battle for Fuel* which is free entrance. On going in one enters a coal-mine very dimly lighted, with dummy miners working at the coal-face and a real live pit pony eating hay. People are warned not to go near as the pony is likely to snap. Through the coal-mine one enters the exhibition proper where every possible way to save fuel is illustrated; it must have cost a fortune to fix up this exhibition, so let us hope that it has the desired effect. I think that the only thing I learned was that a two-gallon bucket holds about 12 lb. of coal or 8 lb. of coke.

Frank Edwards *Saturday, 7th.* Still the news continues very good and Rommel has certainly got it in the neck this time.[41] This week's news has certainly been a tonic to people, stirring them on to still greater efforts and further sacrifices.

As a change from films about the war, I went to see the much heralded American picture *Yankee Doodle Dandy* this evening at the Warner Theatre, Leicester Square. I enjoyed the film very much and there were some good rousing songs in it. There were many American soldiers in the audience – in fact the whole programme was, except for the news, practically American, and even the organ interlude by Mollie Forkes was of American numbers. It struck me that this theatre specially gives an eye to looking after the entertainment for the Doughboys.

Herbert Brush *Sunday, 8th.* Today is fine, the sun quite warm and the baro-meter rising rapidly. The war news is comforting after such

a long spell of doubtful reading. If the west coast of Africa is
to be regarded as the second front, it will take a long time to
get into Germany, but I can dimly see what the move means,
and unless Hitler has more men in Africa than we know of he
will soon be in trouble, even with the help of those devils, the
French. Can we trust any of them?

Tuesday, 10th. A bright morning, but the barometer is dropping back again. The war news makes good reading now, so
different to a month or so ago. I wonder where Rommel has
gone to now; he must be feeling worried as he won't dare to
go back to Germany unless he can shift responsibility to some
other general.

I wonder whether we shall begin now to give Italy hell; I
hope so, though I don't feel for the Italians the same hate I feel
for the Germans. I shall not be surprised if the French fleet is
handed over to Germany for their use in the Mediterranean.

Wednesday, 11th. Suddenly realised the news has become excit-   Muriel Green
ing. I had got so tired of advances and withdrawals in Egypt
for the past few years I did not realise this one was anything to
jump about over. It is marvellous the Americans striking the
other side, I really think things are beginning to happen and
that victory is on the way. As I raked up the Brussels sprouts'
leaves I had it in my mind all the while that next year when the
said leaves wanted raking up the war might be over!

Wednesday, 11th. Today was Remembrance Day. As far as I   Frank Edwards
could see everyone was wearing a poppy or poppies. Lots of
people wore as many as three or four poppies, which set me
wondering if perhaps each one was for someone at present in
the services, belonging to the wearer.

At eleven o'clock Big Ben chimed and was put out on
our factory wireless loudspeakers, and whilst the work didn't
stop, there seemed to be a sudden quietness in our office. The

carpenters who are at present making alterations to our office went on very quietly and ceased their hammering for two minutes. Also there were no incoming telephone calls on any of the six phones in our office during that two minutes. This fact was probably more coincidence than anything else, since the phones are hardly ever quiet.

Herbert Brush *Friday, 13th.* 3.50 p.m. There is some very heavy firing going on somewhere in the distance now; I can't quite locate the point, but it is eastward to southward from here. The only son of Mr Rogerson, the managing director of W's firm, is a pilot in the RAF; a month ago he was shot down in Egypt and reported missing and thought dead. Today, Friday the thirteenth, a card arrived from Germany saying he was a prisoner of war. Great rejoicing in the Rogerson family. What a relief it must be for them, after a month of mourning him dead.

Frank Edwards *Saturday, 14th.* This evening I spent a most enjoyable time for I have seen how men of the Merchant Navy enjoy themselves, when on shore, at their new West End club. This club is without doubt one of the finest service clubs in this country, and it is a revelation to see over this establishment.

Having a free evening I conceived the idea of getting a couple of theatre tickets and inviting a Merchant Navy man who would care to come to a show, to join me. So I called at the club with a parcel of magazines, which I had been saving, and mentioned the idea I had in mind to the receptionist.

It was not long before I had the companionship of a young Dutchman who was at a loose end for this evening, and so went along to see *Aren't Men Beasts?* starring Alfred Drayton and Robertson Hare. This is a scream of a show and we were soon doubled up with laughter. After the show my companion invited me, as his guest, back to the club.

Here I had a glorious opportunity of seeing how these men, ashore for the weekend, enjoy themselves. Each Merchant

Navy man is allowed one guest and there was a very happy crowd present. In the reading room, writing room, rest room, games room, restaurant, and bar they were to be seen. But the big crowd were to be found in the lounge where dancing was in full swing. Well, time soon goes and the evening was all too short, but it was certainly one of the most enjoyable I have spent for a very long time. I came away with an invitation to go along tomorrow afternoon to a tea dance and evening concert.

Sunday, 15th. Church bells ring ... and strange they sound. This   Edie Rutherford
diary a week behind time because I've had Husband at home ill and he can't bear to hear typewriter tapping. But I have not done much or even spoken to many as I have been tied to the house except for daily quick trot to shops or library. However, Himself should be back at work tomorrow so I can pick up diary again. We've had a lot of fog and dark days but the news is so much brighter that one can endure bad weather.

Tuesday, 17th. A nice morning with barometer steady, but it   Herbert Brush
is very cold. I dug and carried leaves in the allotment for an hour or so, but I sweated so much that I had to come home to change. Cold weather does not stop my perspiration when I exercise, and then, of course, if I stand still for a minute I begin to feel chilly. I wonder how long I should last in the Arctic regions, or even in Russia during the winter. There must be plenty of Germans constituted the same as I am, so I hope they will be sent to Russia.

What game do you think Darlan[42] is playing? I should not like to trust him as the Americans seem to be doing. I should not be surprised to learn that it is a 'put-up job' between him and the Germans, who can't trust Laval [prime minister of the Vichy government] to carry out their orders. Personally, I don't feel like trusting any Frenchmen now.

Muriel Green *Monday, 23rd.* We don't often hear the war talked about in
the gardens but this morning Mr S said, 'We've won the first
round in Africa all right. He'll come out of there like a scalded
cat.' I think we all feel we are winning now. P and I frequently
talk of when the war is over and the employment situation
with regard to women gardeners. Before things looked so good
we frequently talked about whether the war would drag on
long enough to conscript us from land to the forces. We both
thought it would, but now we say, 'Perhaps by the time this
job wants doing next year the war will be over.' 'Perhaps we
shall be off the land.' 'How long will they want the women in
the gardens?' Last week one of the unskilled women gardeners
after being lectured on some deplorable gardening error said to
Mr S, 'Oh well, the war will soon be over, then you can have
all men back in the garden and you'll have everything done
just how you want it!' He was surprised, but not convinced of
the certainty of getting what he liked from the men. In fact I
am sure he really prefers the work of the women, as they are
more adaptable, quicker and less dogmatic than his former men
under-gardeners.

Edie Rutherford *Wednesday, 25th.* Labour Exchange sent for me. Would I go to
Income Tax offices in suburbs about a job to replace a younger
woman? I went. Interviewed by a rather nice man in his thirties
and a very old man about seventy who was both ignorant and
silly. I did not go down well because: (1) I am 40, (2) I have
not worked for ten years, (3) I have not worked in Sheffield,
and (4) I had no Sheffield references. The condescension was
pitiful. One would think I was dying to work for them, which
I am not! By the time I came away several more women were
waiting to be interviewed, all junior to me, so I know that's
another job I don't get.

The Russians are still gaining ground.[43] Oh, how I hope
they keep it up and never retrace a step now till the day they
reach Berlin, for of one thing I am sure, we must all close in

on Berlin from every side this time and treat the Germans to a
victory parade of ours for a change.

Thursday, 26th. The killing of thousands of Germans in Russia   Herbert Brush
makes pleasant reading now, and I hope that it will be kept
up for a long time yet. It is the only way to convert young
Germans. I wonder how the Russians will treat the prisoners
they capture; on this will depend our friendly relations to a
great extent after the war; as it will show whether the Russians
are really converted to civilised life.

Sunday, 29th. I listened to Churchill[44] with a shadow on my   Nella Last
heart. It's bad enough to think privately all that he said, without
hearing it on the wireless – to see the long, hard and bitter road,
to feel the shadows deepen rather than lighten, to envy the ones
who think that Germany will collapse in the spring, to have
in mind always the slave labour, the resources of rich Europe,
to remember Goebbels's words 'that whoever starved, it would
not be Germany'. I thought of all the boys and men out East.
How long will it be before they come home? It's bad enough
for mothers – but what of the young wives? I felt my hands go
clammy and damp, and I put my toy rabbit down. I looked at
his foolish little face, such an odd weapon to be fighting with.
I never thought my dollies and soft toys could be used in my
little wartime scheme of life. I don't envy people with money
as I used to do, for most of them want it all for themselves; it's
best to have a little gift of making things. Three-and-a-half-ton
bombs on Italy. I'm sorry it has to be. I like Italian people. I
wonder what would happen if they revolted. I've read a lot of
nasty things about the Fascists, and I wonder if there are a lot
in comparison to the 'nice' Italians.

Monday, 30th. I listened to Churchill's speech last evening   Herbert Brush
and was duly impressed. I hope that we shall soon begin on
the southern part of Italy; though I would rather see bombs

dropped on Germany, more and more of those 8,000-pounders. These must be awful things to be within a mile of when they go off. The blast alone must kill even more than the material of the bomb.

Frank Edwards   *Monday, 30th.* I think everyone asked today had listened to Mr Churchill's talk on the wireless last night. The majority thought it very good and typical of Churchill. A few were a bit disappointed and I think this was because they had been rather misguided by the newspapers, one of which to my knowledge intimated that his speech would contain heartening news, not that it didn't – if only by way of the promised intensified bombing of Italy, but they thought, I think, something special was coming, and that is where some of [the] listeners were disappointed. But Churchill is always rather the other way, for he doesn't make promises and he can't say anything which could be turned to good account by the enemy, and I don't think any newspaper should forecast anything likely to lead people up the garden path.

DECEMBER 1942

Frank Edwards   *Tuesday, 1st.* In London today it has been prisoners of war (Red Cross) flag day. I hope, and from what I have observed, I really believe this flag day has had a great response. Everyone has bought a flag, and many have not just put a copper in the collecting box either. We have heard so much lately about our prisoners that I should say it has stirred one and all to give very generously.

More than once I saw people hurrying to catch buses at bus-stops, when flag sellers were calling 'Don't forget the prisoners', and the would-be travellers at once paid heed, and if they missed the bus – well there was always another to come.

On the radio tonight in the nine o'clock news details were

given of the Beveridge report. I haven't thought much about this yet so I will not, at this stage, pass any comments.

Wednesday, 2nd. Never since I first listened to a speaker on the air have I felt as interested as I was tonight by Sir William Beveridge. I'll feel a bit more hopeful about the 'brave new world' now, and begin to feel a *real* effort will be made to grasp the different angles of the many problems. His scheme will appeal more even to women than to men, for it is they who bear the real burden of unemployment, sickness, child-bearing and rearing – and the ones who, up to now, have come off worst. There *should* be an all-in scheme.

Nella Last

As I listened, my mind went back to the days when the boys and their friends argued and set the world to rights. I seemed to see Ted's solemn face peer up at me, from where he always sat, 'tailor fashion', on the rug. He thought I was a visionary when I spoke of a scheme whereby women would perhaps get the consideration they deserved from the state. Life has lots of puzzles about finances. Suddenly it came to me – if I was left, I'd have a 10s widow's pension, and a few pounds a year of my own, which would barely pay for clothes. My husband never believed in insurance and, beyond a policy of £200, due soon, never made any provision for dependants. I've never had more than just enough to manage on, and so what I *could* save was always for the boys' welfare. He said plaintively, 'I'll have to go on working till I die – I'll never have anyone to work for me, and keep me going like we kept my Dad.' I said coldly, 'Do you think I'd have *let* you retire at 52, and batten on the boys, as your lazy self-seeking old father did? I'd not have that, you know. I'd have worked myself.' Perhaps it was the thought of Beveridge's speech, but I got really wound up – got a few things off my mind.

Trouble with menfolk of my generation, they looked on women as 'to be cared for' – and did not realise how hard we worked, how small an allowance we had to bring up our families on, and when, as in our case, sickness and an operation had to be met and paid for, what a bitter struggle things could be.

Muriel Green   *Saturday, 5th.* A wet night, so too wet for digging. Only P, B and I turned up for work. Mr S gave me a 30-minute talk on the moral strength of coming to work on wet mornings. 'The present generation has no guts; what would happen in the factories if no one went on a wet morning? Ditto in Russia, ditto with all soldiers.' At last I got a job gathering moss off the grassy banks for making the Christmas wreaths. Afternoon after doing the fires, lights, etc. I went to meet Jenny in Gloucester.

We have had a row with our landlady. She hasn't spoken since we came home for breakfast. She is a violent-tempered woman and swiftly accuses us of things for which it is not our fault. This morning she went too far and knew she was in the wrong. We don't usually answer. This morning we did! She hasn't spoken since. Neither have we. She is the one that owes an apology to us. We can hold out as long as her. We went to tea at the home of a young woman we met at YHA meetings and WEA socials. We enjoyed it.

Herbert Brush   *Christmas Day.* The BBC was announcing the murder of Darlan when I got up, and I was not sorry to listen to that bit of news. So far I have not heard anyone express sorrow; Hardy remarked that the murderer ought to have the VC.

I have done an hour or so digging on the plot this morning and it was pleasant there, and I enjoyed listening to the church bells, though I must say, there was nothing much in the way of ringing to listen to from the churches in this neighbourhood.

W has managed to get plenty of Christmas food into the house somehow: yesterday we had duck and green peas, and today there is turkey. A vegetarian must miss a lot of pleasure he might have at Christmas if he could bring himself to eat a slice from the breast of a fat duck.

3.30 p.m. After a rest following my unusual dinner, I listened to the BBC world broadcast and to the King's speech. He
certainly has made a wonderful improvement in his delivery,
and did not stammer once; and even ventured to tell a little tale
of a boy carrying another boy on his back up a steep hill. The
last time I listened to him, it was really painful.

Christmas Day. Got up at 8.30 a.m. and after breakfast hearing   Muriel Green
the church bells in the valley decided to go down to church.
Most of the others were going on a ramble, but we get enough
rambling up and down hills in our work. A nice low church
Christmas service in village church with large congregation.
Christmas dinner began at the hostel at 1.30 p.m. At 4 p.m.
we were still sitting at the tables feeling blown out. It sounds
awfully vulgar and in fact bad taste in wartime, but we really
were in such a state of over-eating to get up. I think we all
felt we must eat everything because it was such a change and
all the rationing rules were defied. We had soup, roast pork,
Brussels sprouts, potatoes, stuffing, the vegetarians having a
large mock turkey which we all *had* to try after our meat. This
was followed by Christmas pudding made from pre-war recipe
(they had been saving fruit all the year for it) and custard, and
a mince pie each. We had non-alcoholic cocktails, etc., then
cheese and biscuits followed by coffee. Then, apples! I drew the
line at an apple. I can eat them any day at work!

After the washing up was over and the room tidied up (we
had a dozen crackers between about fifty of us, but it's surprising the mess they made), we sat round the piano and sang
carols and folk songs. No one knew more than one verse of most
of them but a few schoolteachers (obviously) and several in the
back row suggested popular jazz tunes, but we weren't allowed
to be lowbrow!

About 5.30 p.m. we had tea, Christmas cake and chocolate biscuits handed round and after began games and dancing
for the evening. The company here is mostly young, the men

noticeably under 19 or over 30. They acted several charades, often topical scenes being acted or mimed including Home Guard and Ministry of Labour interviews. We played Murder and other ridiculous games. A running buffet of sandwiches, trifles, flans, coffee and more non-alcoholic drinks was set up during the evening. Everyone was thoroughly friendly by now and a very jolly time was had by all. A certain percentage of the company have a mania for country dancing, which they inflict on the rest each night. We did ballroom dancing too to a gramophone. We did not go to bed till after midnight.

Boxing Day. It has been a grand Christmas up here, but somehow the atmosphere is more 'youth hostelly' than 'Christmassy'. I have always spent Christmas at hotels in pre-war days and then there was more genuine merrymaking and more Christmas spirit. I suppose it is the war that has altered that. I often feel sad when I pause to think during jolliness of young people, because I think, 'How many of these young men are doomed to kill and be killed?' I felt sad this weekend as I thought of a soldier of 30, one of the liveliest of the crowd who is on embarkation leave. He does not want to go. No one has talked 'war' though.

1943 THE TIDE TURNS

The year 1943 marked a turning point in the war. In January the German army in Stalingrad surrendered; from now on the Germans in Russia would be fighting a rearguard action as the reinvigorated Red Army began a remorseless westward advance. Meanwhile Churchill and Roosevelt had met in Casablanca, where they agreed to open a second front in Europe by invading first Sicily, then the Italian mainland. In March, Montgomery's Eighth Army broke through the German bridgehead in eastern Tunisia. Rommel, who was ill, returned to Germany, and in early May his successor Arnim surrendered, with fewer than one hundred tanks and no fuel. North Africa was finally liberated from the Axis powers.

The Anglo-American invasion of Sicily began in July, and within two weeks came news of the fall of Mussolini. By September, Allied troops had landed in Italy, whose new government soon agreed an armistice and declared war on Germany. The German homeland was increasingly subjected to attack by British and American bombers, with heavy raids on the industrial cities of the Ruhr, Hamburg and – in November – Berlin.

In Britain there was now a more confident mood. A fund-raising 'Wings for Victory' campaign was enthusiastically supported, and there were even hopes of the war ending by Christmas. The blackout was still in force and German air raids continued, though the roar of aircraft overhead was now more likely that of British and American bombers *en route* to Germany. By the end of the year, Britain seemed to be flooded with American soldiers and airmen: they were generally welcomed, but there was distrust, even resentment, in some quarters. What most people did not know was that they were 'over here' in preparation for an invasion of northern France, planned for the spring of 1944.

The American presence – and the absence of British men serving overseas – had an inevitable effect on personal relationships.

Women's magazines offered advice, but marriages broke down and single women were often the butt of local gossip. Many felt that the old values of loyalty and fidelity were under threat; equally, many women were beginning to appreciate that their active participation in the war effort had given them a new voice. This was to have a profound effect on the social ethos of post-war Britain.

JANUARY 1943

Nella Last   *Friday, 1st.* Such a dreadful day of battering rain and cold winds. I stayed in bed and rested till ten o'clock and wrote two letters and had a little read and then got up and packed my MO papers and made a sweet for tomorrow when the four Atkinsons are coming. Such a lovely sweet too, I feel so happy about it. I had a sponge sandwich from the grocer at Xmas – I don't like grocer's cakes but nowadays one has not to refuse anything offered in kindness, so I took it, thinking I could use it with custard on it for a hot sweet, but I overlooked the milk shortage. Today I got out a shallow glass bowl and have put in the sandwich and sprinkled a wine glass of port over. I opened a small tin of pineapple and drained off the juice and after cutting the fruit small I mixed it with the juice, made up a pint of jelly square melted and poured it over the cake – keeping back two tablespoons which I 'set' on a plate. When the jelly was set I poured over a layer of custard and tomorrow when I'm baking I'll keep back two whites of eggs and whip them with a little tin of cream I have and after piling it on the 'trifle' I'll decorate it with chopped jelly. I can see Margaret's eyes dance as she looks at it – she loves 'party food'.

Peter Baxter,   *Tuesday, 5th.* Anybody reading this diary will notice that since
25-year-old   I have been on a camp, my comments on war events are becom-
RAF corporal,   ing scarcer, and I am far more concerned with the immediate
Padgate,   facts of service life. I regret that, but it is inevitable. There are
Warrington,
Lancashire

newspapers provided for us in the NAAFI, but it is no exaggeration to say that from the time we get up in the morning until we've finished tea at 6 p.m. we never have ten minutes in which we can legitimately relax and read the paper. The brief breaks we get in the day's work are mostly taken up with discussing arrangements for our syllabus or other duties. By 6 p.m., the morning papers seem strangely out-of-date and in any case by that time they have usually disappeared or become disintegrated. I rely almost entirely, therefore, for war news on the radio, and the BBC news bulletins are not exactly stimulating. They all conform to pattern, and are too often padded out with a lot of blah-blah which I find most irritating, especially when read by that complacent, self-satisfied Joseph Macleod [writer and broadcaster]. I have always held that this lack of contact between the realities of war and most RAF non-operational units is a very bad thing. I should like to see everybody given a couple of short talks weekly by the education officer, on the progress of the war and the general significance of events. How I should love that job! For most fellows here, the real war scarcely exists. Their whole life is choked up with drill and polishing floors and scrounging another helping of pudding. I find myself getting just the same if I don't fight against it.

Friday, 8th. Lately I have several times had pitying looks from folk to whom I have admitted that in rations I get exactly what I'm entitled to, and no more. No matter how Lord Woolton schemes, unscrupulous folk can outwit him, shopkeepers as well as public, and he never will get a fair distribution while such people exist. Later, I went to butcher straight from work, got there at 12.30 to be told no meat left. I asked, where was our ration then? Blank look. I persisted, asked what was the point of coupons then, and surely it was early in the day to be sold out. I got no meat which struck me as rotten bad management. When I told my husband, he had his lunch and then went to see the butcher for the first time in his life. He did

Edie Rutherford

some straight talking and refused to leave till we got our ration. Then a leg of lamb was produced with the remark that it was the butcher's own weekend meat. So my husband said, 'Well, if you are such a poor manager you should go without, not a patient and reasonable customer such as you must admit my wife is.' He agreed that I am so but said I often get more than my ration. I wish I had been there! Never pen'orth over ration have I ever had. I never go near the shop till the weekend and then I get my ration for two and no more. Well, the leg of lamb is twice our ration but I am making the most of it, though I don't know how I'll dare go into the shop again!

Peter Baxter *Monday, 11th.* This evening there was a typical example of RAF stupidity. We were informed that a wretched recruit in one wing had failed to salute the wing commander, and that, as a punishment for this heinous offence, the whole of our wing, comprising some hundreds of men, including NCOs, would spend an hour every night until Thursday doing saluting drill. *That* is service justice and discipline. It makes me choke with rage. We can do *nothing* whatsoever about it.

Edie Rutherford *Tuesday, 12th.* I wish Lord Woolton would ration bread. Apart from it possibly making them eat more potatoes, it would stop the waste which goes on daily. I itched to smack a woman in a shop the other day – the woman behind the counter had turned her back and this customer began to pick up loaf after loaf and feel it, muttering that she often got a stale loaf. I said, 'We don't mind how stale the loaf is. We eat till a loaf is done regardless of how long we've had it. And I don't care to buy bread that has been mauled!' She blushed and said she meant no harm. Maybe she didn't, just another ignorant woman.

Frank Edwards *Sunday, 17th.* Having put the radio on a few minutes ago I noticed it was of poor strength and inclined to oscillate all the time, like it used to be in the blitz days. After a long period of quietness, we have gone back to the blitz for the sirens have just gone, and I can hear a plane coming over. The guns are going, but fairly distant at the moment. Now they sound much nearer and windows are vibrating as in the earlier blitzes.

More planes are coming over and now ack-ack is going from all directions, some distant, some close at hand. Assuming that this raid is being directed on London it is evidently a retribution for our heavy raid on Berlin last night.

Wednesday, 27th. So the big news is that the Prime Minister and the President have met in Casablanca where very important decisions were made.[45] This lunchtime I saw the following chalked on a board outside a small general shop in a busy main street:

NO MATCHES
NO OIL
NO WOOD
NO DYES
NO BEER
NO HURRY
NO WORRY
JOY AT THE END
NO WONDER!

Saturday, 30th. What a climate! Does it ever do anything else but rain and/or blow a gale here? My feet have been wet every day this week. Air force boots are of rotten quality: they have to be excellent to stand up to Padgate conditions. There's not much else to report from here. The dreary routine of training goes on from day to day. Saturday always seems twice as long as any other day now that we're working. I have received a letter from my college at Cambridge, interesting that I can now 'proceed to my MA degree' on payment of £5. I was rather surprised, as I always understood that one had to wait five years from the date of graduation. I must see if I can get a special pass some time to go and collect my MA.

Peter Baxter

Heard today of the daylight Mosquito raid on Berlin, in the midst of the Nazi anniversary celebrations. It is, of course, negligible from the military point of view, but it is a good gesture, and the best sort of propaganda for our side. I wonder how they will retaliate this time.

FEBRUARY 1943

Frank Edwards *Thursday, 4th.* News from the Russian war front[46] is very good indeed and Russia is indeed doing remarkable things. Whilst waiting for the 10.45 p.m. news in the European News Service tonight I was having a run round the radio short wavelengths and came across Haw-Haw who I haven't heard for many months. I don't know the station but from the announcement which followed it was a French radio. Haw-Haw was just as sickly and impudent as ever and was talking about delivering England from the filth of Bolshevism.

Muriel Green *Saturday, 6th.* Half-day and I had a date in town with a young man I met at last YHA weekend. He wrote me this week. He is a CO doing market garden work in a community. We walked round the town and then he took me to their living place, an ex-cricket pavilion. Five of them, an ex-butcher, ex-schoolmaster at public school, ex-carpenter, two others (I don't know what they were but none had previous knowledge of agriculture or horticulture), live with a female housekeeper, an ex-secretary to a town clerk. They are all COs. It was an interesting afternoon, I enjoyed talking to him but I am not sure whether my interest in him lies in his ideals of pacifism or his sex! Anyway, I was not convinced by any of his arguments. I have far less faith in the goodness of human nature since I left my home, worked with others, for others, and lived in lodgings!

Nella Last *Monday, 8th.* I've always been of the opinion that our rations

should be more 'flexible' – we should be able to buy alterna-
tives and those of us not wanting bacon should be able to get
extra lard, etc. After hearing and seeing the way women lost
their silly heads at the sight of tinned fruit I can only think it's
a wise plan to 'protect people from themselves'. I saw women
with several tins – large ones – in their baskets which must
have taken about all the month's points for the family! I met a
woman from centre, a policeman's wife. She was very jubilant
over two small and one large tins of salmon. She said, 'I've not
had first-grade salmon for *months* and I grabbed the chance.'
I'm not too well up in 'points value' for I buy what I think
best and don't remember from month to month, only to know
certain things are 'impossible' off two books. Idly I said, 'You
have four books and can get "luxury items" – how many points
are they?' and got the amazing answer, 'Thirty-two the large
and twenty each the small ones' – she had spent all but eight
points on them!

Friday, 12th. I saw something I've never seen before today – an
'Easterner' of some kind in full navy rig! With the menacing
gaze of one whose ancestors had all worn heelless shoes and
his long slender hands and narrow head with its cap set firmly
and squarely on top. He looked 'all wrong'. He spoke faultless
English and chose a tea exactly like an ordinary soldier would
have done. I always feel a little nervous with Hindus, etc. – I
wonder if our food will 'offend' in any way – no doubt I've a
memory of reading 'Indian Mutiny' books!

Saturday, 13th. For the first time I visited a British Restaurant   Frank Edwards
today. I went there for lunch and believe me was most surprised
when asked, 'Are you hungry, sir?' On replying that I was, I was
given an exceedingly generous helping. Not previously during
the war have I been asked that question in a restaurant.

  The service was very quick and the helpers most courteous.
I was very struck with the most efficient manner in which this

restaurant is run, and I expect the other British Restaurants are run on the same lines. No wonder they are so well patronised.

Nella Last *Sunday, 14th*. The shocking news on the wireless about the murder of so many Jews by the Germans set me off thinking of 'after the war'.[47] One thing the planners of 'Utopia' don't seem to take into account is who is going to buy and *pay* for all this 'vast expanse of trade' we must build up? With the wholesale destruction there has been – and dear God – that which will come – the ones who are losing *all* – even health and spirits to build their lives afresh, the 'gap' in the birth rate caused by potential fathers in the services and last but not least the women who will wither and the ones that 'industry' and too strenuous work will make incapable of motherhood as after the last war. I can only see a fraction of people to 'buy' or 'make' ... If we take America – the whole continent – Britain and her Empire, as yet uninvaded and overrun – the tragic loss of manpower will be apparent – but Europe cannot surely be considered as a market for a long time – it will be a place to help and give, with no thought of return. Will Japan be decimated, or places where coloured people predominate, places where they breed like animals? Will this war see the end of the white people in power and the slow uptrend of coloured races? All this talk of what *we* will do after this war – as if straws set the pace or direction. When the winds of destiny cease to blow, when the 'evil wind' has blown itself out and calm comes again, it will be to vastly different circumstances of present and future than all the 'brave new world' builders as yet visualise.

Peter Baxter *Monday, 15th*. I take up this diary again after a lapse of a couple of weeks. They have been horrid weeks, for me, not worth writing about, filled with unpleasantness, rows, tickings-off and irritating muddling. The spirit in this wing is abominable. The men are weighed down by an excess of useless tasks and deadly routine, by the lack of encouragement and reward they get from above. The NCOs are, almost to a man, angered and exasperated by the ceaseless nagging we get, often in front of the recruits. We haven't heard a word of thanks or praise since we've been here. Before I joined up, in the innocence of my heart I never imagined that the RAF could be like this. It's the stupidity and inefficiency of it that gets me most. This week I have found myself longing more desperately than ever for the end of the war and my return to that golden thoroughfare, 'Civvy Street'.

This feeling has been heightened by the first gleams of hope for an early finish aroused by the stupendous achievements of the Russians. Of course, I am cautious enough to discount a lot of the newspapers' 'blah', but even so it is evident that the Germans' retreat has not been by any means an ordered one. I am pretty sure that they will not halt the Russians; some of the fellows here visualise the Red Army driving straight through now to the German frontier, if not beyond. The NCOs have been talking, quite hopefully, of being back home for next Christmas. They seem to forget that even if the Germans could be beaten this year we should still have the Japs to deal with. I'm afraid that, as usual, the wish is father to the thought. To me, the great question of the moment is, 'When and where will the Allies strike?' It is obvious that it must be soon, before the Germans can regain their breath, and I feel that stretchy feeling of wanting coming upon me that I always get before running or going in to bat. How will the invasion, when it comes, affect me and Dora? Have the Allies really got the strength and the brains and the organisation to put this thing across at the first attempt, without wasting time or men's lives? The next few months will undoubtedly be the testing time. The consciousness of this makes me extra impatient of all the unreal and ridiculous bullshit we have to inflict upon the men here. Our favourite refrain, when ordered to do something particularly stupid is, 'And there's thousands dying in Russia!'

Sunday, 28th. These two weeks have seen a gradual slowing-up of the Russian advance, caused chiefly, I presume, by the unusually early thaw in the south. It is a great pity, as this will probably give the Germans just that breathing space they require for regrouping their armies and forming a new defence line. I pray that the Russians may be able to resume their advance with the minimum of delay. The whole future may depend on their ability to do so.

Events in Tunisia have been worrying and ominous.[48] It has been plainly shown that the Americans, with the best will in the world, have got a lot to learn yet about fighting the Germans, and it is a nasty reminder that if and when we invade Europe we shall be up against troops who are experienced and fearless exponents of the tough trade of war. Directly I heard of the American retreats I knew just what would happen. Our fellows, almost without exception, positively crowed with delight, and announced that the Yanks were all talk and had no guts. Corporal Jack Driver, who was an infantry sergeant in the last war and holds the DCM, said in his stolid Yorkshire way, 'Ay, you see, they'll be putting in British troops to stiffen 'em. That's what we had to do in t'last war.' I scoffed at his suggestion, but sure enough we heard next day that the Guards had 'come up in support' or some such thing. Now they are giving all the credit to the British troops for driving the Germans back through the Kasserine Pass. The old-timers regard all this as another vindication of the British principle that an army must have iron discipline to be successful in battle. They ascribe the American failure to lack of discipline, by which they mean no saluting, absence of petty restrictions and artificial class distinctions between ranks, lack of bullshit and spit and polish. I disagree with them heartily. I think the Americans merely lack training in battle conditions, and maybe aren't too sure what they're supposed to be fighting the Germans for. I still do not understand why the Allies have been unable to launch a major offensive in Tunisia for four whole months. I suspect that the

supply problem must be more acute than we've been told, and
I am mystified by reports that our forces are short of first-class
aircraft. That is surely one thing we should have plenty of by
now. We *must* get a move on in Tunisia soon, before we can
really get started on an invasion of the Continent.

MARCH 1943

Wednesday, 3rd. Meg bought a Hovis [loaf] the other day and
hugging it to her said, 'If only I had half a pound of butter I'd
sit down and eat this now!' She and Roger hope to get married
in June. Have not yet found a house or flat but are slowly collecting things for their home. They attend auctions and pick
up second-hand household ware when they can. Furniture is
the major difficulty. Meg wants everything to be ultra-modern,
Roger favours old oak and copper. Both varieties almost impossible to obtain and prices appalling. At an auction recently a
small, plain oak table which might have cost about £4 before
the war went for £27. Meg is violently opposed to the Utility
furniture – I think she is influenced by highbrow critics in
architectural and art press. I saw it in the Building Centre
and thought that it might have been much worse – in fact
I wouldn't mind betting that if Meg had seen some of it in
Bowmans before the war she would have chosen it without
hesitation.

Friday, 5th. Food situation still excellent. Have steak and
kidney for the weekend. Mrs T has sent me three more fresh
eggs. Have been eating raw vegetable salads, curried vegetables, bacon, and tonight some fresh spinach from the garden.
Milk plentiful – junkets, custards and cocoa all possible this
week. Cooking apples have come from the greengrocer several
times – he told me that there is quite a good supply in the
country but distribution difficult to control. They (and he

Maggie Joy
Blunt

seemed to include himself in that pronoun) watch out for bad
practices and put a stop to them as soon as possible. But on the
whole, he said, we mustn't grumble – we try to make things
as fair as possible.

Frank Edwards   *Saturday, 6th.* Today London kicks off in the 'Wings for Victory'
campaign. From observation I should say it has been a very good
start, with good weather attracting thousands of people. This
afternoon I visited Dorland Hall in Lower Regent St where the
inside of a Halifax is on view and this is exact in detail and a
most interesting exhibit. There is also, in the lower hall, a Spitfire which went through the Battle of Britain. I joined a very
long queue to gain admission to the hall, which I estimate has
been visited by some thousands of people today. From there I
made my way to Trafalgar Square to see the Lancaster which is
on show there. Here I found hundreds of people. Long queues
were formed of people passing up the stairway on either side
to have a look at this monster bomber at quarters as close as
could be allowed.

   An RAF band was playing cheerful music in the square,
and in the pool a diver was engaged in collecting the coins
which you were invited to throw in and which were going to
provide a rescue craft. A million pennies were wanted for this,
the announcer was saying, and the total number then (about
4.30 p.m.) was some 4,000 odd.

Muriel Green   *Saturday, 6th.* Goodbye to Gloucestershire! We have had happy
times and the opposite since we came over a year ago. Anyway
it has been an experience, from the social as well as the horti-
cultural point of view. Some of the queerest folk I've ever run
up against and some of the nastiest have passed my way. I shall
not be at all sorry if I never see H. Manor, or a rice pudding,
ever again. Sixty-six milk puds out of seventy! Everyone was
very nice seeing us off really and it was very thrilling to tell
them we had got a better job. I think most of the staff were

sorry to see us go and Mr S was genuinely upset. I'm sorry for him really. He has more or less got to continue to live with his old woman! We haven't!

Mr B took us into town. We were like a couple of Xmas trees dangling parcels and bags in all available spaces on us. We arrived at our Somerset destination 3 p.m. off the train. [Muriel Green was a head gardener and a shop assistant in Taunton, Somerset.] The hostel is a mass of ready-constructed wooden buildings on new land. It is furnished with every amenity. The bedrooms are in separate houses with a house matron in charge of each. She has a domestic assistant. The bedrooms are fitted up with all new conveniences. Three bathrooms, showers, lavatories, washing cubicles and a common-room for each house. The men and women's houses are separate and I understand grouped into classes of workers all of the same social status, cleanliness, etc. We are at present in one of the women's blocks, but next week are to move into the staff block. The furnishing is the same in all the houses although the workers are graded. All workers and staff feed together in a large central dining-room, serving themselves from hatchways from the adjoining kitchen. The main assembly block also contains a large ballroom which is also a cinema and theatre, a writing room containing library shelves, a recreation room – table tennis, billiards, etc. – a lounge, a shop selling sweets, cigs, stationery, toilet necessities, etc., and the administration offices, also a café. Beside the sleeping houses are store buildings, a laundry where residents do their own washing, electric irons, mangles, etc., a hairdressing shop, a carpenter's shop, a sick bay with matron and nurses, wards private, isolation and general, a surgery where two doctors visit daily and a fire and ARP department. All sleeping quarters have an air-raid shelter fitted with bunks. Our old friend Mr H, ex-holiday camp proprietor from Norfolk, is assistant manager and two women from home are matrons here. After exploring, tea and dinner we retired early exhausted to bed. I notice everything in the hostel is stamped G-R.

Monday, 8th. Today we began work here. Mr B the social director is in charge of the vegetable production and Mr H is our
boss. We soon discovered they know practically nothing about
gardening let alone large-scale food production. They told us
not to start before breakfast which is at 8.30. We did not get
started at all before 10 a.m. Just got started and someone told
us a cup of tea was available for all staff at 10.45 a.m. Lunch at
12.45 and tea at 4 p.m. Mr H told us to finish at 5 p.m., but
we say 5.30 p.m. as it leaves no time for any operations. The
only other official gardener is Jimmy, age 74. He is the chief
drawback. He is not exactly under us, but is definitely not the
head gardener like us! He is more or less the odd job man but
Mr H had put him breaking down some of the rough land for
us to perform on this week. To our horror he was redigging
the ploughed land and removing the turf from the soil. He
has got to be stopped but our first day is hardly the time to
upset him!

Peter Baxter   *Thursday, 25th*. On the fourth day of my leave Dora and I trav-
elled down to London to spend the remainder of our holiday
at my old home at Stamford Hill. We found both my parents
in pretty good health and spirits. My mother, at 55, is now
working a full wartime day as a clerk in the Ministry of Supply,
and is, I suspect, enjoying herself more than she has done for
years. She has a quick brain and an orderly mind, and it is stimulating for her to be using her wits instead of toiling through
a load of housework as she has done for years previously. She is
modest about her usefulness, but from the way she talks I can
see that her department regards her as a considerable asset in
these days when the standard of temporary labour is generally
so low. I can't help thinking that, much as my mother has
loved her children, she might perhaps have been happier all
these years if she could have kept on with a business career
as women do in Russia, leaving part of the upbringing of her
children to others.

By a fortunate chance, Bernard, Dora's brother and my buddy for eleven years at school and Cambridge, now a sub-lieutenant in the navy, was on leave from his ship, and Vera, Dora's younger sister, who is a nurse at the London Hospital, also had a few days off, so they both came to stay a couple of days with us. As young people on leave usually do, we took a trip to the West End. We were all hungry for a sight of Picca-dilly and Trafalgar Square again. I wonder why I always return to London with such affection and pleasure?

Bernard, feeling a little expensive, decided that we must lunch at the Café Royal in Regent Street. I had heard of it only by name. Had I known what it was like I would have taken a big bomb in with me and deposited same in a quiet corner. Vile place – it made me seethe with anger. We went into the lounge first, to have a glass of beer before lunch. It was crowded with people of the kind I detest. The men, mostly officers, were not too bad, but the women … Ugh, they made me want to crawl up the wall! They sat there perched on stools or reclining elegantly in chairs, holding cigarettes in painted fingers, talking in loud strident voices with clipped, affected county accents as they sipped their gin and cocktails. Many of them were young – they couldn't all have been on leave. I felt like rushing out to find Ernie Bevin [Minister of Labour]. What work do these painted parasites do to help the country? Is keeping officers amused a sufficient contribution to the war effort?

APRIL 1943

Monday, 5th. Today is my 26th birthday. I can scarcely believe that I have reached such a ripe old age. It seems no time at all since I was a boy at school. Especially since the war has been on the time has flown by, and I can't help feeling sad, not only for myself, but for my whole generation who are wasting some

Peter Baxter

of the finest years of their lives in the dreary business of war. Our manhood has come to full fruition, but it is stifling and decaying in these wasted years. I know I am one of the more fortunate ones, but even for me, who have at least the happiness of the frequent contact with my wife, and lead a tolerably comfortable and safe existence, the deadening, paralysing influence of service life has blighted my middle twenties and stunted my development. I pray that I shan't have to spend many birthdays in uniform.

Muriel Green   *Wednesday, 7th.* The Ministry of Labour told the hostel staff to expect 100 girls transferred from a Welsh factory this week. They have all been busy opening a new house for them, doing extra catering, etc. Today they heard 47 were to arrive. All the staff were on duty waiting. It was a vile day: very windy and raining. At 5 p.m. a busload arrived, and they were fed, checked in and housed. At 9.30 p.m. when the staff had their snack the rumour went round that nearly all the new girls were in the nearest pub. One matron said one of her men residents had come back from the pub and said the girls were drinking pretty heavily. As we went to bed the singing of male and female voices broke the air.

Thursday, 8th. This morning the staff were in despair. The majority of the new girls arrived in the main entrance hall distinctly the worse for drink after closing time last night. Some were with the working men, some alone. Several were sick on the dining-hall floor and one was so drunk the others carried her. Their house matron was not at breakfast and was reported to be going round with a mop and pail cleaning the mess of vomiting etc. in their rooms and changing the bedding. I don't know what will be done with them; the manager and highest staff on duty last night were disgusted. There have been very few of this class of women and behaviour in this hostel before this and everyone thinks the good name of the other residents will suffer. Another busload arrived tonight and the great majority, a painted 'tartish'-looking crowd age about 22, were again gone to the pub tonight. There are a few fairly decent-looking quiet ones who sat and watched the badminton match. One of these told one of the staff they were ashamed to be with the others and hardly dared show their faces.

Thursday, 15th. We had our breakfast early so as to mind the tractor. They got going and the two girls took turns in driving it. One of the girls and the young man sat down all the morning and watched. I asked if I could ride on it and he said I could drive it if I liked. One of the girls showed me what to do. It is quite easy. In the afternoon the man told the newest of the girls, one who only began tractor-driving yesterday, to get on with the job and left her going up on the hill with the other girls. He lay rolling about the grass with the two girls all afternoon and the newest poor girl was left alone to finish the job. She did not even know how to stop the engine, and could not see to move it from plot to plot over the paths and bridges alone. I got on the tractor with her and helped her. The man never came near all afternoon. At 4 p.m. we took the newest girl into tea and left the tractor, thinking it was about time one of the other girls did a bit of work. When we came back the man and other girls were furious with the newest girl for going off. We gave them a good telling off as we are supposed to be in charge of the proceedings. Anyway, the ground is done at last, so now we can go ahead with the planting.

It is two years today since I took up gardening. I did not expect to be a head gardener at a war hostel in two years when I began it. We are so happy here I'm glad I began it. It has its rough patches, but now we have come to a smooth one, and it's been worth it. The weather is marvellous. Like June.

Wednesday, 21st. Not only left light on in bedroom in February but again about four weeks later and the whole performance   Maggie Joy
Blunt

of policeman climbing in after dark when I was out, to turn
out light, was repeated. Excused myself from attending court
for first summons and was fined 30/-. On the second occasion
was charged with breaking blackout regulations *and* wasting
fuel. When these summonses arrived all the men at the office
set on me saying that the second fine was likely to be very
heavy and that I ought to obtain legal advice. They got me so
scared I phoned my old schoolfellow and present Red Cross
commandant, J, and was invited to call on her father. He was
very sympathetic – advised me not to call in a lawyer as there
were no reliable ones in the district and there was nothing in
my case that I could not say for myself. But attend the court
myself this time I would have to. He is an old and influential
resident of the area and (because I had been to school with his
daughter!) would, he said, if the case had been at the S1-court
have probably been able to get it withdrawn for me. But I come
under B——m where he knew no one. J, however, thought she
could bring influence to bear on the inspector who brought the
charge, and promised to do her best.

I attended court as bidden last Monday morning, quaking. I
was expecting to have to pay out £5: at least £3 for the second
blackout offence and £2 for the fuel charge. I pleaded guilty,
accepted the policeman's evidence and explained in a small
voice that I worked from 8.30 to 6 every day, was alone in the
cottage, had no domestic help, had to get myself up and off in
the morning by 8 o'clock, had not been well and in the early
morning rush it was easy to forget the light. The bench went
into a huddle and then I heard the chairman saying, '£1 for
each charge.' £2 in all! I paid promptly. What wires J and her
father have been pulling I don't yet know but I have to thank
them for this I am sure. Everyone at the office is as astonished
as myself and thinks me very fortunate. But Heaven help me
if I do it *again*. At H's suggestion am now making a habit of
turning off main switch before I leave every morning.

Tuesday, 27th. A windy and rather cold Easter but not a wet one. N spent the weekend with me. We sat in the garden on Sunday and got quite brown. For food we had salads, a tin of sausage meat (present from America), fresh eggs, cheese, stew, spinach from the garden, rhubarb – stewed and jellied – junket, milky rice, honey, marmalade, cakes, although the scones I bought were dusty and tasteless. I was short of nothing and gave N 1 lb. of sugar as an Easter egg as she does not get enough sugar and has no means of saving any. This is not as generous as it sounds, I am sometimes rather ashamed of my 'hoard' of food. I sent about 1 lb. of lard to E and Aunt A – I have my 2 oz. every week but have no time to use it – they are using it in cakes now.

Wednesday, 28th. My ATC lads have finished their training and passed out. They earned great praise, and for the first time in all the two years I have been on this job, I was complimented on the efficiency and smartness of my men. It makes *such* a difference to get a bit of praise occasionally. RAF officers realise this all too rarely, I'm afraid. The boys will be posted away in the next few days; I'm going to miss them badly.

Peter Baxter

The rupture in Russo-Polish relations is most unfortunate.[49] I suppose it was bound to come some time with a Polish government composed of aristocrats and army officers. People of that type can never, I'm afraid, remain on amicable terms for long with the Soviet, and the problem of the Polish frontier is indeed a thorny one. It's a sort of Eire v. Ulster business on a much vaster scale. The actual incident of the Polish graves is, on the face of it, a typical Goebbels lie, cleverly designed to play upon the popular conception of the Russians as semi-barbarous savages. It will, I'm afraid, be believed by many millions of people in all countries simply because people like to believe stories of mass murder and atrocity for some obscure psychological reason, and because they have been fed for years with similar fairy-tales about the Russians. Myself, I do not rule out the possibility of there being some foundation of truth in the story. Men fighting wars are not constrained by the usual consideration of mercy and decency. Russians are capable of such an action, so are Germans, and Japs and British and French and Americans and any other nationality you care to think of. But for the good of all of us I hope the British and American governments will have the sense to repudiate the story entirely. Any breach with the USSR on such an issue would be an overwhelming catastrophe.

MAY 1943

Peter Baxter *Sunday, 16th.* There is great optimism here among the fellows, and great hopes that a successful Anglo-American invasion coupled with a summer offensive from the Russians may finish the war off, at any rate by 1945. I'm afraid they all tend to lose sight of the fact that even then Japan will still remain to be dealt with, and that may take anything from one to three years. And there will also be a long confused period of abnormal conditions after the actual fighting is finished. Yes, it will be a long job yet. That, at least, is my opinion, and Dora agrees with me.

In the light of all this we've been reconsidering the question of starting a family. Dora is older than me – she will be 28 this summer. If we wait for me to get back into civilian life before we have any children, she will be at least 31, possibly older, before the first one is born. We both think that would be a wholly bad thing, so we may decide to chance our luck some time soon.

Frank Edwards *Monday, 17th.* In the early hours of this morning there were three alerts, the second one lasting something like two hours. There were no incidents in this neighbourhood.

The breaching of three of Germany's biggest dams[50] by the RAF was indeed a remarkable piece of news, and it is a blow, which is likely to have devastating results. It is a new kind of blow – the kind which I confess I hadn't thought of before, and it seems to me that it is the kind which above all others cannot be hushed up by the Germans, though no doubt they will do their best to keep it from the public. Anyway, we shall see how things develop.

Monday, 17th. Heard tonight the news of the destruction by the RAF of the three big dams in NW Germany. I don't like it. The action will, I know, cause immense dislocation in this vital centre of German war industry. It will bring everything to a standstill for miles around, it will wreck communications and cause untold damage. But, it will also drown thousands of non-combatants – women, children, old people and many of the wretched slaves working in Germany who have come from the occupied countries. It will render many, many families homeless, and, I feel, it is calculated to create bitter rage and hatred against we British which will not easily be forgotten. In its way I consider it to be as bad as using poison gas or germs. Bombs can at least be aimed at a military target with a fair likelihood of hitting it. Rushing water cannot distinguish between a factory and a hospital, cannot discriminate between soldiers and children. I know this is Total War, but are we to abandon all standards of mercy and humanity? An act like this makes us all barbarians.

Peter Baxter

I'm sorry to say that I haven't yet found anybody to agree with me. The other fellows say, 'The more Jerries we wipe out the better', or, 'It's just too bad for the people who happen to be in the way', or 'They'd do the same to us if they got the chance.' It's very saddening. When one's fellow countrymen are so callous, one can't feel over-confident about the chances of getting a peaceful civilised world in the future.

JUNE 1943

Maggie Joy
Blunt *Thursday, 3rd.* This week at the office all is bustle and hustle for
our Wings for Victory week which begins on Saturday. Mr O
is finishing off a large number of posters, and an exhibition is
being arranged in the canteen under the direction of the works
manager. Posters are to be displayed in all the offices and corri-
dors. Photographs of various personalities have been taken and
are to be shown with a suitable slogan persuading the reader to
buy National Savings Certificates. Our target is £15,000. P has
decided to take a few days' holiday this particular week.

Changes in our department are imminent. H has at last left
us for the labs. P is going into the army. Mr O may not stay.
The publicity staff will be reduced to myself and B. There will
be little but routine work to do but probably quite enough
of that to keep us busy. MOL [Ministry of Labour] officials
have been round interviewing members of the staff in various
departments personally. I was in London when they paid their
first visit to us. P was away too, but when they came again they
saw him and were evidently satisfied that there were no super-
fluous workers in our department. I was not visited.

Saturday, 19th. Meg and Roger married this morning. Ceremony at Paddington register office, and reception at Grosvenor
House. Meg radiant in powder blue and navy accessories. Frock
was from Galeries Lafayette. Hat was made for her too but not
sure where – with veiling bunched at the back and flowers. She
carried orchids and pink roses. She went away in Cumbrian
tweed jacket and a grey skirt just made for her. They have gone
to Salcombe for a week.

Marriage is not very easy for the young these days as Mr O
was saying yesterday. Housing shortage acute. Furniture scarce
and expensive, much domestic ware quite unobtainable, and
crockery and cutlery very limited. Coupons required for furnishing fabrics and linen besides the bridal trousseau. Short

holidays and many husbands of course in the armed forces. Roger wanted to join the RAF but has a very slight defect in his hearing – it does not inconvenience him at all in civilian life, but the RAF turned him down because of it. He has quite a good job now in our firm – was recently put in charge of the press shop at our new works ... but Meg is keeping on her full-time post in the production department because they need the money. It is a wonder, really, that so many people do get married with all these difficulties facing them. There is little incentive. I'm afraid I should live-in-sin, but the majority of Englishwomen seem to prefer the security and social standing which a wedding ring bestows. (There was some difficulty in obtaining Meg's ring too. Roger wanted it to be 14 or whatever carat it is that wedding rings should be and only a very small percentage of these are now produced.)

Monday, 28th. When I got back here this morning I found the camp in a major panic in expectation of a visit tomorrow from Air Marshal Sir Arthur Barratt, the new C-in-C of Training Command. For the last few days, training has been almost-at-a-standstill, as the men have been engaged in scrubbing and polishing, and digging up gardens, and mending roadways, and painting, and generally giving the camp such as it never normally bears. I hope the Air Marshal will like it!

News received today suggests that something is going to happen in Greece. In response to leaflets dropped by our planes, Greek patriots have sabotaged the main railway leading south from the Balkans to Athens. Maybe this, then, is the beginning of the fireworks, or maybe it is just another decoy to foozle the Axis. I hope, if it proves to be the latter, it will not expose the Greeks to serious reprisals such as the French suffered after their premature rising at St Nazaire.

Peter Baxter

JULY 1943

Nella Last *Wednesday, 14th.* I felt exhausted and hoped my husband could get in to go and see a picture I had looked forward to seeing: *Tomorrow We Live.* I've finished reading *Thirty Million Gas Masks*, most interesting even if I did not really enjoy it. Made me go back to the time when I tore my nerves to shreds with wild surmising, fears and conjectures. Now I don't think a great deal about the 'war in general' – try to *only* think about day-to-day – even hour-to-hour – problems and now dear yesterday has flowers on its grave and the raw wild grief has died and tender memories of what has been. Tomorrow seems to merge into today so quickly – I sometimes pant a little in my efforts to keep up – and as for 'next week', 'next year' – they are in God's pocket as Gran used to say.

Peter Baxter *Friday, 16th.* The end of the war in Europe now seems likely within the next couple of years, and people are beginning to think more and more about the post-war world. The government still shows a most serious dilatoriness in drawing up concrete plans for the future. A number of commissions are sitting and inquiries being conducted, but what use are they going to be? The latest 'blueprint' is that issued today as a White Paper on education. I have only so far heard the BBC report of it, and I mustn't judge prematurely, but it sounded pretty half-hearted to me. The leaving age is raised only to 15, with a vague promise of advancing it to 16 at some unspecified later date. Every child, the scheme generously says, is to proceed to a secondary school at the age of 11, irrespective of ability to pass an examination. This sounds good, but some of the 'secondary' schools turn out on inspection to be more or less the same as the 'senior' schools recommended in the Hadow report of 1926, and put into fairly general commission before this war.

Nella Last *Friday, 16th.* It was so irritating at canteen, few cakes, no butter, half a pound of marge to do all afternoon and not a thing for sandwiches. We made up the marge with cornflour but this afternoon it looked more like blancmange! I put a pint of milk in a pan with ½ teaspoon of salt and when it boiled added three tablespoons cornflour mixed to a paste and boiled till stiff, then poured it, cut up ½ lb. marg and beat and beat it. It was amazingly good and not at all 'dodged' tasking, no one grumbled and we had no complaints.

Monday, 19th. Wrote up a list: '*What I can do with an odd spoonful of sugar*'

    2 tablespoons – week's supply of salad dressing
    1 tablespoon – a milk sweet
    3 or more tablespoons – stewed loganberries
    4 or ¼ lb. – small cakes
    8 or ½ lb. – large cutting cake
    1 lb. – bottle (a pound jar) of fruit in 'syrup'
What about that sugar in tea? Saccharines are just as good in coffee and cocoa.

Another letter from Jack in this afternoon's post and none from Cliff. My mind wanders to him whatever I'm doing – is he in this 'push', what is he doing, is he well? It's such a 'cruel' war, few escape, bodily or mentally we are 'all in it'. I often wish I was a bit more 'credulous'. I was talking to a woman in the shop today and I felt envious of her confidence in Petulengro [a fortune teller] whom she had heard while on holiday. He had 'foretold the crack-up of Italy in July, that of Germany in August and peace bells in September'. It must be a good thing at times to 'believe' and not to feel deep down in one's consciousness a cold stone which only grows heavier and no 'gaiety' warm for more than a fleeting hour.

Thursday, 22nd. Worked full-time today and was fagged out at   Edie Rutherford
the end of it. Nice to come home with double pay and a week of loafing ahead. The Pope makes me tired. He has no love of

humanity at all. All he cares about is his villainous Church and the relics and rubbish connected with it.[51] Well, the war will teach him and his followers some lessons as well as the rest of us. Rotten dull day and cool. I do wish we could do more to help poor China. The Japs have accomplished all they set out to do and all they want now is time to make good on their conquests. And that is precisely what we are giving them. One presumes we are obliged to give it them. Surely there can be no other reason? How galling it must be for all interned civilians and prisoners of war to watch Japan consolidating her gains, raising that dock of ours that we sank at Singapore, and similar clever tricks ...

AUGUST 1943

Frank Edwards *Thursday, 12th.* This evening I saw a very thrilling and awe-inspiring sight. It was just dusk (10 p.m.) and there was the roar of plane engines. I looked out of the window and saw, flying fairly low, three big bombers followed by more and then more again until the sky over our end of the road seemed to be full of these mighty bombers. Some had their lights on; some had just the tail-light; and some just a white light on top of the plane. All these planes, although well apart, were going in the same direction and no doubt would join up in formation when further out. Evidently, starting at this hour they were going on a long journey and I should say we were seeing the start. We watched them going over until after blackout time when we had to light up, but the roar of these planes lasted for over an hour.

Peter Baxter *Thursday, 12th.* The Russians have swept westwards almost to Poltava, completely outflanking Kharkov, which now seems certain to fall.[52] Meanwhile, Churchill has gone off on another trip, to Canada this time. The reason generally propounded for this visit is that he and Roosevelt have to speed up the whole Allied programme in view of what has happened in Italy. It's a pity they couldn't have speeded it up a fortnight ago, when the whole Axis structure seemed about to totter if only we could have struck a shrewd blow or two in the right place. I am perturbed by the absence of Russian representatives from the conference once again. I wish I knew whose fault this is. It seems senseless to me. How can one plan for war and the peace to follow without close personal contact between *all* the Allied leaders? The differences between Anglo-American and Soviet policies are unfortunately most pronounced at the moment.

Tuesday, 24th. Today the Quebec conference[53] ended, and a joint   Frank Edwards
statement has been issued, which, though it does not convey any details as to what has been arranged yet it most certainly will not be likely to warm the cockles of the Axis heart.

Great news about the monster raid on Berlin last night,[54] that is to say for us, not Berliners, for I should think they were scared stiff. Perhaps after so much waiting and expecting, they are glad it has at last arrived, yet they can hardly seek consolation in this fact, because last night was only the opening round in the battle of Berlin, and they don't know how much heavier the rounds to follow will be, and there are certain to be many such rounds. I expect they will be wondering if we are going to visit them again tonight.

Sunday, 29th. During the week, I saw, with great enjoyment,   Peter Baxter
the modernised edition of Charlie Chaplin's film, *The Gold Rush*. I have never forgotten it since I saw it as a youngster, especially the parts where he stewed and ate his boot, and where the cabin perched on the extreme edge of the precipice. Chaplin is undoubtedly a great genius. Watching his perfect clowning, I realised yet more strongly how feeble and amateurish, by comparison, are the George Formbys of this world.

SEPTEMBER 1943

Frank Edwards   *Wednesday, 1st.* Today is the fourth anniversary of Germany's
invasion of Poland. To mark the occasion there was this evening
a special edition of the BBC European News Service which
lasted 45 minutes instead of the usual 15 minutes. During this
news we heard Polish personnel of the services broadcast from
New York, Cairo, from Scotland and from an RAF station in
England. The Pope broadcast to the world today, speaking
for 14 minutes, and he expressed his hope that peace will be
restored to the world before the end of this year.

Peter Baxter   *Friday, 3rd.* Fourth anniversary of the war. This morning, at
long last, British troops landed on the toe of Italy.[55] There
is no news yet of how the operation is progressing. Resistance will be stiff, we've given rather a lot of warnings of our
intended arrival, and the Germans have had time to organise
their defence. Our attack, I'm sure, will succeed, provided it is
conceived on a bold enough scale.

Muriel Green,   *Friday, 3rd.* Can it really be four years today? I must have been
Snettisham,   quite a child when it began! I was certainly far less experienced
Norfolk, on   of the world and its peculiarities in those days. Now I am home
leave   again I am convinced that those carefree pre-war days can never
come again. Home will never be the same to me. I hope to
remember it always as my happy youth when tennis, swimming and dancing were regular happenings and the rest of the
world was uncared about. I don't think I could ever settle again
in this village. I used to think I would never get on so well with
people who had not known me and my family for years. Now
I know that friends are soon made and that in life people come
and go and in a fresh place a start can soon be made.

Peter Baxter   *Monday, 6th.* This invasion of Italy is surely the most extraordinary military operation the world has ever seen. All accounts

1. A crowd watching Big Ben strike eleven o'clock in London on 3 September 1939, as Britain's ultimatum to Germany expired

2. A child waiting to be evacuated

3. Outside a Royal Navy recruiting station, 1939

4. Clearing up after a bombing raid, London, August 1940

5. Bomb damage at the corner of Tottenham Court Road and Oxford Street,
October 1940

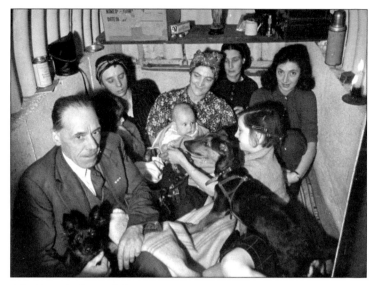

6. Inside an Anderson shelter

7. 'Business as usual', 1940

8. Bidding farewell to loved ones

9. Reading – a popular wartime hobby

10. RAMC stretcher drill, Leeds

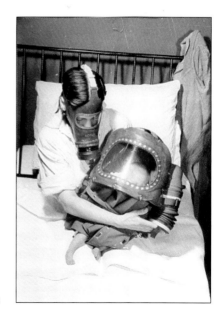

11. Gas masks for newborns

12. Recruiting women for war work, Liverpool

13. 'Digging for Victory' on Clapham Common, London

14. Remembrance Day

15. Children playing as air-raid wardens

16. Queuing for horse meat

17. A victim of a V1 flying bomb in Aldwych, London, 1944

18. Wartime cinema, providing entertainment and news

19. A V1 flying bomb about to land on a residential area of southern England

20. A bomb crater beside a garden air-raid shelter

21. German POWs marching to their internment, 1944

22. Dancing and singing on VE Day, 8 May 1945

23. Waving at soldiers returning home

concur in saying that the Sicilians turned out to wish our troops good luck and speedy victory, and that on the undefended mainland the Italians have welcomed the invasion of their country with great cordiality. I suppose the truth is that Italy is now a German-occupied country, just as much as France or Norway, and the great majority of the Italian forces make no attempt now to keep up the pretence of fighting for the Germans. The invasion is going well, but we haven't yet come up against the German defences: I hope to see the maximum use made of our command of the sea to execute outflanking landings every time the enemy make a stand, just as the Japs did so successfully in Malaya. The Italian campaign mustn't be allowed to draft out, and absorb all our strength throughout the coming winter.

Tuesday, 7th. Yesterday as I was preparing tea there was a knock   Edie Rutherford
at the door and there I found a 26-year-old wife living in one of these flats with whom we are on cordial terms, her husband a bomber in the RAF. Her face was wooden and she jerked out, 'Mrs Rutherford, Henry is missing,' thrust the telegram into my hand. Of course I just opened my arms and took her in and let her have a good weep the while I cursed audibly this blasted war. 'He isn't dead. I'm sure he isn't dead. He was home only last Wednesday. He's alive somewhere and worrying because he knows I'll get this telegram to upset me.' It read, 'Regret to inform you your husband missing operations night Sept. 5/6 letter follows squadron leader.' A little earlier in this diary I had commented on planes lost the previous night not knowing poor Henry was one of those missing, though we knew of course he was on operations these days. It is difficult to know what to say to a wife in such trouble. I did my best, poor lass. Felt myself as if my inside had fallen out. I wish to goodness this war would finish. There was always enough in the world to worry conscientious folk without all this on top of it.

Peter Baxter   *Wednesday, 8th.* Italy's surrender[56] came as a great surprise to me
at six o'clock this evening. There had been so many rumours of
peace during the last three weeks, that I had come to the conclusion that Badoglio was only stalling, and that no settlement
could be expected while he remained in power. The news was
received with great jubilation, and many remarks like, 'Won't
be long now', and 'Back in civvys for Christmas.' The fellows
thought me a proper old misery because I contended that Italy
would still have to be conquered from the Germans. I agree
that the moral effect of Italy's collapse is enormous, but if I
know the Nazis, they won't be caught napping. I expect them
to turn northern Italy into an occupied country, and fight a
stubborn delaying action up from the south, on the model of
the Etna campaign.[57] The wretched Italians may find themselves worse off than they were before, unless the Allies act with
boldness and imagination to attack the Germans at once in the
north before they can get thoroughly organised there.

What, I wonder, will happen to the Italians in Germany and
the Balkans and Dodecanese? The Germans will give the poor
devils a rough time of it, I fear. I am slightly amused to see
how the Allies have managed to save their face over that stupid
Casablanca declaration. Officially this surrender is 'unconditional', yet in the same breath it is admitted that there are
conditions to which both sides have agreed. Personally, I think
the sooner we make it clear that we *will* accept certain conditions of surrender from Germany also, the sooner we shall get
the war finished.

Edie Rutherford   *Thursday, 9th.* What glorious news at 6 p.m. last night. Now
let us hope we clean up the Italy war soon. All this talk from
Germany about setting up a fascist government[58] strikes me as
just laughable. Oh yeah? Well, our lads will be up against the
real thing again by this time. It seems to me the repercussions
of this incident are endless. No wonder certain other countries
have been having cabinet meetings and such. Musso must be

feeling mad ... so he deserves. Everyone is jubilant of course, though the people of this island take joy very soberly. BBC made rather pathetic attempt to celebrate last night, but they just don't know how. No doubt this is partly because we have got so used to bad news. I know many people were amazed to hear the news that Italy had packed up and could not take it in for some moments.

Tuesday, 21st. Most of the national daily newspapers have now published a picture of Musso after his being rescued from Italy by Hitler's paratroops. Most people have displayed a rather marked interest in this photograph and to say the least of it only about two in every ten think it has any likeness of him. Of the remainder 60 per cent don't definitely believe it is Musso. The others express a doubt, but one and all say, 'He looks so different.' In this picture I have heard him described as looking like 'an old josser', 'an old farmer', 'an old frump'.

Frank Edwards

OCTOBER 1943

Saturday, 2nd. I have just been listening to Tom Harrisson on the radio, discussing and playing his choice of eight records in the *Desert Island Discs* series, and I much enjoyed the programme. For one thing it was rather unique to have a broadcaster who had really had the experience of being on a desert island as Mr Harrisson has because this morning we had an 'experienced' choice, instead of 'imaginary' ones as is usually the case in this series. Secondly, of course, being one of MO's observers, I was particularly interested in listening to Tom Harrisson, as I am sure all observers, who were able to listen, would be. Incidentally, as a point of interest, I always read Mr Harrisson's radio column in the Sunday *Observer*.

Frank Edwards

Sunday, 10th. I was interested to hear in the news the other

Edie Rutherford

night that half the population of this country has moved since the war began. Seeing no new homes have been built, we have presumably been doing a lot of exchanging! And of course that is so. I have friends who have been obliged to move two or three times and each time have had much difficulty in finding someone who also has had to move.

My husband has been asked to attend a meeting at ARP post in our basement tonight to hear helpful advice in case our dams are busted. It seems that enemy planes have been looking at the dams a little too carefully lately, hence our odd daytime alerts, and dirty work is suspected. Of course all this is not for general discussion, as some folk would panic at the mere idea, though Husband and I have wondered about the possibility ever since we did it to them. Special water sirens are being installed to distinguish from the ordinary. They reckon that it would take ten minutes from the busting for water to reach these flats. We lie low so would be sure to take in plenty water. Belief is we would be safe above the third floor. We are on the third so would be unlucky though presumably our stuff stands a better chance of survival than the lower floors. One imagines the experts don't know exactly since this has never happened, but anyway, let us hope the eighth floor will remain dry! But if the foundations sag ... ooooer. And what of the thousands of private homes for miles round? Fortunately Sheffield is plenty hilly and it seems to me that the water siren should be the signal to get to high ground at once and not attempt to maroon oneself in top floors of places where low-lying. Not a nice prospect with winter just due as it is sure to be done at night. What a mad world ...

Peter Baxter   *Monday, 11th.* Preparations and speculations are in full spate for the forthcoming Three-Power Conference in Moscow. The American press keeps printing an awful lot of rot about Russian ambitions, which makes it painfully obvious that the Americans as a whole still haven't the faintest understanding of the

USSR, and are still very frightened of the Communist bogey. The USA is also getting horribly imperialist in many ways. Recent speeches about post-war aviation, shipping, retention of bases, etc., make sad reading. Politically, the Americans are about a hundred years behind the Germans, and that's saying something. The Russians, for their part, are suspicious about our actions in North Africa and Italy, and justifiably so. I'm more than suspicious myself!

Sunday, 24th. There took place today the biggest defence test   Frank Edwards
which has yet taken place in London. The army, every unit of the Home Guard, and elements of the navy, air force, civil defence, NFS, and police took part. The regular army were the 'enemy' and the Home Guard were the main defenders. From all accounts the whole test was a great success and the Home Guard very successfully saved London from the 'invaders'. I was called out, as a local member of the Home Guard, and we were defending this district, or part of it, I should say, but the 'invaders' did not get to this area, and so we did not come into contact with them, which disappointed a great many of us.

NOVEMBER 1943

Saturday, 6th. I think the magnificent courage and devotion   Frank Edwards
to duty of 21-year-old Flight Sergeant Richard Aaron, who, it was announced last night, has posthumously been awarded the VC is perhaps the greatest example of its kind I have yet read of during this war.[59] In appalling conditions and although terribly wounded and dying, yet he was all out to save his plane and crew from falling into the hands of the enemy. And, one reads, this young man once said to a friend, 'I'm not one for heroics.' Truly, this war has shown us that we have indeed some wonderful young men, and it is a million pities that in many

such instances these grand fellows have lost their lives, though their great example will live for ever.

The Russians are still making great progress and news of their capture of Kiev comes today.

Maggie Joy Blunt

Saturday, 20th. When the new ration book period began in the summer I changed my grocer not because I was dissatisfied with the one I patronised but because the other one in the village still runs a delivery van and to have one's goods delivered is such an enormous help. I now give an order about once a fortnight. The greengrocer (also newsagent), butcher, baker, milkman all still deliver, so that I only have to do personal shopping for points and clothes.

The long evenings have begun. The kitchen blackout I leave up all the week (and the cottage *beams* on a Saturday morning when I take it down before going to work because it knows that the kitchen will have two whole days of whatever sunshine there is and that there will be a fire in the range!). The outside painting has been done and the gardener has been digging and clipping and sweeping and weeding.

There always seems a lot to do in the evenings during the winter and I wish it were the other way round in a way because of getting home in the blackout when nights are dark and cold and wet. The London Symphony Orchestra was performing at the centre on Wednesday, for war factory workers only. I should have been one of them but for somebody's error: ENSA sent 2,000 vouchers which were allotted to the various factories including ours, but the hall holds only 1,000 people and at the last moment all our vouchers were recalled.

Peter Baxter

Monday, 22nd. There's a colossal rumpus going on over the release from gaol of Mosley and his wife,[60] and rightly so, in my opinion. The worst possible impression has been created by the way the thing has been done, while Parliament is in recess, and without prior authority from the people's representatives.

Herbert Morrison 'takes the can' for it, of course, but he can't have acted without permission or instructions from Churchill. The only person I have met so far who defends the release is Hannen Swaffer [a prolific and outspoken columnist], who maintains that Mosley is a broken man, sick and bitterly disillusioned, more to be pitied than feared, and that his continued detention would be cruel and undemocratic. All that may be true, but Mosley was not merely a theoretical Fascist. He adopted the full technique of street gangs and beatings-up and thuggery, and a man who could turn that stuff loose on a democracy cannot be treated generously. It is too bad an example to future aspirants to Fascist power. What must the peoples of occupied Europe, and the Russians, think of it? No, I consider the release a major blunder, however ill the man may be. Gandhi, after all, was not released even when his death was daily expected.

Saturday, 27th. Berlin again last night ... I hope Hitler remembers how he in the past ordered certain places to be rubbed off the map. I'm sorry for the Germans though I can believe I might not be if they had done to me, or if they ever do to me, what they've done to many. Husband has no pity for them whatever – says they wrecked his career and health 25 years ago which is true. Even though that has affected me, I am not bitter about it. Husband says if we will only leave Joe Stalin to settle with the Germans they will be settled with properly after this lot. That Joe has no Christian ethics to upset his actions, whereas they always get in the way of our doing what should be done. I don't wholeheartedly agree with that: when it comes to ideas on God and Life I never do entirely agree with Husband ...

Edie Rutherford

I dislike the mention on BBC and in paper that pork goes well *with* turkey. Surely it will be fairer if those who don't get a turkey get a bit of pork? I find it hard to believe there will be so much of either that anyone will get either for sure. As for

our 29th, or is it our 30th, egg ... they are so stale these days
that I have got to like dried as much, as I never had a packet of
them that was stale.

Our men in Italy are having a poor time, weather must
be awful. I wish it would improve for them. Somehow when
told about the steps we are taking to preserve pictures and
monuments and suchlike as we come to them in Italy I want
to shout, 'Is that really necessary – let's get on with the war!'
Let the Italians rootle out their own treasures ... if we persist
in helping they'll accuse us one day of looting their stuff or
something low that only such low minds stoop to.

DECEMBER 1943

Frank Edwards   *Monday, 6th.* Now that the mornings are so dark it is a case of
going to work in the blackout and coming home from work in
it. Yet a few days ago when the blackout ended earlier, it was
rather nice to see curtains pulled back from windows of rooms
in which the lights were on. Going up Park Lane, past the big
hotels and flats one would see, from the top of a bus, beautiful electric light fittings in rooms, or sometimes just a lovely
standard lamp throwing a warm light in the room. Sometimes
curtains would just be drawn back, a window would be opened
outwards or perhaps pushed up whilst the occupant took a look
across the park opposite.

This evening, some three hours ago, a communiqué was
broadcast by all the Allied radio stations of the decisions
taken at the meeting last week of the Big Three – Churchill,
Roosevelt and Stalin, and I imagine there will be a great outburst of rage and insults by the Huns now they have heard the
splendid results of this meeting.[61]

Edie Rutherford   *Sunday, 12th.* Sidelights on this war – girls at office yesterday
very interested in a case they discovered in the back of one of the

women's weeklies where free advice is given to those in trouble. The case in question is that of a woman whose husband was a prisoner of war, and she got too friendly with *two* Allied officers and got pregnant, she doesn't know by which man. Then her husband is repatriated ... whatever shall she do? He is critically ill and she has enough regard for him to want to spare him a bad shock. Well, the woman in the paper said it was hard to advise, she had to say how awful it was for her to go so far with *two* men at the same time. Advised her to write to the hospital matron where her husband would be sent on landing, explain matters and ask for a case to be made out that he could not get leave or visitors until he is strong enough to take such a shock ...

The girls started condemning such women, cited many similar cases, so after a bit I asked them what they thought servicemen went to VD hospitals for? Reminded them that of the two sexes men lapse more than women – to date. One girl told of a friend of hers with a husband in Middle East who got too pally with an RAF officer with wife and child. Suddenly one day she heard the lover was killed and her husband returning home ... she is now in a fever wondering if incriminating letters she sent her lover are with his kit which will be returned to his wife, and if so, will she turn up when her husband is there?

Wednesday, 15th. I am reliably informed that a woman living in one of these flats with an infant son is selling the orange juice she gets from the clinic. This woman has two boys under 14 as well as the baby so one would have thought that in the event of the juice not suiting the mother or baby, the boys would have had it. A bachelor living in another flat boasts he gets all the orange juice he needs ...

Still terribly rushed at work, no matter how much overtime one does, the mountain of work still remains a mountain ... I wish I knew a fairy with domestic leanings who would come and do my housework for me while we're so hard-pressed at office.

Our draughtsman friend is still out of work and fears now he'll be thrust into army. I must say as I looked at him last night, his shoes dirty, face unshaven, I felt not much pity, rather a desire that he should be put somewhere his ideas would be smartened up a bit. Imagine a man loafing round for weeks at a time like this. He lives next door to the secretary of local YMCA, surely he could have got some voluntary jobs in connection with Xmas for the forces had he had the desire? This man leans a lot to the Left and rails against capital, etc., but there is not much evidence of co-operation in his own life.

Thursday, 23rd. I consider it rotten of us, and bad propaganda, bombing enemy-occupied territory during this Xmas week. We know from the past the awful aftermath of a blitz and those folk have enough to endure as it is, and it is the Germans who have spoilt our Christmases in the past, so let their towns have the aftermath now. We want the help of people in enemy-occupied territory soon ...

I have just finished reading Tom Harrisson's *Savage Civilisation.* He has a queer style. I don't mean his sarcasm which I rather enjoy knowing from first hand how the whites do treat blacks. At times the sentences don't seem to me to make sense – but maybe I am at fault. Anyway, the book was a Herculean task, and having lived in Queensland a couple of years I could get a grasp of that side of things better than if I had never been there.

Frank Edwards   *Christmas Day.* It has been a very pleasant Christmas Day for me. I was up early to attend the first Mass of Christmas, which, as there was no midnight Mass again this year, was at eight o'clock this morning. There was a big congregation. Later in the morning the postman arrived and he brought me a message which was tremendously welcome, a postcard from my cousin who is a POW. I write to him regularly and send a monthly parcel of cigarettes, but because of the camp regulations on the number of cards which a POW can write in a month, I cannot hear from him direct very often. Perhaps you can guess therefore the great joy which this card gave me (and my family) particularly being delivered on this day, when our thoughts are so specially with our absent ones. Incidentally I think the post office did a special good turn to deliver this card on Xmas morning because in doing so I got it exactly one month from the day (November 25th) it was posted.

Wednesday, 29th. Christmas is over and gone, all too quickly. **Peter Baxter** Dora came and stayed at the Buchanans' in the village here, from Friday evening until Tuesday. I had to go into work on Monday morning, but was free the rest of the while. There were two other couples present, besides Mr and Mrs B, and their daughter Eunice, so that made up quite a party of us, and we were able to have plenty of party games and competitions. We usually got back to cards eventually, as Barney himself is a real card fiend: Newmarket Chase the Ace, Put and Take, Pip, and Call your Partner were the favourites, but we also had a lot of fun playing Up Jenkins (or Tippit) and Hokey Pokey, a variant of the time-honoured game Grunt, Piggy, Grunt.

The food was excellent, considering present difficulties. Christmas dinner consisted of roast goose, pork sausage, savoury stuffing, mashed swedes, boiled potatoes and brown gravy, followed by Christmas pudding and custard. We would have preferred sprouts to swedes, and we missed the usual roast potatoes, but in somebody else's house you can't be fussy. The goose was admirable. Wine and spirits completely unobtainable, so we contented ourselves throughout the holiday with ale, Mackeson's milk stout and orange crush cordial. Many of the accessories of pre-war Christmases were inevitably lacking – no bon-bons, no grapes, no nuts (except salted peanuts) – but there was no shortage of cigarettes, and we managed to make up a few chocolates and sweets between us. Altogether we did exceedingly well, and the time certainly sped by much too quickly.

The news over Christmas was good. On Monday came the announcement of the sinking of the *Scharnhorst*.[62] The Germans didn't stand much chance against our superior strength, but somehow it seemed to help wipe out the nasty memory of that foggy day last year when that ship, with her two companions, impudently sailed straight through our home waters. Tonight comes further satisfying news of the sinking of a blockade-runner and three destroyers in the Atlantic. Nice work, navy!

Muriel Green   *New Year's Eve*. Work all day and the shop was shut early for the dance. It was great fun, several had hired costumes, but the majority were home-made. There were about 40 in fancy dress. J made a rather doubtful variety of Russian peasant girl outfit from all sorts of odd clothes and paper which looked very pretty. I was a Dutch girl in a checked frock, Austrian peasant apron, a cap made from a white table napkin, two raffia plaits of hair and a pair of real Dutch clogs which I bought at the beginning of the war from a contraband load which was captured. It looked quite a good turnout. Four of the residents came together as a hospital ensemble, a man as a nurse and another as a surgeon and two girls as patients which the nurse and surgeon pushed on the dinner wagon. This caused much amusement, also a policeman and Nellie Wallace [a much-loved music-hall performer] who were one pair. There were several period costumes, gipsies, a Hoola-hoola girl, another Dutch girl, a tennis player, and about six or seven forms of sheik or Eastern costume made up from sheets, towels and dressing-gowns. The whole evening went off with rather a grand swing and we all enjoyed it. We danced until 2 a.m. The bar was very busy and many were worse for drink. At midnight we sang in the New Year with 'Auld Lang Syne' after listening for Big Ben on the radio.

1944 THE BEGINNING OF THE END

Increasing confidence at home was bolstered during 1944 by increasing success abroad. Although the Italian campaign was bogged down for months by strong German resistance, Rome was finally liberated on 4 June. Two days later came D-Day, the Allied landings on the beaches of Normandy. The Germans had been deceived into believing that the landings would be in the Pas de Calais, but the invading troops found the Normandy terrain a difficult fighting ground and it was two months before a break-out was achieved. Paris was liberated on 25 August. Ten days earlier, French and American forces had launched a diversionary invasion in south-eastern France.

On the eastern front, the Russians pressed on and by August they were in Rumania, Poland, East Prussia and the Baltic countries. In the Far East, the Japanese were retreating as US forces began to recapture occupied territory and British and Indian troops fought their way into Burma.

In Britain, news of these successful campaigns was welcome, but there was now a new threat from the air. In June the Germans began a flying bomb offensive: V1 pilotless planes, packed with explosive, were launched across the Channel. The whirring roar of these 'doodlebugs' was unnerving enough; even more so was the moment when their fuel ran out and they crashed to the ground. On the ground, people were instructed to fall flat, a precautionary measure regarded with some cynicism since no one knew where these flying machines would fall. Many were destroyed before they landed, but civilian casualties – particularly in London and its suburbs – ran into thousands. It was, wrote Evelyn Waugh, 'as though the city were infested with enormous, venomous insects'. Then, in September, came the V2 rockets, monster missiles which carried a ton of explosive. Unlike the V1s, they were a silent menace – until they exploded.

Despite this new aerial bombardment, the British people remained confident that the war would soon be over. Towards the end of the year the blackout was lifted and the Home Guard disbanded. There was now a certain war-weariness, along with a growing sense that the post-war world would have to offer a new deal for ordinary people. In Wales the miners went on strike, in London the bus drivers. There was a restlessness in the air, a general wish to get the war over and done with and begin a post-war reconstruction. Aware of this, the government responded with proposals for education and housing. The prospect of peace was widely discussed, but any hope that this would be the last year of the war was rudely shattered by the Arnhem disaster in September and the German counter-offensive in the Ardennes in December. It was not over yet.

JANUARY 1944

Muriel Green   *New Year's Day.* What will this year bring, I wonder? Last year brought several things I never expected. I really do think this will be the last whole year of war if it lasts as long as that. I wonder a great deal where I shall be next New Year's Day. If the war is over I don't expect we shall be here, as I expect this place will close, though perhaps not at once. I think I have had a happy year and nothing I have done I regret. I was probably nearer death than ever before but never worried about that. This year will probably bring more hardships and great losses to the country, but if it finishes the war successfully it will be worth it. Very tired today after all the celebrations.

Frank Edwards   *Monday, 3rd.* This week we shall really have to get down to brass tacks once more. I am afraid last week seemed hard going after the four days' Xmas holiday, and I personally found it difficult to get the spirit for work, not but that I did plenty nevertheless. I shall be glad when the mornings get lighter as at present I go to and come home from work in the blackout. From tonight's papers I see that Berlin has had a couple of big-scale raids in the past 21 hours. This battle of Berlin must be getting the Berliners down, one would think. Anyway I should think the raids must take some enduring.

Tuesday, 11th. An excitement of magnitude occurred on this front about a fortnight before Xmas. I came home from the office one evening as usual about 6.30 to find the cottage in chaos. Someone had prised open the kitchen window, removing the blackout, opened every cupboard, drawer and box in the place, turned most of the contents on to the floors and walked off with my fur coat, an electric iron, two clocks, miscellaneous pieces of jewellery (nearly every necklace he could find, most of them quite valueless, and an old rosary which has been in our family as a curio for years – we were none of us Catholics – but no earrings of which I have a great number) and various other odds and ends. I rushed to the neighbour's, telephoned the police, took the next morning off (a Saturday and snowing, the only snow we have yet had here) and was a heroine for at least 24 hours. Of course none of the articles or the thief has been traced, although the police suspect a man of 60 who has done several similar jobs in this neighbourhood. A cunning old devil. They say he has an appalling police record. He goes about as a jobbing gardener asking for work, then watches the surrounding houses. Several people have said to me, 'But if the police know him why don't they go and arrest him?' which in England you cannot do without evidence. They never seem able to get evidence.

The most serious items are the fur coat and electric iron. I am covered by an all-in policy but not for the wartime increase in values. The iron, for instance, cost me in 1939 between 13/- and 15/-. Now, if you can get such a thing, they are about

Maggie Joy Blunt

30/-. As for the fur coat, I have applied for more coupons but doubt very much if I shall get them – the Board of Trade, someone has warned me, expects one to go around in a Lady Godiva condition. And then the price! My coat was a good dyed squirrel, bought in 1936 and had just been cleaned and remodelled (£10/10 had gone on that). The furrier told me it would sell like that today for £150. It cost me originally about £40. With the jewellery and all the other items I could not with any honesty make my claim up to £100. The insurance company are sending someone to see the house this week – but what I am to show him beyond a cracked kitchen windowpane and a practically empty jewel box I don't quite know.

Peter Baxter *Wednesday, 19th.* I returned from leave last night – an extremely enjoyable ten days, which we divided between London and Blackpool. The first weekend we were in London, and met Private Paul Fischer, a friend of my Uncle Joe in New York, who was staying for a 48-hours' pass under the parental roof. He turned out to be 6'4", and 16 stone of simple, good-natured humanity – not at all the slick, streamlined smarty I had imagined would be produced by that rather formidable metropolis. When we were introduced he shook me firmly by the hand, looked me straight in the eye and said, with unmistakable sincerity, 'Glad to know you, Peter.' He was like that all through – straightforward, honest, simple, and we found that it was we, denizens of old England, who were the sophisticates, and not the son of modern America. He is an excellent card-player, and a devotee of swing music. He hates walking and rides whenever possible. But in the social sense, there is nothing artificial about him at all. I got him to talk as much as I could about his home life, and the US army. He said he is having the time of his life in England. The troops get better food than they did back home, better living conditions, more leave and travelling facilities. The American idea seems to be that their fighting men are entitled to the best of everything. I couldn't help

comparing it with the traditional British attitude that anything will do for the troops. They'll grumble, but they'll put
up with it. Two small comparisons: Paul, a PFC (equivalent to
our lance-corporal) gets paid about £17 a month. I, a corporal,
get about £8/8, 28/- of which is deducted for my wife's allowance. Paul pays 3d for a packet of 20 good American cigarettes
at the Army Post Exchange. In our NAAFI I pay 1/6 for 20
adulterated 'Virginia' cigarettes. Another noticeable difference
was in our respective attitudes to officers. Paul regarded them
with a friendly, but quite undeferential respect. (He said their
food is often not as good as the men's, and their expenses higher
in proportion to their pay.) We, on the other hand, are supposed to tremble and bow and scrape when an officer appears.
Usually we regard them with a mixture of pity and contempt.
The gap between the living conditions of British officers and
men is vast. Paul couldn't understand that at all. He couldn't
see, either, why I was so impatient to get out of the RAF, until
I made him realise the difference between the forces of the US
and of HM. He loves the army. He is comfortable and well
cared for. The discipline is light provided you behave yourself.
He likes the fellows he's with. He likes England, and altogether
he's very happy. Of course, that's partly accounted for by his
own temperament, but I'm sure the whole atmosphere of a US
soldier's life is very different from the prevailing atmosphere
in our forces. I liked Paul, and he brought home to me several
of the good points in the US outlook and way of life which I
had rather lost sight of in my aesthetic impatience with their
cultural immaturity.

Saturday, 22nd. We had a return visit of the raiders at 11.30   Frank Edwards
this morning. Again there was a very heavy barrage and the
planes could be heard diving about in an endeavour to get away
from the barrage, but I think without success. There was a
considerable amount of shrapnel and at times it seemed to be
just raining down. This raid and that of last night had everyone

talking this morning, just like we used to do in the days of the blitz.

It is good to learn of the big new Allied landing in Italy and rather staggering to read that we sent out last night a force of approx. 1,000 planes to bomb Germany and the most Germany could collect for raiding this country was 90 of which he lost 10 per cent.

FEBRUARY 1944

Frank Edwards   *Saturday, 12th.* There are so many Americans around just now that I am sure at times you wonder whether you are in England or the States. There seem to be three or four American soldiers to every British Tommy and just now I am seeing quite a lot of US navy men around. I suppose it will seem quite funny after the war is over and they all return home. Anyway, by the time it's all finished we shall have shown them a few things they will like at least to mention back across the herring pond. Our silver threepenny bits they think are 'cute' and these they are collecting as fast as they can get them. Our pantomimes are all right but they 'don't get' what a pantomime is all about. And this week I see the American servicemen have just been going crazy on buying Valentines of which they think a great deal in the States. I am afraid we over here don't think very much about Valentine's Day of late years but our 'buddies' have helped clear stocks which have been on some shelves for many years.

Peter Baxter   *Monday, 21st.* I have recently seen two of the specially made American films in the series *Why We Fight*. The first I saw was no. 2, entitled *The Nazis Strike*, dealing with Hitler's pre-war activities, his Fascist imitators in other countries, Munich, and the invasion of Poland. It was very well done, the commentary and maps were excellent, but I couldn't help feeling that it had been made four years too late. We have learnt its message now in the bitter experience of total war; it should have been hammered home in late 1939 and early 1940. Here is one stupid, benighted idiot who failed completely at this time to see the big issues involved, and to recognise Fascism for the filthy scourge it is.

The other one I saw was no. 3 of the series, called *Divide and Conquer*, dealing with the months October 1939 to July 1940, covering the period of the 'phoney war', and the invasion of Denmark, Norway, the Low Countries and France. It was most impressive, and made one realise more fully than ever how miraculous was Britain's escape in 1940, and how the Russians must have fought to resist and finally fling back such colossal military might. Reverting to the earlier film, for a moment, it contained the most pathetic sight I have ever seen on the screen – the full scene of Chamberlain's return from Munich, waving his silly little piece of paper, his face beaming with pride in what he obviously believed to be a great act of statesmanship, and no trace of any slight shame at having perpetrated one of the most shameful betrayals in all history. Did Britain really deserve such a leader in such a perilous period of her history?

Tuesday, 29th. Local morning paper gives space for my appeal   Edie Rutherford
for playing cards for submarine crews, as requested by *Reveille*.
I hope the publicity will mean that plenty of packs are sent.
Snow is melting, what a mess the streets are. But the sun shines on it as beautifully as ever, though it has a coating of Sheffield grime now. How dogs and kids enjoy the snow!

All this discussion about civil aviation after the war … the Tories obviously want private enterprise, Labour wants government concerns apparently. I don't know enough about it to have an opinion but I do think that competition far from being healthy in many directions is just plain idiotic. As Husband says, he was quite a small boy when he asked his mother why one milkman could not serve their street and several other streets round, and how dissatisfied he was with her explanation about it being a free country, and we've had it from Mr So-and-so for years, he followed us from this and that street, etc... . Zoning is a good thing in the main, and as I see it, till every belly in the world is assured of enough food, and every head a shelter, there should be no waste in the world.

MARCH 1944

Maggie Joy
Blunt

Wednesday, 1st. Air raids last week were noisy here but there were no incidents. Gunfire is terrific. My cottage shakes like a jelly and I wonder when the ceilings will collapse. I lay in bed one night watching the flares. Various relatives and friends in districts near London tell of damage and fires. One or two people I know saw planes shot down. Some complain of 'nerves' from which they have not suffered before, others say they find these short, sharp raids easier to endure than the old blitz. June has moved with her baby daughter to Gerrards Cross and Stella who was living with her has gone back to live at S.M. and travels to her job in London daily. N, at Swiss Cottage, who is suffering from colds and sinus trouble and much the same debility that I had, says that she feels much more likely to die of illness than under a bomb.

Wednesday, 8th. Received full amount from insurance for burglary, and to my astonishment, eighteen coupons from Board of Trade for fur coat. The fur coat I have been lucky enough to replace with a kitten musquash which my London tailor and furrier happened to have in stock. He let me have it without coupons – I did not enquire too closely why but assumed it to be second-hand, cleaned and remodelled. It is quite a success and many people say they like it better than my old one although I am not passionately fond of musquash. Cost me £60, which some folk think much too expensive but most of the amount was covered by insurance money and tailor has given me a replacement value certificate for £100 for insurance. Have replaced nothing else. Still using old flat iron and will get an electric if I can. The other items stolen I consider lost to me.

Thursday, 9th. Yesterday in town I saw something happen which I have up to now only had happen to me in a nightmare … I was in a shop, standing a pace or two behind another woman at a counter. Suddenly her pink silk knickers flopped on the floor. She gave a wild glance round, I suppose to see what sex I was, being vaguely aware there was another person in the shop. Then with a red face, she grabbed the pants, and wildly stumbled round the counter and through a doorway behind, the assistant meantime asking, 'What?' which I of course cleared up, and made my purchase quickly and came away, to save the unlucky lady further embarrassment. I bet they were Utility pants, said she who has no time for Utility wear.

Edie Rutherford

This morning I have an airgraph from my sister in South Africa dated February 17th. All of us females at work are doing far too much overtime. The men staff don't do any, and the workmen get paid if they do. It is all wrong, and yet the work is there to be done, and being conscientious we do it, but, again, *it is all wrong*.

Thursday, 16th. I begin to wonder these days if this will after all be the last blackout winter. We don't seem to *get on* with this war, despite all the weight of bombs we threw at Cassino[63] yesterday. News this morning is of the big defence Jerry is putting up there – he seems invincible – shall we ever break the Nazi heart?

This afternoon there was a knock at the door – a woman living in the opposite wing of these flats said, 'Would you accept these?' holding out a paper bag. 'This' proved to be four eggs, huge ones. I said with pop eyes that of course I would accept them! She said she had had some sent her and thought she'd like me to share … what a beautiful thought!

Dear God, 40 planes lost last night ... we watched over 100 bombers pass over us last night at dusk, such a noise they make. It made me quite ill for the evening, just thinking of the poor lads, the risk they take and what they would be doing to fellow humans, for we *are* all fellows of each other. What utter folly war is. The day will dawn when those who are sorted out to have honours bestowed on them will be the ones with *no* war service.

Husband's nephew, fighter pilot, who left England a few weeks ago, is in North Africa, quite happily camped in a wood and will no doubt soon be in the thick of things. How will all these young men, those who survive I mean, ever settle down to humdrum life after the war? Oh well, with civil flying the way it looks like being, many of them should get jobs of a kind they'll like.

Maggie Joy Blunt

Thursday, 16th. Last night another big raid on London, according to the papers. Guns here were active and I got all my Red Cross uniform ready. We are not being called but have to use our own discretion about going to the point. Can hear our bombers going out now. A continual hum, like the dynamo of some fearful machine. I became conscious of this noise about a quarter of an hour ago. Mr O went home tonight prepared for another enemy raid. They come now only when there is no moon ... which does not rise until 1 a.m. tonight. He and his wife live in a top flat near Paddington and he has seen many fires recently. This evening he was going to collect some sand which is being issued again to householders in London, and has a garden hose ready to attach to his kitchen tap.

I am sick of this war. Sick of everything. Of the waiting, and the sound of bombers, of my work and my clothes and the general dullness of my complicated and unfruitful existence. Having caught up on the routine work which had collected while I was ill am left now with nothing to do and very little in view. Our department is dead and apparently buried. On Saturday I had a chance to speak to our general manager when he asked me point-blank what I was doing and how I was getting on. I said, 'Frankly, nothing,' and managed to imply I was restless and bored and wanted to be doing more. Had intended to get this across to D but he is so much away with our film and when he is back seems to spend most of his time at the main office doing what no one knows. He does not appear to have any plans for his staff or any ideas for his department at all. He puts me on to routine work which B could do and the amount of work she has to do for him she has herself admitted could be done by our junior Miss C who is learning shorthand and typing at night school. B may leave – she has been talking of doing this of course since I came two years ago – but now her petrol is being stopped and after March she will have to come a long and difficult journey by bus so is quite seriously asking for her release to join the WRNS.

Friday, 17th. Today being St Patrick's day has been different. **Muriel Green** We have about 70 Irish residents, many of whom took the day off from work. Tonight we had a dance and the majority of them got at least merry, some more than merry. All week boxes of shamrock have been arriving from Ireland, and they all wear bits of it pinned on their coats and emerald green ribbons. The fact that Eire isn't very popular diplomatically just now did not make any of them wish to hide their nationality. Tonight they did Irish reels and sang Irish songs. It made a jolly evening.

Monday, 20th. It has been one of those awkward sort of days **Frank Edwards** when you seem to do plenty yet have nothing or little to show for it. All day the air seems to have been full of the noise of planes and at one period this afternoon the noise was so great that I could not hear a subscriber on the telephone. It is unusual for us to hear so much activity whilst at work, for whilst, of course, planes do pass over – and I expect in big numbers – it is rarely that we hear much of them. The Russians are still progressing at a terrific speed, and the aerial war onslaught by the

Allies gathers momentum. Home progress continues with the land fighting in Italy which is being carried on with violence, but it seems a difficult and slow job due to so many difficulties of one kind and another.

Wednesday, 22nd. I did not seem to have been asleep long last night before being awakened by the sirens and found it was nearly one o'clock. I dressed and with other members of the family went to the shelter across the road. We thought we had been very quick, but found many people in the shelter. AA defences were going pretty strongly and in the shelter we could hear the rocket shells going up, and planes diving about to try and evade the defences. There were no incidents in this borough. I would say that since the new series of raids started about a month ago we have been using the street shelter and so have many other residents in the road who, like us, have not a shelter of their own, and because of the considerable bombing which this borough has lately received.

Maggie Joy   *Wednesday, 29th.* People are seething. Nearly everyone I have
Blunt   spoken to about it was disappointed in Churchill's speech (the one broadcast last Sunday). Many want to know why he spoke at all – they resented his cracks at his critics when no one could answer him back, and felt he was trying to win the country's sympathy for a possible coming election. We are restless and anxious about the second front – some people think it will start in the Balkans, some favour Norway and few think we shall try through France. And we stick in southern Italy. While Russia moves from strength to strength.

APRIL 1944

Maggie Joy   *Tuesday, 4th.* Last week Shinwell MP came down and spoke to
Blunt   our discussion group. Over 300 people came to hear him. His

subject was 'Post-War Britain'. He said that he thought world economic and political unity an excellent ideal but we must be realists.

He could not see how we could achieve this perfection while such differing ideologies as that of Soviet Russia and that of individualist, capitalist USA existed together in the world. We must realise the competition that would face us from these enormous empires after the war, and also possibly China and India, and that we must organise our industrial resources to the very fullest extent if we did not want to fade to a fourth- or fifth-rate power. It could be done if we willed it. We had the resources and the skill. All the more mature industries and the public services he thought should operate under state direction, but not Civil Service direction, as we know it today, but by personnel drawn from the workers and technicians in industry who thoroughly understand it. The smaller, newer industries might be left to private enterprise. And so on. It was a stimulating speech, given impromptu, without notes, and was received with tremendous enthusiasm. Many questions were asked afterwards and the meeting would have gone on indefinitely but for the chairman's firm closing of it.

Wednesday, 12th. Work again today. A lovely sunny day, nicer   Edie Rutherford
than any day of the Easter holiday, drat it. Sirens at 1.30 a.m., All Clear 2.10 p.m. and no noise, so we stayed abed. Went to town from work, to get hair done. Town crammed. A friend whose cat we cared for over the hols and who went to Newcastle, said it wasn't too bad going up on Friday, but the crush getting back yesterday was awful. She stood Newcastle to York, and York to Sheffield and felt lucky at that. The trees have already started to sprout and these few days' good warm weather have made a tremendous diff. to their progress. The birds also are singing joyously.

Brains Trust last night was good. For the first time we had two women. Hope they do that more often: must break down the idea women haven't as much sense as men – many haven't, but then many men haven't as much sense as many women!

Maggie Joy Blunt

Thursday, 13th. At the office today I had to take under my wing an artist sent from the SBAC. He is doing painting and drawings of aircraft production all over the country and has already visited our Birmingham factory. The paintings are for propaganda on British wartime industry for distribution abroad.

Arrived this week to help Mr Thrush, in the room opposite is a man blinded by blast in an air raid. He is not quite totally blind – can see objects at a distance but nothing close to. He takes down shorthand on a Braille machine and types from that. How he sets his material out we haven't discovered. But Thrush says his work is excellent. He is what is known as a 'gentleman', i.e. obviously comes from the better-educated sections of the middle class and seems a very likeable person. I commented today on his courage (he does not seem to mind discussing his handicap at all: in fact he tells you at once and quite cheerfully, 'I am practically blind') and he replied, 'I don't know that it doesn't take more courage to stay at home and do nothing …'

Frank Edwards

Wednesday, 19th. Coming home from work this evening something seemed to be strange when I got to Hyde Park Corner. Here was a huge crowd of people and at first I thought there had been an accident, since these people seemed to be one big crowd and not in a queue. But it was no accident, just people trying to get on buses. Anyway in the Underground the same thing prevailed, the platform being crowded three deep. Whatever could be the cause of these exceptional circumstances, I wondered. Then I arrived at Hammersmith. Outside the station and across the road I went to my bus stopping place. Here was a queue of people – about 300 in number, and it was here I learned there was a bus strike. Only some buses running – but none on the No. 9 service which is my home service. Seeing the

strength of the queue which continued to grow, I, in common
with many others, decided to walk the 2½ miles. Tired after
the day's work, the prospect of this wasn't too exciting. But I
had to get home and I wanted my meal, so I made the best of it
and walked. But I might say there was a general air of discontent amongst the public from many of whom I heard opinions
expressed about this strike as I walked home.

Thursday, 20th. I expected to have to walk to Hammersmith
Underground this morning as the bus strike was still on.
Instead I found the military had taken over and were running a
service of army lorries between our local bus garage and Hammersmith. The service was very good and we had every courtesy
from the drivers – very much more I might say than we are
used to from bus drivers on the normal service. There was no
conductor, but I was very glad to note that very few people
failed to forget the driver. The bus strike has spread during
the day, but on our service – No. 9, and also on Nos. 73 and
33 – I found the army had taken over the LPTB buses and were
driving them. A mate was on the conductor's platform to look
after the setting down and picking up of passengers but not
in the capacity of conductor since there were no conductors,
no fares, and no grumbles. There were plenty of expressions
of thanks and gratefulness for the splendid work these men of
the RASC were doing in helping us by keeping the transport
going. Few people failed to express disgust at the bus conductors and drivers being on strike at a time like this.

MAY 1944

Friday, 5th. Business has got very slack with my firm, steel,   Edie Rutherford
annealers, heat treaters and forgers. Boss says he has been told
by a steel man who thinks he knows, that we have enough stuff
piled up for six months, and that we hope to end this part of

war in that time. However, if after a month or two that looks unlikely, we can all set to with a will again. Sounds feasible. Anyway, yesterday the boss said everyone must decide on a week's holiday whether they can get away or not ... Husband and I had decided we would not even think of hols till this invasion business got going. All at work had taken the same view.

Curtin [the Australian prime minister] is talking a bit about emigration to Australia. I doubt if he'll get 100 per cent backing at home. But it is clear we'll have to do something about our Empire if we are to hang together. Empty continents and overpopulated lands can't exist in the world without wars resulting.

One of the 21-year-old girls at office who has been deferred up to now, has to go at last. She chose land army. Yesterday the woman who recruits for that did her best to put her off, painted the job in its worst light, but Peggy remained keen, so she has her medical on Sunday morning. The office girl leaves next week to join telephones at PO [Post Office]. The girl who lost her husband two months ago is restless ... if something doesn't stop the rot soon I look like being the oldest employee before long!

Frank Edwards *Saturday, 6th.* This afternoon I paid a visit to the *Daily Telegraph* Prisoner of War exhibition being held in the grounds of Clarence House in the Mall. This is an intensely interesting exhibition and represents an internment camp. It is of course being run in conjunction with the British Red Cross and in consequence everything is as near to the real thing as possible. There were a great many visitors – I estimate there were something like 800 people in the queue ahead of me waiting for admission; and I was on the end of the queue for a very short while, and in a matter of about ten minutes there was upwards of a further 50 people on the queue, which constantly grew in size. The whole length of the queue, people were in

most instances three abreast. It was, I think, the most orderly
queue perhaps I have ever seen, for there were no police on this
queue.

I heard some passers-by say, 'How cheered our prisoners
would be if only they could see this huge queue and the patience
of those waiting for admission.' The hut showing the various
sketches, drawings and paintings done by the prisoners in their
weary hours, together with many items they had made from all
sorts of bits and pieces – chiefly saved from the packing of their
Red Cross parcels, aroused the highest admiration. Another
hut of especial interest dealt with the food parcels sent every
week by the Red Cross, whilst another depicted living quarters
including sleeping bunks.

Tuesday, 9th. Coming home from work at midday today, an   Edie Rutherford
old woman got on tram, carrying two heavy shopping bags. A
woman said to her child, about ten years, 'Get up and give your
seat to the lady.' The child shook her head and turned her face
round to look out of the tram window, to indicate clearly she
was not interested. And that was that. Contrast – my mother
would have said nothing but would have looked volumes, and
when I got home I would have *felt* volumes. And I realise today
I would have *deserved* volumes.

Another sunny day but cool wind persists. Just finished
reading [the widow of the Liberal prime minister] Margot
Asquith's book, Off *the Record*. It is eminently readable, her
books always are, but I bet she makes some folk mad! I agree
with Margot in many things, for instance her attitude to
Neville Chamberlain, and Roosevelt. But I disagree with her
over many things, hunting pre-eminently, and dislike folk she
dislikes but for other reasons than hers. She always amuses me
– speaks of herself as not rich and calmly mentions she and her
son lived at the Savoy for two years after being blitzed. She does
know that to millions on earth, one who affords the Savoy is
as near a millionaire … If I knew Margot Asquith I believe I

would love her for some things but that she would infuriate me for others, so it is as well I don't know her!

Government getting down to equal pay question. Not before time though it depends a lot who handles it what results we get.

JUNE 1944

Muriel Green   *Monday, 5th.* This morning about 8.30 p.m. while I was still doing the letters the head housekeeper told me that a man had told her the second front had started and we had landed in northern France.[64] Last night the sailor's wife had told me that her husband thought it was starting this week. Also she had heard lots of Americans had gone from the locality and other parts and leave was stopped. As she had told me similar tales before about when it was starting I did not take much notice but it did occur to me that as Rome had fallen it would be a good day to make the pounce while morale had been affected on both sides.

At breakfast at 9 a.m. there was some talk of the invasion and the social directors put the radio on so that the news about 10 a.m. was broadcast in the hostel dining-hall and foyer. The general reaction was excitement because it would hasten the end of the war and thought for all the brave men that were to be killed and wounded every minute to bring it about. Everything in our remote spot went on as usual all day and we all said there was a feeling of unreality about it when it was so near and nothing here had altered. Even all the trains ran all day, and D arrived at 6 p.m. It was grand to be with him again and another whole day tomorrow.

Frank Edwards   *Monday, 5th.* Back to work today after an enjoyable week's holiday, and to the tune of our big Allied victory in the capture of Rome. This is the first of the three great Axis capitals to fall. Especially am I pleased that the Vatican and all the many monuments of the city have escaped damage. Everyone today has seemed in a happy mood over the good news, and undoubtedly it has done us all good. But we are a very calm-minded people and there have been no salvoes fired, no church bells, and no flags – at least I haven't seen any. But I guess any other country would have celebrated such a victory – most assuredly Russia.

Tuesday, 6th. Well 'D-Day' is now nearly over and it has been a great day in the history of the war, second only, I suppose, to the day of declaration of the war. The first inkling I had was when a colleague boarded the bus I was on *en route* for work, at 8.15 this morning, and said to me, 'Well, have we started or haven't we?' Further on the journey another colleague joined us on the bus and sitting down, opened conversation with practically the same words, explained the German reports which had been given in the BBC news. Then at 9.30 a special announcement was made over the loudspeaker system at work confirming that the invasion had begun. Arrangements were made that all the BBC news bulletins throughout the day would be broadcast throughout the works.

The news was certainly received with some excitement although this didn't amount to anything in the nature of high spirits, for all our thoughts were with our boys in their great and hazardous undertaking. Many of us breathed a deep sigh for at last this was 'it'. When we had some idea where the landings were taking place, some of us in our office studied the *Daily Telegraph* invasion map, of which we have a copy. At lunchtime we were keen to hear the one o'clock news, prior to which we had had lunch and during this time there passed over the restaurant where we were a huge flight of planes which made so much noise that we all went out to have a look and a lovely sight it was. They looked to us to be Marauders.

Coming home tonight I saw the biggest queue I have ever

seen – it must have been somewhere near 100 strong, single file, of people wanting to buy an evening newspaper. A lorry driver's mate leaning from his cab, whilst waiting for the traffic lights to change, shouted to some men in a bus queue, 'How are we doing, mate?' Another man in the bus queue I was in said to the fellows at his side, 'How far in are we?' and so it went on. Then some army vehicles passed us and the drivers smiled and winked at us. Before the 9 p.m. news the King broadcast from Buckingham Palace, calling the nation to prayer. The news was particularly interesting and wound up with various observers' commentaries on the start of the invasion, after which a short intercession service was given.

Edie Rutherford   *Thursday, 8th.* Weather a bit better yesterday and even more so today, praise be. We seem to be going on all right with our invasion. The whole thing is so stupendous that the stories of eyewitnesses are various and endless. Fancy old Howard Marshall [BBC broadcaster] going over and coming back and getting dipped in the Channel twice, at his age …

In town yesterday in shop window I saw two small straw hats with an odd bit of trimming on them, each ticketed £9.5.0d! I still have to meet the kind of female who pays that price for a hat. I know they exist but thank God, not in my orbit. Plenty of people waiting to give blood. Was told there has been a big move up in numbers yesterday and day before – invasion news bucked folk up. One still has a dreary wait, but it is little we do compared to the men who fight. I had a sea letter today from my nephew near Cairo dated April 24th. He had just had leave which he spent in the Holy Land and seems to have enjoyed it very much. Says his boat was held up three days in Suez Canal and they were just thinking of giving up and returning to spend leave in Cairo when they moved on again. So we must have plenty of Canal traffic these days.

Frank Edwards   *Friday, 9th.* An airmail letter received today from an RAF friend

written on 28th May; winds up by saying, 'I hope the second
front won't be long starting now as then we shall feel that home
is just around the corner.' Well, progress of the invasion continues to be good and gives us good heart. In my evening paper
tonight is an article, 'Will Cherbourg be Freedom's Gateway?'
It would be interesting if this should be so, for I have happy
memories of a day visit to this port made whilst staying at a
South Coast resort shortly before the war.

Tuesday, 13th. So Churchill has been over the Channel. He
would. I bet he's itched to get there all the time. I hope we can
believe all we hear about enthusiasm of French people. Seems to
me, reading between lines, that the Germans have not treated
them at all badly, and if we want to impress them we'll have to
do more than be just courteous as they seem to have been. And
isn't it time Roosevelt either acclaimed de Gaulle, or said why
not, or acclaimed another?

Edie Rutherford

Tuesday, 13th. The battle in Normandy continues to go well
and we are all in very good heart about it, especially all the
fellows doing the fighting for they are absolutely full of beans.
The newspapers are very interesting to read just now, and the
BBC news bulletins equally hold the interest, very particularly
the war reports which follow the 9 p.m. news, and everyone I
know has expressed great interest in these. I don't think any
one of us was very much surprised to hear that Mr Churchill
paid a visit to the Normandy beaches yesterday, for I think we
all gathered the opinion that he intended to do so, when he
made no reply to a question raised on this possibility in the
House last week.

Frank Edwards

   In the early hours of this morning there were two alerts
– the second one following a short interval after the first All
Clear, about five minutes after to be exact. These were the first
alerts we have had for a considerable time. There was no gunfire
and no planes in this district.

Edie Rutherford   *Thursday, 15th.* Last night we went to local cinema to see Dis-
ney's *Victory Through Air Power* which Husband has been keen
to see ever since he read first reviews. There is no doubt at all it
is a good film and splendid propaganda for the Russian–American Seversky's ideas.[65] (I may not have got that name spelt right
but that matters not as he cannot be mistaken.) (Incidentally
I bet the Soviets are mad he didn't like them well enough to
stay behind and help them. He is just the sort of man they have
needed and do need and will need.) Mind, that film strains at
truth to get its points. But there is no doubt there is a lot in
the contentions made. Only, the film misses as usual the FACT
of our appalling poverty of war weapons back in 1939–41 and
even '42 and '43 for that matter. It seems as if no one outside
this island will ever appreciate just how unequipped we were
for war and what a time it took us to get enough stuff to keep
the enemy off our shores, let alone set out to whack him as we
are at last doing today. Thinking it over afterwards, one realises
that when the killing is over we must make some international
agreement that no one is to make any armaments individually
as a nation, no one build a submarine, and so on, and if any
nations start doing it, the rest must at once set about them
and force them to desist. All this must be done so publicly
that every man, woman and child in the world is aware of it,
so that they will back up the majority in their dealing with an
offender, as it is never the masses who want war.

Muriel Green   *Monday, 19th.* Morning went to town in the firm's taxi bor-
rowed from the factory. Rest of day on duty. I forgot to say on
Saturday there was as much excitement in the hostel over the
Derby as over the second front. I had never had a bet before in
my life but as most of the staff and residents were doing horses
I had a bob each way on Mustang and Garden Path which I
was assured were dead certs. We had great excitement listening
to the race and when they did not come in I was quite disappointed. I felt ashamed afterwards to think that while such

vital issues were at stake and men's lives going with every snap of the fingers we should be betting on racehorses.

Thursday, 22nd. At teatime today the girl who works with us had a telegram to go at once to her sister's in London. She thinks she has been bombed so decided to go tomorrow. That means I cannot have my day off but will have to save it up for another time. I am very disappointed as I had wanted to see *Jane Eyre* and I shall be on late duty the night it comes to the hostel. We have heard a lot about flying bombs[66] lately at the hostel as several of our residents have been to London, one or two returning before their time was up because they could not get any sleep and it was so dreadful. It is so quiet here it seems unbelievable.

Wednesday, 28th. Today there has been a lot of low cloud and it has been very dull nearly all day. In consequence it has given the flying bomb a good chance and we have been pestered with them all day since 8.30 this morning. Alerts have been going all day and so have the morning signals from our spotters at work – they have certainly had a time of it and no less than eight times we have had to drop flat. They have been well over the district – NW London where I work – today and whilst we have had no incidents there have been some pretty big bangs fairly close, and they have made us jump a few times. Thank goodness for our sense of humour which has enabled us to have some laughs at *ourselves* during the day for really we have looked funny at times when the signal warned us to drop flat. You really couldn't help but laugh and that certainly helped us through a difficult and trying day.

JULY 1944

Monday, 3rd. The best news today comes from Russia with the   Frank Edwards capture of Minsk which they have celebrated by the firing of one of the biggest salvoes yet. It has been a very trying sort of day with flying bombs causing constant interference more or less all day. Coupled with this the weather has been depressing, pouring with rain all day, and we have all felt rather tired and a bit on edge.

Edie Rutherford   *Tuesday, 4th.* Good that the Russians have got Minsk. Surely the Germans have taken men from that front – it seems too easy now. Husband says their yard foreman's married daughter was waiting in town on Sunday evening to meet her husband at an arranged spot. An American negro soldier went up to her and said, 'You take me home – I pay £2 – no baby?' She said, 'You'd better get along or I'll call a policeman,' and off he ambled, grinning unconcernedly.

Sunny today but of course the wind must return. Flying bombs still coming over. I should think Mr Churchill is going to say something about them soon. We'll have to retaliate some way. Oh I do hope the weather won't stay rotten and bog our efforts to end the war. Already our men are having discomforts through the weather, which they could well do without, there being enough discomfort in war anyway. At work today we have packed several hundred Poldi Hardness Testers for shipment to Russia. Sounds good to me.

Frank Edwards   *Wednesday, 5th.* What a day! What a life! At night we trek down to the shelters looking like a lot of refugees, with our blankets, cushions, etc.; in the day we spend our time between work and ducking, dropping flat under tables or whatever else is handy, or diving elsewhere for shelter from the flying bombs. One came down in the lunch-hour today very close to the works and in fact actually circled over the place twice. Luckily it just cleared us and fell in a nearby road. Damage caused on the houses where it fell was considerable and there were a number of casualties, some fatal, and we had employees amongst the casualties.

Sunday, 9th. Wet. I feel quite glad we're not going away for our   Edie Rutherford
hols this year as it seems to be a set-in wet summer. More flying
bombs in the night. One wonders if our bombing has done
some good, so that they now send by night only with what they
have got left, when we can't so easily shoot them down. We are
going on well in Normandy. Lovely postscript in *Sunday Express*
today: 'It must be very irksome to some of our sentimental-
ists that they cannot offer a cup of tea to a flying bomb.' Nice
picture in all papers of Monty with two pups, though why he
should inflict them with such names as Hitler and Rommel, I
don't know. A dog is far too fine for such indignity.

Wednesday, 12th. Last night was the first raid-free night we have   Frank Edwards
had in London since the Germans started launching their flying
bombs. But to make up for it they have been quite busy today
– in fact very busy this afternoon, and at work we seem to have
done nothing else but get 'imminent' danger signals from the
spotters including two 'instant' danger signals when we had
to get down quickly. Three bombs came over in quick succes-
sion and the second one fell fairly close to our works, seriously
damaging houses in the road where it exploded. The Russians
are making great strides and so are we, and every day makes it
harder for the Huns.

Thursday, 20th. The big news today has undoubtedly been the
attempted assassination of Hitler.[67] I am sure the idea of it has
not surprised anyone though I do not think we thought there
was much opportunity for ever carrying out such an attempt,
having regard to the strict watch of the Gestapo and Hitler's
personal guards. For all that, it seems the attempt has been
made, if we can believe what the enemy says, and the best
caption for the affair appears to be 'Missed him!'

Friday, 21st. Wet and cool but oh, what good news for us from   Edie Rutherford
Germany ... what a pity that bomb didn't get Hitler yesterday.

Surely this upset within Germany will shorten the war by months. Killing off the leaders won't help any, it is the old way with dictators but helps none. Only makes matters worse. A system founded on fear and upheld by fear cannot last and the rot has at last set in.

Hitler sounded like the maniac he always has sounded like, though not at first, but when he had got himself worked up he reverted to the maniac again. What a horrid language German is and what horrid-sounding surnames they have. Ugh ... what are we going to do with these unsavoury sycophant Germans? Yet if we leave them as we did last time they'll upset the world all over again. They seem as if they can't help it, as they have been educated up to now. Well, it should keep thousands of folks busy – educating Germans. Ha ha. I suppose it is worth it. Let's hope we don't go to the other extreme and allow decent nations to suffer ...

Friday, 28th. Russians sweep on and on and Moscow must be a racket to live in. The Americans also prosper but the British and Canadians seem to be up against it. And still the missiles come over ...

In flat beneath us they have one evacuee from London aged six. The mother, aged 23, with her other *four* children is parked in a nearby street ... Teacher next door who has a class of five- to six-year-olds says she is sure they're all little criminals ... this week alone these felonies have been committed by her children: thrown stones at train and smashed windows. Climbed up railway signal and put same out of order. Entered pigeon cote, killed one sitting bird, scared others off their eggs, stolen eggs, cooked and eaten them and been away from school sick afterwards ... needless to say detectives are for ever visiting the school. Artful little monkeys they are too ... one didn't go for school dinner one day two weeks ago. Yesterday spent his dinner money and then told teacher she owed a dinner from 21 weeks ago. She has a good memory and said his dinner had been ordered and paid for and that was the end of it. He was given a meal but made to sit on the floor and given a rap on each hand just to help him remember. He is one of the bad boys of the gang mentioned above. The head of the school, a man, will never chastise a child physically. I wonder if he is right or not.

Friday, 28th. Great Russian advances again – why don't we do the same in Normandy? People are asking if Monty is failing or if someone else is holding him up.[68] The papers are full of it – evidently it is hurting some consciences. Last night I was very miserable. I had time to think of Tom – today I was thinking of what he had to live for – of why he should have lived. Fire-watching again – surprising how a couple of drinks help brighten it up – and also surprising how conversation amongst men seems always to drift to sex.

Kenneth Redmond, 23-year-old civil servant, Bridgend, Wales

AUGUST 1944

Thursday, 3rd. During the twelve hours ending midday there was a heavy attack by flying bombs. The alert sounded before midnight last night and since then there has been an almost continuous stream of the missiles, and I seemed to have very little sleep in the night. Two incidents occurred not too far away which made everyone in the shelter jump. All this morning they have been coming over, too, but after lunch it was a very clear sky with brilliant sunshine, and since this came about there has not been a single alert. Everyone I have spoken to has been very pleased with Churchill's speech, although of course we don't like the idea of the rocket-bomb which Hitler may use against us.

Frank Edwards

Tuesday, 15th. Papers in from South Africa. We get letters when censors have done with them. I'm not surprised to hear birth-rate is up. One sees so many pregnant women with prams ... I wonder if we're going to bring off something big in France:

Edie Rutherford

General Eisenhower was guarded in his Order of the Day yesterday. I know he has to be cautious.

Yesterday I went to the basement and cleared the firewatchers' cupboard of cups, Oxo cubes, etc., which have been there for years. Reckon we won't need 'em now and if we do, they can soon go back.

Lovely day yesterday and looks like being another today. Of course I know it is now what this country calls a drought. Must admit I've never seen our various rivers, etc., which we pass on our walks, so low. There is a distinct autumn touch in the air already and leaves have begun to fall. But not many.

Later Tuesday. What news! A landing in southern France.[69] Splendid. And comparatively easy, too. Not that we expect it so all the way, but just to have done it, and how it helps close in on the enemy. God help all our men, they need all the help they can get, every one of them, and the women too. Surely this war won't go on much longer.

Kenneth Redmond

Tuesday, 15th. Another grand day. News of landing on south coast of France by hearsay (2 p.m.) – then said to be between Florence and Nice. Did not hear news as out on bike in evening – reading *The Iliad* (peaceful relaxation?). Landlord said the landings were between Marseilles and Toulon – and going well. Good job – show Jerry how little hope he has. Nestlé's milk with tea – wedding in dairyman's family so he couldn't supply milk. I notice he delivered around the richer area of his round. Just had to pinch some of the tinned milk – I could have eaten the lot.

Wednesday, 16th. The news from France has completely routed Russia from the front pages of some papers for the first time since 1941. The southern front hasn't made so much impression as the second front. Poor weather today – still we've had a good spell – especially seeing we're still supposed to be under the influence of St Swithin. Stayed in in evening and finished writing up my notes on *Theory and Practice of Socialism* (John Strachey) – a good job well done.

Wednesday, 23rd. Rain again this morning – a bad week for holidays. In all morning. One p.m. – Paris free – news electrifying – and has had most noticeable effect since D-Day. Comments: 'One in the eye for Smuts' [the South African prime minister], 'Even the sun shines now that Paris is free.'

Saw *Lifeboat* (Hitchcock). Marvellous photography – start – smoking funnel – sinking – turmoil – debris drifts past – a dead body – the lifeboat appears in the mist – four-star and some. Home in evening – listened to *Salute to Paris*. One can't complain that the BBC lets many occasions pass without notice. News at end was startling (Marseilles and Rumania[70]) and as the war ends some are taken away (Preston school disaster[71]).

Thursday, 24th. The best news today has been of the fall of Paris. Soon after midday I heard cheers going up in our canteen but thought nothing untoward of this. Then I heard the announcement about it in the one o'clock news. Everybody hailed the news with great enthusiasm and once more there was a big rush for the evening papers.

Frank Edwards

Tuesday, 29th. Glad Churchill is speaking straight to Italy. No worthwhile foundation can be laid for that nation without frank acknowledgement of past folly. I used to like Maurice Chevalier but that doesn't mean I'm not glad he is now getting what he has asked for by being a traitor, and that goes for [playwright and director] Sacha Guitry and several others also. Are we expected to believe that young Michael of Rumania's courage in defying Hitler had nothing to do with having the Allied nations at his back? Ugh, let us not be praising folk who fought us till the eleventh hour.

Edie Rutherford

SEPTEMBER 1944

Edie Rutherford *Saturday, 2nd.* Wet, windy and cold … North wind. How it rained in the night, woke me three times, but left window wide as rain was not blowing in. How well the war goes for us. Vimy Ridge ours now – that was where Husband copped it in the last war.

My cousin serving in France, in his letter to Husband this week, said the war seemed to go slowly, with the end far off. I was able to reply sincerely with the remark that to us they seem to go fast, and the end seems to us not far off therefore.

A nice surprise today – parcel from my boss in South Africa. He has never done this before and I'm quite overcome. *Most* kind of him – contents list for Customs sent with this series for MO. A tin of South American roast beef – what *can* it be like? We'll have to go into a huddle about it when we have that!

Frank Edwards *Sunday, 3rd.* Today is the fifth anniversary of the war and by desire of HM the King has been a special day of prayer throughout the country. To me, September 3rd 1939 seems a very long time ago and yet it is only five years and even though it does seem much longer I can remember it as plainly as if it might have been, say, only yesterday. Of course, so much has taken place in the five years that I don't suppose anyone can remember a complete history of events, but it is interesting to look back and recall some of the things you can remember.

That first alert, for instance, which followed immediately Mr Chamberlain's declaration of war on the radio. I expected nothing short of heavy bombing to follow this, but nothing happened. This seemed to herald something terrible about to happen and I remember how we all seized our gas masks and fled downstairs. Then we got muddled up in putting on our gas masks and no wonder because Mother's which was small got picked up by Dad and he requiring a big size, had a job trying to get in one, whilst Mother who had grabbed Dad's found equally it wouldn't fit being too large. In the worry of the moment there was much puffing and blowing and amazement that the respirators wouldn't fit until the mistake was found out, and then we had to laugh about it, as we have done lots of times since.

Then there were the awful first weeks of the blackout – I was working in Birmingham at that time. I remember going about with a white handkerchief tied round my coat sleeve. And I remember the dimming of the lights on buses and trams and the difficulty at first in trying to make out their destination and number. And I well recall on one occasion falling over a heap of sandbags and nearly pitching head first up an arcade of shops. Yes, the first days of blackout were pretty awful, and I think gave me one of the biggest worries.

And then one by one nearly all my friends became absorbed in the services. What of the Battle of Britain? I remember that marvellous episode well and how much is owed to 'the few' who made it such a great victory. And then later those dreadful air raids by day and by night, especially by night – and *all* night many of them. Yes, during these raids, the cellar, which had been reinforced, in this house, was our nightly shelter for something like three months.

Rationing, fire-watching and Home Guard are other memories. As you will see the memories I have recalled are personal ones and don't include our setbacks and victories as to try and recall all the five years' events would take some time and much more space than I have available.

Sunday, 3rd. What is the good of a day of prayer? People who never otherwise go, crowd to church like the hypocrites they are, and then when the war goes well by the sheer ability of the mass of workers and soldiers they say God is good, and then forget all about it. Pity some of the Church funds aren't disposed of to help the poor and aged (I think I should say all of its funds).

Kenneth Redmond

Frank Edwards *Monday, 4th.* Further great news today in that amongst other big events Brussels has been liberated, this being the fourth capital to be freed from Nazi occupation. And to top all the setting free of Brussels is considered the most dramatic coup of the war, and further the Nazis are leaving Holland. By Jove, is Jerry on the run? I'll say – as he has never been before! This afternoon I paid a visit to a West End news theatre and was most interested in an exciting newsreel of the liberation of Paris and the story of the French Forces of the Interior (FFI) – all these pictures were taken by a cameraman at the risk of his life.

Wednesday, 6th. To many thousands of men in the home front the best news of the day has been that as from Monday next all compulsory parade and training in the Home Guard will cease and such duties as are necessary will be purely on a voluntary basis. This announcement was given tonight by Sir James Grigg [Secretary of State for War], after the nine o'clock news, and it is indeed good news at least for the majority of us as members of that force – and I am one.

Actually, I have been a member of the Home Guard for two years having been 'directed' into it in September 1942. I am sure all its members have been very glad to have helped in every way they could and to know that their help has been considered so valuable. Nearly all of us have given up hundreds of hours in parades, training and pickets – in many, many cases the only time which would have been free to us after working hard for long hours. Yes, we really do appreciate that we can now relax – at last we shall be able to from next Monday and this concession is indeed most welcome.

Edie Rutherford *Wednesday, 6th.* Russia declared war on Bulgaria and at once Bulgaria asks for an armistice – wise. I feel the Germans won't crack until/unless Hitler either flees, commits suicide or is killed. Their unbounded faith in him and his miracles is still alive. Flying bomb lull continues, praise be. In any case it can't be much that they do in that direction now.

Thursday, 7th. Home front news this morning is really most exciting containing as it does news that the blackout is to be cut to a minimum. Home Guard compulsion is ending and fire-guard duty is nearly ended. And the item which will affect us all is the relief from the blackout. Everyone I have spoken to is most thrilled about this and are just longing for the arrival of the 17th. As London's lights are not operated from a master switch we shall only get partial lighting until the blackout can be entirely done away with, but even so it will be a case of the lights go up again, and I shall have more to say about this when the time arrives.

Frank Edwards

Some of the newspaper headlines today were:

Daily Express	BLACKOUT TO BE DIM-OUT
Daily Mail	BIG BLACKOUT CONCESSION
Daily Herald	BLACKOUT TO END SEPT 17
Daily Telegraph	LIGHTS GO UP AGAIN AFTER FIVE YEARS

Sunday, 10th. Mother broke down today – and insisted on Val telling us how Tom was killed. Quiet day – and so seems London – Connie anxious to go back.

Kenneth Redmond

Saturday, 16th. The Russia–Poland business[72] goes on. Churchill had much to say yesterday about what we think ... where does he get the idea he speaks for 'this country'? I don't personally agree with Churchill and I know others who don't. In any case, why should *we* have a say? I agree with Eden it is time Stalin came here. I have no silly ideas about it being undignified for Churchill to go to the others. I just think he must be sick of careering round and Mrs C also sick of it, so let the others have a turn. I make allowances for Roosevelt! As he is lame, but that able-bodied Stalin ... faugh ...

Edie Rutherford

Frank Edwards *Sunday, 17th.* Today has been another 'D-Day' for there has been a huge airborne landing in Holland[73] by the Allies and from radio reports this operation was a truly masterful piece of work. Today has been Battle of Britain Sunday in memory of 'The Few' of the RAF who so marvellously won this battle. Special services have been held in many churches where people went to remember the pilots of the Battle of Britain. Collections were given to the RAF Benevolent Fund. Double summer time ended at 3 o'clock this morning, and brought with it that lifting of the five years of blackouts which is now being replaced by dim-out.

Kenneth Redmond *Tuesday, 26th.* The situation of our airborne forces still gives concern. I'm glad the news of last night was not as bad as it seemed to be.

The government social insurance scheme has not caused much comment. I'm afraid people are apathetic when White Papers are concerned. I think that for all the difference between it and Beveridge, B could have been law now – we would have gained two years. The release of Captain Ramsay [of the anti-Semitic Right Club] is a kick in the pants to those fighting Fascism and Hitler.

Wednesday, 27th. Wrote to our federation about protesting at Ramsay's release. Tom was killed fighting those who stand for what Ramsay stands. Why did he have to die if this country is to tolerate such things? Some thought is now being given to social insurance and post-war housing. I only hope they act as swiftly on this as in the Ramsay case.

Muriel Green *Friday, 29th.* The news of Arnhem these days has been depressing. We all thought the war was so nearly over and now we hear of such sacrifice of lives it makes me miserable. I suppose we are taking victory so much for granted it makes such disasters seem worse.

Saturday, 30th. Work all day and tonight I distinguished myself by being chosen from the ENSA audience to go up on the stage to assist the conjurer. It was great fun and he gave me chocolate and cigs at the end of the act. Dancing afterwards.

Saturday, 30th. Nothing much to report today. There is a   Frank Edwards
24-hour truce between the Germans at Calais and the Canadians, for the purpose of evacuating the 20,000 population, and that armistice ended at midday today. Hitler has told these men at Calais to hold out to the last man, but after assisting in the evacuation many of these men do not want to go back, but want to be taken prisoner. I can't quite see what happens in an instance like this since with there being a truce one cannot take these men prisoners, though presumably when the 24 hours has expired we could do so.

And so another month comes to an end; a month which has brought us appreciably nearer the end of the war. A month which has shone with the success of the Allied armies (and air force) and been crowned with the valour of the men at Arnhem, and in addition a month which has carried the war right on to German soil.

OCTOBER 1944

Sunday, 1st. We start the month off with the good news that   Frank Edwards
Calais has now fallen, and so at long last the people of 'Hellfire Corner' can return to their normal routine and be free from the very trying and dangerous times to which they have been subjected by the shelling from Calais. It must indeed be a grand relief for them and should be a happiness to everyone in the knowledge that this cannot happen again to the people at Dover, Deal and Folkestone.

And judging by *War Report* this evening the people of these towns have every reason for celebrating the occasion. But from what I can see of it, many will still have to carry on living in the caves because so much property has been damaged. I think they are a great people and I highly admire their determination and pluck through the whole affair.

Kenneth Redmond *Tuesday, 3rd.* Work from 8.30 a.m. to 8 p.m. – not much time to think of anything but work. The Poles seem to be trying to put over the Warsaw rising as a piece of heroic resistance rather than a sideshow that Sosnkowski hoped to turn to his own ends.[74] The people are to be pitied that they have had such terror thrust upon them by one man's ambition.

Frank Edwards *Thursday, 5th.* It is sad news today to learn that the Polish home army's resistance has been overwhelmed at Warsaw for they have made a most heroic stand against gigantic odds under the most dreadful conditions of hardship and they have fought marvellously for 63 days. The battle of Warsaw has brought terrible damage to that city and the heroic population has undergone untold suffering. We shall not forget this epic of Warsaw. From the other side of the picture we have good news in that British paratroops and seaborne infantry have made a landing in Greece[75] and Albania, and are harassing the Germans.

Kenneth Redmond *Saturday, 7th.* The news that Greece and the Greek islands are being freed is very heartening. This corner of Europe has seemingly had the worst of a bad time. The only comment I could get from a friend of mine on the social insurance was, 'They (the government) should take over the insurance companies.' She is a teacher. Later in conversation she did say it was time they could get something during illness – they are only allowed ten days a year with pay under the Glamorgan County Council, and this can soon be exhausted.

Connie (our evacuee) has gone back – she has been itching to go back for some time. She took the first excuse she could get – her husband was home on leave.

Saturday, 21st. As I passed a shop window this morning I noticed some toys displayed. Another fellow standing nearby remarked that they were out early – but the most noticeable thing to me was that none were priced. I should mention now that for three nights this week I have dreamt of Tom. Each time I have been assuring myself (in the dream) that he was not dead. Were I at all influenced by dreams and spirits I might start hoping – despite the factual evidence against such a thing. Only this week I heard of a woman who had been to a spiritualist meeting and was advised her husband was safe, although a chap who was saved from the ship and had seen him drown had written to her. This mumbo-jumbo being dished up by people who claim to sensibility is unfortunately being swallowed by the more credulous of our fellow citizens. Unfortunately our organised religions are too deeply in witchcraft and graft to be either a means of exposure or liable to exposure itself.

Thursday, 26th. Went to King's Lynn today. The same murky town as when I went to school, only more so. It seemed strange, when we sat for lunch in the same restaurant we used to sit in when Mother and Father met me out of school, to think of the things I had seen and done since then. It seemed strange to think that the war had been on over five years and how little different it was for us in spite of the ravages of the war and what some had gone through. There was I eating at the same table looking more like a million dollars than ever, when you think of the picture we all visualised of ourselves after five years' war. I thought we should be more or less uncivilised in way of life in rags amongst ruins if we had survived the first six months. Of course our family is one of the lucky ones, having so far lost no near relations, the home is still intact and we have still means of livelihood as good if not better than pre-war days. Of course it will never be the same again, but there are many families with far greater losses than our petty grumbles.

Muriel Green, Snettisham, Norfolk, on leave

Kenneth   *Friday, 27th.* Some German prisoners were brought here today.
Redmond   As they were being marched through the town one of the girls
             from the office passed them. Of course she had to tell us all
             about it: 'There were some nice-looking fellows amongst them
             – especially the German RAF. I felt quite sorry for them. One
             of them smiled at me and I smiled back.' Of such breed are
             collaborationists. I felt like kicking her backside. I hold all
             Germans guilty of Tom's death – I can't forgive that.

NOVEMBER, 1944

Muriel Green   *Saturday, 4th.* The review went off tonight with a grand swing.
             It really was good. Far better than the last. From the opening
             chorus 'Merrily we roll along' and 'She'll be coming to the
             hostel, when she comes' to the tune of 'Coming round the
             mountain' the audience was delighted. We had a packed house,
             I know we amazed them. The eight chorus girls had different-
             coloured peasant costumes which made a flashy combination.
             There were numerous short sketches including one I did with
             the housekeeper, 'The Dangerous Age'. There was a ballet done
             by four girls in blue ballet frocks to the tune of 'Where the
             waters are blue'. There were numerous solos done by the more
             talented members of the cast: 'Follow the Van' and 'Out in the
             Cold Cold Snow', 'My Hero', 'The Kerry Dance', 'Friend of
             Mine' and a skipping-rope dance. A series of lightning sketches
             called 'A day at the hostel. It won't happen here' which was a
             take-off of hostel life, the scenes coming from the reception,
             the canteen, the shop, the bedroom, etc., were very popular.
             This ended with all singing to the tune of 'This is the Army,
             Mr Jones', our version written by myself:

             This is the hostel, Mr Jones,
             You're sure to have your moans and groans,
             You've had your breakfast in bed before,

But you won't have it there any more.
This is the hostel, Mr Green,
Soft feather beds we've never seen.
Where you've had feathers and springs before,
You'll find wood like you've had on your floor.
Cushions you miss, we know well,
But this is a hostel, not an hotel.
This is the hostel, Mr Brown,
Bus every hour into town,
You've had a bus every minute before,
But you won't have it here anymore.

The finale was 'Shine on Victory Moon' done by all with a moon lighting effect. Of course having proper stage lighting and hired stage costumes makes these amateur shows. J and I thoroughly enjoyed the performance which made us happy as there was not a hitch and we could feel the audience liked us all. Afterwards we had a good supper spread for us in the handicrafts room. Now we look forward to Thursday when we are putting it on again by request of the shift workers who missed tonight's show.

Thursday, 9th. The general election in America[76] has caused a **Frank Edwards** lot of excitement there – and here so far as American servicemen and women are concerned, which, of course, is quite natural, but I think the USA makes a great deal more of a general election than we do in this country. There has been good news today in that London is to have its lights up. I expect some time will elapse before all the boroughs get lighted up, but no doubt a start will soon be made.

Saturday, 11th. I must first record the fact that Hammersmith, a nearby borough, has already put into effect its improved street lighting following on Mr Morrison's announcement on Thursday that London's lights were to go up. As a matter of fact they went up actually on Thursday night in the Broadway at Hammersmith which was indeed quick work, and since then other roads have been lit with the improved lighting and it is expected that by the time the weekend is over the whole borough will have its lights up. Today has been Poppy Day. I should imagine sales have been excellent for I don't think I have come across anyone not wearing one or more.

Churchill and Eden seem to be getting a great reception in France where they arrived last night.[77]

Kenneth Redmond

Saturday, 11th. This day only means Remembrance of Tom – War and its horrors, Peace and the best of life that it can bring – all these things will mean to me Tom. I get very morbid when I think of it. The two minutes' silence did not take place – the majority of the girls are really too young to remember or care. One even asked what was Poppy Day.

Monday, 20th. When I arrived in Bridgend a scene of desolation met me – the river had broken its banks and flooded the town. It had gone down now but the mess was still there – nine feet of water in one cinema – at one shop you could look through the window of the basement and see firewood floating near the ceiling. The NFS was out in strength to clear the cellars. At lunchtime most of the office staff went out to see the damage. Perhaps now the council will move to have the river attended to, and not merely pass resolutions. Most of the conversation at the club was about the flood. A number of the members could not get home and had to spend the night with friends. In rushing down the water had washed away the wall of the local Palais de Dance and a bakery. It looked very much like bomb damage but for the fact that the glass round about was still in. The grand piano had been hanging over the edge of the floor and eventually slid off – 'Water Music' – but not by Handel. There has been nothing like it here since 1877.

Sunday, 26th. Quiet day – despite baby. During evening conversation got round to Home Rule for Wales. Although I do not agree with severance of connections with England I do believe Wales needs autonomy in connection with internal problems. Dad just said, 'Do you think Wales could pay its way?' – this is a point that needs working out. I said I did not think anything was done in Wales that could not be or had not been paid for by Wales. Of course if a policy of increasing Wales's industrial strength was pursued, instead of draining away its best workers, Wales would undoubtedly become far richer.

DECEMBER 1944

Sunday, 3rd. Today is a date which I shall always remember for   Frank Edwards
it has been the day for the official stand-down of the Home Guard. And a great day it has been. A big ceremonial parade in Hyde Park this afternoon of 7,000 guardsmen drawn from all over Britain and Northern Ireland. HM the King took the salute in Hyde Park and he was accompanied by the Queen and the two Princesses. The parade was two miles long. In it were men of all ages. The saluting base was Stanhope Gate, Marble Arch, and from there, there was a grand march through the West End by way of Hyde Park Corner, Piccadilly, Regent Street, Oxford Street, back to Hyde Park (Ring Road).

Great crowds of people saw the parade – the police estimated the crowds at one million. I saw the parade – the men marching six abreast – from a spot in Regent Street, and it took 40 minutes to pass me. There were 11 HG Bands. Amongst the spectators were hundreds of HGs in and out of uniform. I was one of them. To finish up a great day there was for the visiting HGs a grand variety concert at the Albert Hall this evening, organised by the *Daily Mail*, *Sunday Dispatch* and *Evening Standard*. HM the King broadcast to all guardsmen at nine o'clock this evening, his speech being sent out to the

world by the BBC medium- and short-wave transmitters. It
has indeed been a memorable day.

Muriel Green   *Saturday, 9th.* We have raised our blackout here and funnily
enough we are not sure whether we like it or not. The police
said we could leave the curtains undrawn to guide people
outside, but inside it seemed uncosy. In the foyer and dining-
hall the uncovered windows seemed to play on our unconscious
mind as we found ourselves constantly looking towards them
with the sort of feeling that we were being naughty. We looked
away remembering it was all right and within a short time the
same thing happened again. The rooms seemed colder and less
friendly.

Frank Edwards   *Sunday, 24th.* And so Christmas Eve has arrived and this time
it falls on a Sunday which will make things quieter than if it
had fallen on a weekday. Anyway I think Sunday is a nice day
for Christmas Eve. This morning I went to eleven o'clock Mass
and the rest of the day I have spent quietly at home. Then this
evening there is Midnight Mass for the first time since the war,
and for me the first opportunity of attending since becoming
Catholic in 1940.

Edie Rutherford   *Christmas Day.* Mail came eight-ish, brought me letter from a
friend in Durban dated 23rd November, censored, and a maga-
zine from a friend in Port Shepstone.

We woke to fog, quite thick. Frost too. About 10 a.m. a
band came along the street, all out of tune, Ted Bedspread
come to life, we could not see them for fog but we heard them
all right. Also church bells. Child in flat below woke early,
five-ish and we heard excited sounds. About 10.30 sun began
to break through and the world looked lovely with frost on
trees, shining.

A peaceful night. We think the fog would have put off
flying bombs had they meant to come again, so thank God for

peaceful night. Seems that the air was clear yesterday at the
front and that we jumped to it with air activity.

Have done a few bits of washing. Seems an awful lot of it
this week. Bird ready for oven. Husband says lunch at 2.15 so
gives me heaps of time. Heard one roar from Sheffield Wednesday ground so the men there have had some excitement for
their going to a football match on Xmas Day. Yesterday before
lunch I was looking over balcony and saw a picture fit for a
magazine cover – two girls with peasant scarves, bright ones,
tied under their chins, with arms full of chrysanthemums, not
less than 50 each. It really was a picture. There are heaps of
chrysanthemums about this Xmas, weather has been kind this
year. Incidentally I have never before known fog at Xmas in my
ten years over here.

Boxing Day. We have certainly got the 'White Xmas' we have   Muriel Green
been dreaming of. This morning when we went for a walk it was
a perfect sunny icing-sugary spectacle. The world seemed such a
beautiful place and it isn't. At the least the folk that are in it spoil
it from being beautiful. This afternoon we rested in the lounge
and played table tennis. Tonight we had more games, dancing,
charades and did the much-talked of Lancers in the more-talked
of dresses minus underskirts. Even E was so charmed with her
success in the 'briefs' that she kept the unrationed creation upon
herself. The evening ended at 1 a.m. and we had a cup of tea in
the canteen on our way to bed. It has been indeed a very happy
Xmas; love and pleasure going hand in hand with amiability
and goodwill. If only there was peace on earth! Speaking peace
reminds me that I have noticed here the word peace has replaced
the word victory. On Xmas night one of the main toasts was for
'Peace in the new year'. Again when the staff toasted with cider
in the office tonight the word was 'Peace'. The hostel new year
printed cards emphasise that we are all wishing for 'Peace'. I
think it is a great thing because the war seems to have got to the
stage where more fighting only seems waste.

Civil war in Greece,[78] strikes in other liberated countries and set-backs in the fighting line seem to indicate that muddle will ever be emphatic and no nation is faultless. Fighting seems to spread fighting; there is no real victory. Over five years of hell let loose is enough for civilisation and more of it will gain nothing. When you see the Italian prisoners happily wandering in our streets and enjoying our pleasures I think it must be fruitless. These men killed and maimed our brothers, sons and husbands two years ago and now they are accepted as co-operators, and there seems little ill feeling towards them. If their black record can end in so short a while, to 'they both lived together happily ever afterwards', so can our other enemies.

Frank Edwards   *New Year's Eve.* The last day of 1944 and mighty cold it is. Perhaps a few degrees warmer than the past few days, but it is still freezing. Lots of skaters were on the pond again this morning. We saw the old year out which we didn't do last year. We spent the evening quietly listening to the radio and reading, and also talking about the kind of year it has been and what we hope for in 1945. Certainly 1944 has been a remarkable year with many things, and especially the war, very different to this time a year ago. All the same we say goodbye without regrets, to 1944, hoping and believing that things will be better still and victory will be ours during 1945.

Kenneth   *New Year's Eve.* Another year over (nearly). Usual quiet Sunday
Redmond   – most of the spare time spent in looking after baby – a very disturbing influence in a home – especially if disturbed. Intended going to bed early but failed – first *had* to listen to the *Review of the Year* on the radio as it was by Louis MacNeice. Victory of the Common People – yes – but they are going to have to fight to keep it.

Went up to bed – but stayed up to write a letter. About midnight all the ships started sounding their sirens – a hell of a noise – they seemed almost on top of us – A Happy New

Year. Mother says, 'I hope it'll be better than the last!' That is the least we can hope.

The year has not been a good one for the family. Father started by being ill and I followed up – and then Evaline was ill for three months. Just after that Tom was killed. Evaline's baby when born was very ill and Evaline had a relapse. Now things are looking brighter – let's hope they really will be.

New Year's Eve. I had the morning off and afternoon Mr J and   Muriel Green
I did stock-taking. Tonight we saw out the New Year in a big way. We had a light orchestral concert with variety turns. We had dancing until 11.30 p.m. and then the company assembled round an electric campfire in the assembly hall and lifted the rafters with community singing. At midnight the old year with cotton wool beard and scythe appeared on the stage and a large plywood painted stork descended from the roof of the stage with a 'baby' in a napkin. One of the youngest girls in a white frock said a little verse about the New Year. The 'baby' had a large label on it, '1945 Peace?' We then sang 'Auld Lang Syne' and everybody kissed everybody else wishing them a 'Happy New Year'. It was all very matey and I found myself being kissed by all sorts of impossible people, some who lost count of the number of times they had performed the ceremony! We retired at 12.30 after a few more dances, the huge bunch of mistletoe in the centre of the floor working overtime.

1944 has been a happy year. I am sure that this year of hostel life will be one of the happiest in my life. I have had good health, good friends, good working conditions with money to spend (if there had been anything to buy) and a jolly time. The war has progressed and left many scars. I am one of the lucky devils who have no scars. Our boss attributed our bad tempers last week to war-weariness. We are certainly that. Let us pray that this year will be the end of war. Nothing could be more wanted.

1945   VICTORY

Britain was still being bombarded by flying bombs and rockets in early 1945, but there was now a general optimism that the war would be over within months. On all fronts enemy resistance was crumbling. In January the Americans broke through the German lines in the Ardennes, the Russians entered Budapest and Warsaw and by the end of the month were forty miles from Berlin. In the Far East the Japanese were now in full retreat, though still resisting fanatically. Germany was under siege from blanket bombing. In February the city of Dresden was obliterated in a massive Anglo-American attack: asked to comment on the effect of the raid, 'Bomber' Harris told Churchill's private secretary, 'There is no such place as Dresden.'

Any misgivings about the devastation of German cities were somewhat tempered as Russian, British and American troops stumbled on the Nazi concentration camps – Auschwitz, Bergen Belsen, Buchenwald and the rest. Films and photographs revealed to a stunned world the mass extermination of millions of Jews and other 'undesirables'.

Hitler's suicide on 30 April and Germany's surrender a week later marked the end of the war in Europe. The British people celebrated the victory on 8 May, their euphoria mingled with grief for those who had not survived to witness the day. Now, many felt, there was a need for change, a need to replace the old duplicities with a brave new world. Churchill misread the popular mood, and in the general election in July the Labour Party under Clement Attlee won a landslide victory. As is amply revealed in the Mass Observation diaries for 1945, the war had given many British citizens a sense of their own identity, a belief that they were no longer pawns in a political game but had a voice in public affairs – and wished to express it.

On the world stage, too, there was a desire for change. In June the United Nations charter was signed by fifty nations. A world which had endured over five years of war now craved an era of peace and international security. The atomic bombs dropped on Japan in August 1945 and the increasing political domination of Eastern Europe by Soviet Russia were harbingers of an altogether different future.

JANUARY 1945

Friday, 5th. 4.45 p.m. Another rocket came as I was writing, **Herbert Brush** and that made the windows vibrate. This rocket business is becoming more trying every day.

5.05 p.m. Another rocket, which shook us up badly. W rang up the Hutts to find out whether they were all right and was told by Bill that Maggie was injured and the house wrecked again. W and I went in the car as quickly as possible and while W took Maggie to East Dulwich hospital, I helped Bill to sweep up some of the broken glass and plaster which covered all the floors. The rocket had fallen about 100 yards away and done a lot of damage to all the surrounding houses, and men were digging in the ruins in Court Lane for people who were known to be buried. All Bill's ceilings were down and all his windows broken and everything in the rooms scattered all over the floors. All Bill's work has been undone in a moment and I think that he feels it very badly. Maggie has to stay in the hospital, at least for tonight, as she is badly cut, and Bill is staying here for the night.

The effects of a bomb-blast are strange. Some of Bill's cupboards were blown open and some of the things left inside were untouched while others were scattered over the floor. In one case a couple of books had been put under the floor carpet, preventing the door of the room being opened.

Monday, 8th. A sprinkling of snow on the ground this morning.

Bill did not sleep here last night, as he preferred to stay in his damaged house, to make sure that no robbers paid it a visit. As there were neither doors nor windows it would be easy to enter and there are plenty of people in this locality willing and anxious to get something for nothing. Maggie is still in hospital, waiting to be X-rayed, in case any bits of glass are inside her. Bomb-blasted glass is the most dangerous thing there is: it seems to go to dust and yet penetrates anything.

Thursday, 11th. W and I went to the plot this afternoon to get some green food if possible. Deep snow lies on the allotments and it was not easy to find anything worth bringing home but I cut a couple of miserable-looking cabbages and managed to dig up a couple of roots of celery. Then we went to look at the bomb-hole, which is about 60 yards away in the school playground.

Huge boulders of clay are scattered all round the crater, which is the largest hole I have seen for a long time. I don't like to guess at the size as it's difficult to estimate with so much snow around, but when standing on the edge, the far side seemed to me more than 20 yards away and looking down the bottom of the hole might be 20 feet below. When the snow melts there will be a decent-sized pond there which will take a lot of filling up.

I think that if I had been working on the plot I should have stood very little chance of escape, as huge lumps of clay have been scattered far and wide, and I noticed several snow-covered lumps on my plot which I did not investigate, but feel sure they are lumps of clay from the bomb crater. The wooden fence between the plots and the playground has been swept away and some of the large trees have been smashed and twisted about as though they were small branches in the hands of a mischievous boy.

The men, so far, have repaired the back door and fixed what they call Essex board on the ceiling of my bedroom, not that I have any intention of sleeping there again until V2 bombs are a thing of the past. After seeing what a V2 can do I think that the best place is a hole underground.

Friday, 12th. Snowed most of yesterday but temperature went   Edie Rutherford
up towards evening and the thaw made such a mess which is still going on, ugh. How men manage to make war in winter, I do not know. However bad it is for us, it must be a hundred times worse for them.

'A truce has been signed in Athens'[79] – first item in news at 8 a.m. Good.

My cousin in Holland writes that he would not mind a Communist regime here if the men at the top were not out for personal ends. Nephew in Cairo writes that something must soon be done about the Communist menace or we'll find ourselves at war with Russia, and adds that the Pope's recent broadcast only said what he (aged 21 this year!) has said for long enough! If I remember rightly the Pope didn't speak out, he spoke about Russia without naming names, in his usual sneakish fashion. Very clever I don't think.

FEBRUARY 1945

Saturday, 10th. My 24th birthday! I feel frightfully old. I   Muriel Green
thought a girl of 24 was a middle-aged woman when I was 17! I thought then that by the time I was 24 I should have finished having a good time and want to settle down. Now that is the last thing I feel like. I suppose the war has taken a chunk of the best years of my life, not that I haven't had a good time during the war because I have, but it has taken the carefreeness from life and made me realise how beastly life can be made. I don't think this last year has been very outstanding, I have had a good time, been taken out plenty, enjoyed my job, my health, my food and also I have become much more confident

and bolder. My job has made me that and I suppose it shows also I am a woman now and not a giggly girl. Not that I've gone off my giggliness exactly, but I have learnt to take more responsibility and I'm sure I am more sensible. I am not in love enough to want to settle down, in fact on my 24th birthday I realise I am getting more involved!

Edie Rutherford   *Wednesday, 14th.* Birds are lovely this morning again. I must say it was a fitting end for the German general at Budapest to surrender from a sewer – the rats. So the Poles are NOT satisfied with the Big Three's arrangements.[80] Well, I don't really blame them, as it isn't right for outsiders with the whip hand to sit down and make decisions which vitally affect others and only secondarily themselves.

Methinks 'twd have been better all round had D-Day been in winter – of course I grant this may have been impossible – but if it had been done and we would have liberated countries in spring and summer, how much easier would it have been to feed *and keep warm* all these folk we liberate. This cruel winter has made the task of caring for them doubly difficult.

Muriel Green   *Thursday, 15th.* My day off and O took me to town to the pictures, tea and back to the hostel for dinner to go out to a factory dance. It's no good pretending any longer, O is very much in love with me and I am (temporarily) in love with him. And that's that! The old, old story of hostel life and married men. Most of the girls here get tarred with the same brush in the end, that is fallen to going out with a married man and being responsible for more or less encouraging them, not necessarily to going further than just running around and flirting with them, but the hostel gossips always think the worst!

Herbert Brush   *Friday, 16th.* 4 p.m. I did a couple of hours on the plot this afternoon, but only managed to plant one row of artichokes. A blitz worker came by and wanted to know if I was putting in leeks as he apparently was an expert in growing leeks in Northumberland, said he grew them 14 inches round and 9 or 10 inches long. But as he confessed that he bought six loads of farm manure to make them grow, I don't think that I will try this year, with manure at 20/- a load.

MARCH 1945

Wednesday, 7th. Saw O off at the station this morning. That is the end of that romantic chapter I think. I don't know if I have been foolish getting so fond of him, because he is over 40 and married even if he doesn't live with his wife. We've had happy times and no harm has been done. I expect O will get someone else in time though he is very much in love with me. I'm in love with him, but then I'm 20 years younger and have got D. Life is very complicated.

    Meanwhile the war goes on. Bigger issues are at stake than my love affairs. The war news is pretty good these days and an end seems in sight at last. How soon, oh how soon?

    I have been amused at the controversy in the hostel over the 'Cleft Chin' murder case.[81] It amazes me that in the midst of the world's greatest war two such futile lives should cause such controversy. I'm not in favour of death sentences, but with millions of innocents being killed in war it seems to me a very trivial point as to whether two low characters should die for killing another.

Muriel Green

Tuesday, 13th. A peculiarity about rockets and doodlebugs is that the people who are close to them when they explode and escape with their lives, don't even hear the sound of the explosion. I have been told this by so many people, and judging by my own limited experience, this seems to be a fact, but I can't explain why it is so. The noise seems to grow in volume up to a distance of, maybe, a couple of miles, and there is probably an easy explanation but at the moment I can't put it into words.

Herbert Brush

Edie Rutherford   *Friday, 16th.* My husband isn't at all well, hasn't been for some time. Can't put his finger on any special thing. Drags his way wearily through each day. I think his giving up smoking must have something to do with it. But I feel that if he will stick it and just peg away, he will eventually benefit. He never is well, being a last war wreck.

Quite a lot of publicity to the Sheffield boy who has married a German girl. Well, Cupid must laugh heartily at all the stupid human comment.

Monday, 19th. I am reading Vera Brittain's *Testament of Youth* – have meant to read it for years. All young folk should read it. She writes with such simplicity and sincerity that I weep and have to put the book aside.

Airgraph today from boy in RAMC, SEAC [South-East Asia Command], dated 1st March. Beryl and George Formby are out there, or were, when Ernest wrote. They have to go into long pants from now on, malaria prevention. Are not going to like it in the heat, and, he says, he won't have brown knees to show us when he returns, which he hopes to do towards the end of the year.

Wednesday, 21st. First day of official spring and a beautiful day too. Hurray for Mandalay,[82] and for the sea battle with the Jap fleet. I hear that the black-eyed one at office told her husband when he came home on short leave that she had walked into a door. And does he believe that, one wonders? The other says her husband is thrilled at the idea she may be pregnant. Sure – he goes back to RAF, and she has the baby and all the work ...

Edie Rutherford   *Friday, 23rd.* Letter today from bro-in-law in Italy. His trench feet still not fit but he says according to army they are. Was at a British hospital and has nothing but praise for care. Going to work this morning met a friend on tram and she told me a friend of their family has never done a full week's work since last war due to trench feet. I do hope it won't go so badly as that with my bro-in-law, as he has all his future yet, with a wife and small children to bring up.

Thank God the weather is at last with us in the war. Looks as if the enemy has wind up about a new push by us. The final? Please God, YES. And may men who attend San Francisco[83] (I haven't heard of any women delegates yet) get down to something worthwhile for the future of this sorry world.

Good Friday, 30th. Two-thirds of the residents are booking out   Muriel Green
for Easter as all the factories are closing. We shall be very slack, and there is no excitement in the way of entertainment. We are all expecting the war to end any day. It really is smashing the way the Allied armies have smashed across the Rhine. It seems too good to be true that it could end any day soon with such victory. I don't think any of us quite know what we shall do on the day it ends or after the war. The general expression is that 'I'm going to get drunk that day', and 'I shan't do any work that day.' I certainly shan't do any work, but I'm not sure if I want to get drunk … a trifle merry maybe, but not drunk!

Saturday, 31st. Hostel life has changed nearly all the girls here to wife-pinchers. There are very few real romances in the sense of boy and girl affairs, because practically all the men are married! The men want company which leads to other things and eligible bachelors are so short, the girls' real boyfriends being abroad or away, it brings natural affairs of the eternal triangle. We all blame the war and go on enjoying life as it comes which in this place is life with other women's husbands. The couples go on enjoying one another's company while they are here and going home to their wives for holidays. Some have stopped doing that. After the war I expect the majority will settle down with their wives again while others have paired here for good.

APRIL 1945

Herbert Brush   *Wednesday, 4th.* One o'clock. I have been working on the plot
awhile this morning and have just come in. Someone is singing
a song about 'The White Cliffs of Dover' on the wireless which
reminds me that many alterations have taken place in the cliffs'
face since I first saw them 50 years ago: especially Shakespeare's
Cliff which had a hut and flagstaff on the summit when I first
looked at it with interest. But cliff falls have lowered the peak
considerably since then, and now it does not appear to be as
high as the Western Heights behind it.

Muriel Green   *Friday, 13th.* I was stopped this morning at 11 by the news
of Roosevelt's death.[84] It is a bitter blow, especially when the
fruits of victory are ripe to be picked. He was badly needed to
form a just peace and his passing is a loss to the world.

Sunday, 22nd. Tonight D and I had a serious talk. He is getting
very lonely down in Devon by himself and wants me to join him.
He cannot afford to marry me yet unless I work as well. The
thought of this frightens me because I don't think there would
be much security in that. We might have a child which would
put us in financial straits and as the war appears to be nearly over,
married women in jobs won't be welcome. I love him and would
marry him if he could keep me which is what I want. I would
rather remain as I am if I am to go on working. I don't want to
leave the hostel, which makes him think I don't love him.

Perhaps he is right. I am more in love with myself and my
own comfort to want to lose my independence. I think no other
man I know would make me a better life companion, as D is so
kind and tolerant and we like the same kinds of things. Marriage is a state which I am more cautious to enter than many,
because I don't want to think afterwards I didn't know when I
was well off. We did not quarrel about it, but I agreed to think
it over. At present the M of L [Ministry of Labour] would be

a hindrance to me moving as a single woman, but if we were married it would not. I would rather wait for M of L restrictions to be lifted than marry for the sake of these. D will be disappointed if I do not go, but if I lose him through it I shall merely regard it as fate and hope for someone else. I am not one to think there is only one man to make me happy. I would rather stay single than marry anyone, but there are as good fish in the sea as come out.

Tuesday, 24th. I can't understand what all the trouble about   Herbert Brush
Poland is about. It was for Poland we first went into the war and yet we can't agree with Poles who agree with Russia. Personally I should have thought that if those two old enemies, Poland and Russia, could agree, it is no job of ours to make them fall out, or to fall out with Russia over the business. Probably the hand of Hitler is somewhere in this pot trying to stir up mischief.

MAY 1945

Tuesday, 1st. Important hours, important as those days at the   Maggie Joy
end of August in 1939 preceding the declaration of war. This   Blunt
is tension of a different kind, expectancy, preparations being made for a change in our way of living. But the tempo is slower. We wait, without anxiety, for the official announcement by Mr Churchill that is to herald two full days' holiday and the beginning of another period of peace in Europe. We wait wondering if Hitler is dying or dead or will commit suicide or be captured and tried and shot, and what his henchmen are doing and feeling.

Tuesday, 1st. VE Day expected at any time – but some people   Kenneth
forget the German forces in Norway – This morning I had to   Redmond
remind my landlady that all these had to be disposed of as well as those in Germany itself. Hitler's death seems rather peculiar – I wonder how much is a put-up job.

Wednesday, 2nd. This evening went into the local for a quick one after finishing work – and while there heard the news of the surrender in Italy. A cause for celebration of course – but none of the news is giving that feeling of exaltation that even D-Day gave. I don't know whether it is the speed with which good news is coming in or the general feeling of horror and disgust at the Germans.

Herbert Brush *Wednesday, 2nd.* 9 a.m. Good news this morning. Hitler is really dead.[85] I wonder what kind of reception his astral form has received on the other side.

> I can imagine when he came
> And when his victims heard his name,
> They gathered round him, not to miss
> So good a chance to hoot and hiss.
>
> But those on earth may all agree,
> From torture he must not go free,
> That God Almighty has some plan
> To punish such a naughty man.

Muriel Green *Thursday, 3rd.* The surrender in Italy is grand.[86] I was afraid the Germans fighting there would hold out the longest. It is all over now really, only the celebrations are to wait until the fighting ceases which is only right. What a pity the lads in the Far East aren't finishing too!

Most people I have asked what they are going to do on V-Day say they don't know or they are going to wait and see what everybody else is doing. As far as the hostel goes I'm sure it is going to be in turmoil, because half the staff are stopping work and none of us know whether the residents are going or coming. The executive staff are keen for as many people as possible to have holidays, as they don't agree with too much double pay for the juniors. There is a lot of arguing going on about arrangements. There is going to be a bonfire which they have begun to build.

Friday, 4th. Every day people are expecting VE Day – I think their hopes are being built up too much – are we going to be left with such a relief from war that there will be a swing away from the necessity of a firm peace and punishment of war criminals? Commander Locker-Lampson [outspoken Conservative MP for North Huntingdonshire] and the *Daily Mail* are already trying to work up a feeling against justice being taken against Fascist beasts. In the evening I went to the pictures and saw the newsreel of Belsen and Buchenwald. Things looked bad enough in stills – but to see it in motion it is far worse – especially Kramer [camp commandant at Belsen] and those women. At ten a rumour was going round town that the war in Europe would be over at 8 a.m. tomorrow. I wanted to believe it – but wouldn't – but certainly stayed up to listen to the 11 p.m. news headlines. After that I had to get some more information – so tried all stations – but they all seemed to be broadcasting in German – telling the Germans the story now – of how they are '*kaput*'. Funnily enough although the news is so good it doesn't give me any feeling of exaltation. As my landlord said, 'The Jap war is still to be won.'

Kenneth Redmond

Monday, 7th. (Written at the end of the week. Pure elation having prevented concentration to write during the time written about.) This afternoon we were supposed to be putting up the decorations for the anniversary or whatever else came but hadn't done more than get them out, look at them and say how dusty they were when one of the residents came along and told us the three o'clock news said the Germans had agreed an unconditional surrender to the three Allies. We were very pleased and really began to hang up the decorations.

Muriel Green

After Churchill's speech saying that by Thursday we should

have had V-Day, there was a lot of speculation about it. Most people thought Tuesday.

We listened to the 6 p.m. news and still we weren't sure. Tuesday was my day off anyway and tonight we had a Ladies versus Gents cricket match which J, E and I were playing in. After dinner I had the radio on and heard the 7.45 p.m. announcement that it was really settled and Mr Churchill would speak at 3 p.m. tomorrow. We still weren't sure if we were to work up till 3 p.m. and felt sure some people would take the day off anyway. Everything seemed frightfully exciting and I felt I wanted to jump about and sing and felt ten years younger!

We had the cricket match. The wireless had been put on out of doors and was going throughout the cricket match. When Big Ben chimed at 9 p.m. everyone stopped playing and waited in tense silence for the news. A general cheer went up when Tuesday was announced a holiday.[87]

Kenneth   *Monday, 7th.* Headlines of papers suggest the end is near.
Redmond   During the afternoon there were rumours that it was V-Day. At
5 p.m. we saw several groups of children carrying flags. During the evening we had a dozen pint bottles of beer in the office and we all gathered in the chief's room to celebrate VE. That was the end of work for the day, but it was 7.30 before we left the office. There was little sign of joviality in town – a friend said that the reason for the 'build-up' was 'to knock the bottom out of celebrations'. At the youth club at 9 p.m. everyone listened for the news – but as soon as the news of tomorrow as a public holiday came through there were some cheers and most went out to shout the news. Later I went out with some friends for a walk round town – it seemed then that most of Bridgend was out to look at the flags (how quickly they've been dug out and hung up). A few US and Russian and one or two other countries with single representatives. In about 11 p.m. – and discussed with my landlord whether tomorrow was a day off – I certainly

think it is and won't be going in to work. As I was going to bed I thought of Tom – how he would have enjoyed these days.

VE Day, Tuesday, 8th. Up at 8 a.m. just in time to hear end of news and beginning of *Programme Parade* – 'details of some of the programmes for today – VE Day' – good enough for me – no work. Washed, dressed and down for breakfast – 8.30 – boiled egg, bread and butter, tea.

About 9.30 it started to rain fairly heavily – went back up to my digs to see if any letters had been delivered – but there were none. The flag had been hung out from my bedroom window – quite a good-size one – my landlady gave 4/- for it – in some shops as much as 14/6d was being asked for the same thing – about 4ft × 6ft. Lunch – cold meat, chips, bread and butter, biscuits and tea – listened to radio and read my papers. Once or twice I thought of the good things that can now come – but always two things would intrude – Tom and Belsen – how soon will people forget. I wondered how mother was feeling about things now. I feel introspective: thinking of nothing in particular, but wondering how I feel and getting nowhere. VE Day is almost an anticlimax. By 2 p.m. it was quite warm – went out for walk wearing open-neck shirt and cycling jacket (trousers, etc., of course). Met two of my pals and after strolling round for a bit went into a small café for a drink and more especially to hear Churchill – by now it was nothing startling. Everyone listened intently but it did not draw comments.

Went for a walk later – but by now we were again being treated to showers. In the window of one shop narcissus, iris and carnation blooms had been worked into a display of red, white and blue. Further on I saw a tiny flag on top of a very long bamboo – from the sublime to the ridiculous. A quiet walk – dashing out of the rain, and carving initials on tree trunks – but still, quiet. 'I didn't imagine we would be spending V-Day this way,' said one of my friends. On the way back into town we noticed a crowd by the Town Hall – some women

and men, just a little bit too drunk, dancing and singing –
what will they be like by midnight?

I had a snack in a café and then fetched bike and went to
catch train – it was almost on time, and nearly empty – surprising for a London train. After we had started it was the little
things I noticed. The countryside seems to have taken on a new
freshness – a new sincerity – and the sound of a bird singing
in the trees beside the line comes out above all others. At Pyle
goods shed someone had hung out 'Wings for Victory' and even
at an isolated farm a little further on there were flags. A peal of
bells could be heard as we pulled out of Port Talbot – perhaps
because the steel works – active for so long – were quiet for
today. All the way there were signs of street parties and races.
At Briton Ferry I heard a bell tolling – is that for victory?
Everything red, white or blue is being hung out – some even
made up into quite fantastic shapes.

About 10.30 p.m. I was at the fair in the Recreation Ground
– but it was almost deserted. At the Civic Centre there was a
drunk threatening to fight a youth – about the only case of
drunkenness I saw throughout my walk. There were crowds
about here waiting for the floodlighting. Fairly discernible
were the flags of the Allies around the green – but the pride of
place about the main entrance was reserved for the town flag.
The lights went on about 11.15 to accompanying 'Oohs!' of
the crowd. At last, after nearly six years, I'll be able to see the
finger of the Civic Centre tower as I go to bed each night. Some
of the side-streets were full of life – with bonfires and their own
floodlighting and amongst the flags strung out in one street
was a line of 'smalls' (but not very small). The town itself was
almost empty, and I made my way home at 12 – in a way glad,
glad that I had not made a fool of myself, in a way sorry, sorry
I had made no effort to get outside of myself. I thought of how
it all seemed a part of another world – that I passed through
it, but was not of it. I'm afraid the memory of Tom will damp
my enjoyment of anything for a long, long time. This, though,

is really no time for celebration, but for dedication of our lives to work for those things we have fought for, and for which so many have died. Shall it be in vain, again?

VE Day, Tuesday, 8th. At 11 the staff had coffee, biscuits and   Muriel Green
cigarettes given them in place of the usual tea. After this J, E and I decided to cycle into the town to see the decorations as the sun had come out by then. The town is decorated well considering the five years' shortage of flags, bunting, etc. Most of the shops which were closed had red, white and blue window dressings with a number of photographs of Churchill, Stalin, Roosevelt and the King and Queen. There were a lot of people walking the streets. We decided to take ourselves into the best hotel in town and have a drink. We had a glass of good old sherry which made us feel just too jolly. We drank to 'Peace in the future'.

We returned to lunch at the hostel and spent the afternoon until 3 p.m. in the sun on deckchairs on the lawn. Churchill's speech was broadcast in the foyer where I was listening along with about 40 others. One interrupted frequently with such comments as 'Good old Churchill'. Immediately after the speech a thanksgiving service was held in the assembly hall, with about 50 present including some of the drunks.

When the silence for the memory of the dead took place there was not a sound of an eyelid. I ran through in my mind all those I knew who had been killed and realise how lucky I am for none very near or dear to me are gone. I noticed the housekeeper was crying during the proceedings. She has lost her dearest son.

After dinner J and M went out for a walk to the favourite country inn about two miles away and E and I arranged to follow them. We talked about the future most of the time on the way there. We found J and M already there drinking. We each had Pommia, a refined bottled cider, and the strongest drink I know. E never stopped talking and each time I spoke

I thought what a silly thing to have said, as I found myself speaking without thinking! We walked home by way of the woods still very talkative but quite sober by the time we got back to the hostel for a snack and to see the bonfire lit at 10 p.m.

It was a roaring blaze and seemed to have a significance in saying 'goodbye' to many wartime restrictions. We stood watching for a long time and about quarter to 11 went in the dance hall. People who in the usual way never unbend were simply romping like healthy children in circles with joined hands. Some had had the necessary amount of alcohol to make them like this, but most of them were drunk with the spirit of victory. The romping continued till the end of the radio music and then with exhaustion the circles were broken up. Dance records were put on and dancing began, but jitterbugging and the 'conga'-type of dancing was the rage, most of the crowd being at a pitch too high to concentrate on serious ballroom dancing.

Several people today have said that as they had relations in the Far East they could not celebrate properly. That has been in everyone's heart that more fighting, more dying and more atrocities are still to come. Also that all the flag-wagging and dancing will not bring alive the dead to their homes. Men that have lost their sight and limbs cannot be the same. Life will always be the sadder for those of us who think. If we knew this had been war to end war we would feel more jubilant but when it may happen again without extreme care, it makes life seem a dilemma.

Kenneth   *Wednesday, 9th.* I think many people have an idea we are going
Redmond   into another world from today – a world of ease, luxury, plenty.
How soon they will come back to earth. I've enjoyed tonight –
in with the crowd you're inclined to forget your own problems.
I didn't want to join in, but once started I was caught up in
the whirl. I believe I know why Hitler rose – he knew how to

keep the minds of the masses off the real problems confront-
ing them – and gave them bright lights and vivid colours and
promises instead.

Thursday, 10th. I read the letter from Regional [WVS] and Nella Last
thought, 'Umph, we will soon all be out of a job' – it was
not with any sense of exultation. It's been a long and often
trying road, but I found comradeship and I bought peace of
mind when otherwise I'd have broken. The knowledge that I
was 'keeping things running in the right direction' in however
small a degree steadied me, helped my tired head to rest peace-
fully at night, with strength to begin again when the morning
came. I wonder if it's the same feeling some of the lads have
when they think of being demobbed!

I love my home dearly, but as a 'home' rather than a 'house'.
The latter can make a prison and a penance if a woman makes
too much of a fetish of cleaning and polishing – but I will not,
cannot go back into the narrowness of 'I don't want anyone else's
company but yours – why do *you* want anyone else?' I looked
at my husband's placid blank face critically, thinking with a
slight sickness, how dreadfully like his family he was growing,
their utter 'mindlessness', their fear of anything different in any
way. I marvelled at the way he had managed to so dominate me
for all our married life, when to avoid 'hurting' him I tried to
keep him in a good mood – when a smacked head would have
been the best treatment. His petulant moods only receive indif-
ference now. I *know* I speak sharply at times; I *know* I'm not the
'sweet woman' I used to be, but then I never was! Rather, I was
a frayed battered thing, nerves kept in control by efforts that
at times became too much and nervous breakdowns were the
result. No one would ever give me one again, *no* one.

Friday, 11th. Where to begin? Well, we came home from work Edie Rutherford
on Monday evening 'bewitched, buggered and bewildered' as a
friend of ours used to say. We had had office wireless on hourly

without getting any satisfaction. Then at 9 p.m. we got the news that the next two days were hols. That was enough for me. I had promised to go after work to help my friend who is still clearing up her home, so Husband came with me. There were bread and fish queues everywhere all along the bus route and our tram route to town.

A neighbour brought in her portable radio at 3 p.m. so that we could listen to Churchill. He spoke well and seemed in good form. Everyone agreed that we have been well blest in having such a leader. I felt once again great gratitude for being born British.

Left at 5 p.m. and walked to nearest tram so that we could come home via town centre. Walked that bit. Thousands round City Hall for a service. More thousands just wandering about.

We got home and had a meal and sat quietly till 10 p.m. when we decided to go and have a look round. These flats had a neon 'V' right on the top-flat roof which looked effective. Our corridor balcony lights were on for the first time since blackout began. At the street corner a radio shop had fitted up loudspeakers and music blared out. We saw many people the worse for drink, in fact most that we saw were in that state. Either looking very sorry for themselves or just merry, and we also saw vomit about, ugh.

Came home about 11 p.m., decided we were hungry and what about looking at reserve food put by years ago. To our surprise and pleasure found tin of asparagus tips and tin of tomatoes. Had these with cheese and water biscuits and marg.

I thought, as always, that the King's speech was marred by his speech, but on the whole his stammer wasn't so bad. Maybe if he were to speak to us more often he would learn to relax so well that he would not stammer at all. Seems to me possible. I have decided these last few days that 'Rule Britannia' is a far better tune than 'God Save the King' which is a poor thing even if our own.

Goering need not imagine he can get away with it by calling

his ex-colleagues nasty names. He is an arch-villain and should swing for it. As to all the reasons for defeat given by various German generals – it is clear they lost because material might is NOT right, never was, never will be. The pity is that they don't see it as simply as that, for it is as simple as that.

There are several Nazis not yet accounted for. And I shan't be happy about Hitler till the body is found. What guilty consciences they have who commit suicide. Is it possible they really thought once that they'd get away with their villainy? I find it hard to believe. I must have had a rigid upbringing, with a stern respect for right and fear of wrong. Good.

Sunday, 13th. Mother told me a friend of hers had said a preacher had told her that President Roosevelt had done so much good in the world that his death was an act of God to compensate for all the evil in the world (Belsen, etc., and the war). Mother wondered if this friend felt compensated for the death of her son.

Kenneth Redmond

Monday, 14th. At times I've a really peevish urge to burn all odd-looking items, patched and mended woollen and darned stockings and socks. I get so tired of our simple meals, I think cream, fresh butter, fresh salmon and 'good' fish, chump chops and fillet steak with mushrooms, shellfish, prawns, crayfish and lobster, cream cakes, rum butter, Kio grapefruit crush, fruit salads. The very thought of seeing them on my table makes me long to take a big shopping basket and make a tour of the stalls in the market.

Nella Last

Tuesday, 15th. Shops now display notices that they have plenty of torch batteries … GOD BLESS OUR LADS FOR THIS VICTORY is painted on sides of houses near where I work. Others thank Monty, Churchill, Roosevelt, Stalin. Clear that decorations were planned some time ago as all show Roosevelt; or is it that folk feel he should get the credit?

Edie Rutherford

Wanted to buy sponge in town today – only from £4 each. Used to be 18/6d before war. I did NOT buy. Also wanted a pair of shoe-trees, 3/- – used to be 6d pair before war. I did NOT buy, will stuff shoes with newspaper rather than give in to such wicked profiteering.

One shilling for small lettuce … oh well … No cress about just now. Nice when we get new potatoes and peas. There are suggestions that we are going to be worse off than ever for food. I believe I would not mind that if the VARIETY could be improved. My husband is quite definitely suffering from poor nutrition today. He NEEDS more milk, butter, cream … I'm terribly worried about him.

Thursday, 17th. Yesterday in a rash mood I bought myself two bunches of pyrethrums, 3/- the two. One bunch would not have made a decent vase-full. It is an outrageous price but when I've been without flowers for months, as I often am these days, I break out …

Just done a wonderful make do and mend with pyjama coat of Husband's. Jamas were bought in Durban 13 years ago so must have been good when new. They had gone where Husband's shoulder blades always cut open his clothes, and at top of sleeves. Now he will have elbow-length sleeves and the good bits from top of sleeves, joined together, have made a new top half of back.

Wednesday, 23rd. I really must make an effort to attend to this diary – what with Husband being ill in bed, Whit holiday … somehow my more or less routine has been proper messed around. The world seems in a mess. All reports that come are of unrest and at home we have all this acid between PM and Labour Party, with an election looming, goodness knows if it *is* wise to go into it. Husband considers Monty just the man for his new job. I am not so sure – he is such a one for Christianity – I wonder if he will emphasise justice and soft-pedal mercy? If not, he isn't the man for the job, as I see things.

Communist friend surprised me last week by saying she'd
rather a Conservative got into Parliament than ILP [Independ-
ent Labour Party] man. Husband reckons Labour isn't fit to
rule. Well, whoever gets in, the voters put them there, and you
can't get away from that. All I want is good men and true and
damn what party they belong to, but I know that is asking a
lot. (Good women and true also!) Was interested to see that
Bevin admitted women had turned out the equal of men in
industry in this war.

Wednesday, 30th. I'm a Conservative – not as staunch as I was   Nella Last
maybe ... I'll never vote for a party that wants things run by
the government. After over five years of dos and don'ts and I am
more convinced than ever that state-controlled things with all
the overlapping, knitting typists, innumerable leaflets no one
seems to read, petty restrictions and hold-ups, irritating forms,
etc., are not my idea of the life beautiful – or even liveable, besides
Churchill is a grand man. I'd like him to steer us, past every rock
and into the clear harbour of peace before he gave up.

JUNE 1945

Sunday, 3rd. A thing and a thing, TWO ugly things – who will   Edie Rutherford
tell us where to dump civilian gas masks and fire-guard tin
hats? They just take up room now. I'll be glad of the space in
this flat.

I wonder WHY de Gaulle blames us? Sounds like Hitler's rea-
soning – the way he used to vituperate about the British when
anything went wrong inside Germany. What a good job we
ended the war when we did. The horrible things the enemy was
preparing to hurl at us ... we should have to be very vigilant
in future if we are to prevent wars. In my heart I feel we won't
manage it. I feel there will be more war and of a far worse kind.

I hope we aren't expected to feel sorry for the Swedes if they go a bit short of food in order to help Finland and Norway. It is their job to help their neighbours. I shall never regard Sweden with anything but contempt for the rest of my life, along with all other so-called neutrals.

Tuesday, 5th. The slanging has begun, and Churchill at his worst doing it. I did not tremble at his bogeyman, Socialism, because I know the other side to the picture. Only the ignorant will fall for that, Mr Churchill, but unfortunately there are plenty of ignorant folk who have a vote. Ah well. The way I feel now, I shan't vote at all. A friend says that is wrong. I say no – if one can't vote for any candidate because one doesn't like their ideas, it is better not to vote, then when someone else thinks of putting up for Parliament, and looks over a constituency, surely the one where most don't vote will be considered a possible place where they want someone good to vote for? If not, it should be so.

One of the grand things about life these days is hearing all the time of ex-POW men returning home. The joy of it. I hear this morn that my cousin Nellie is to be wed on Saturday. Her boy has been POW since Dunkirk. Poor kids.

Kenneth Redmond *Tuesday, 5th.* Today some interest was expressed in the office about the election. Most people mentioned Churchill's speech in an awed and wondering way.[88] I thought it betrayed an utter lack of consideration of the problems of peace and a most violent attack on the common sense of people. It was almost a case of telling everyone they were blockheads and couldn't think unless they had class or money and were labelled 'Tory'.

Wednesday, 6th. My thoughts and actions are all rather muddled. People talk of anniversary of D-Day. What is it to me but the anniversary of Tom's death? When they talk of fraternising with the Germans I feel like screaming, 'Kill them!' Possess their women, but stamp on them and show them what they are, the scum of an era. If the welfare and leave arrangements are really working there would be no need for such talk.

Wednesday, 6th. Well, we reckon Attlee walked rings round Churchill. He was constructive and lucid.[89] Man at work said to me yesterday that he would always vote Tory because he believes in freedom. He wants to be free to walk out of his job to another when he likes. So I just said, 'And free to walk into the dole queue when there isn't any job?' and left it.

Edie Rutherford

A year since that momentous news of the landing on the Normandy beaches. That yarn about the sheep which landed first has not yet been confirmed. I wonder if it was true. The man who told it to Husband said he was there on D-Day so we took it as authentic … I wonder.

Friday, 8th. One short at work yesterday. What a mess we're in when one is away now we are already short-staffed. In my next incarnation, if I have a say, I'm going to be male. They leave dead on time always; draw the big salaries; sit down to meals prepared for them and put up their feet while some female clears away … talk about equality of the sexes, women are for the most part far superior to men.

I have a hunch we shall have the Tories back in power – folk are torn between fear and ignorance, and will vote for no change. I hope I'm wrong, but …

Sunday, 17th. Now the Big Three are to meet in Berlin with a parade too. I'm all for the parade but think a visit to London by Stalin is years overdue. Ribbentrop [German Foreign Minister] in the bag now, apparently feels he is innocent. Haw-Haw in England safely locked up – also seems to think he has a good case. Leopold returning and so the rumpus is on in Belgium.[90] Sometimes I feel a desert island is the only fit place to live these days.

Looks as if I shall have to vote for A. V. Alexander – anything to help this country to a change. Meantime we close in on Japan steadily, and rumours of peace feelers persist.

Tuesday, 26th. San Francisco affair winding up now. I wonder if it has achieved anything worthwhile. One hasn't heard much, nothing clear anyway. Meantime Joyce is pleading not guilty. And when are we going to tackle the Nazis? And why not withhold the drugs from Goering, let him go mad, he has sent plenty mad in his time ...

Why hasn't Leopold the sense to go quietly away? What a mess the world is in, whichever way you look. However, I suppose we have to have these ghastly upheavals to get anything done. I say this – if the Tories get in here next month, they'll have to alter them now to make things damned uncomfortable if they don't play the game at the top. They'll be holding a lid on to a boiling cauldron and it will boil over no matter who governs, if justice isn't done, and quickly enough to suit the men who fought this war for them.

Wednesday, 27th. Last night Albert Victor Alexander came to speak to us. He looks older than his photos and knows his stuff. He got a fair hearing (opened up with the remark that it was the best setting yet, after so many schoolrooms, etc.), only one woman at the back kept interrupting with comments about letting Churchill down. Questions were asked for – Dorothy Holmes (whose cat on fifth floor we care for when she goes away – spinster and clerk) sitting next to me, asked would it not cost a lot of money to finance all the nationalisation, etc. Alexander said it would but that the money was there and would be better invested by government than left to private folk who bungle and contrive and scheme with the profit motive, etc. Another tenant, woman, asked him if he believed in equal pay for the job, and he said, 'YES I DO' in his very loud voice.

The extra tea ration leaves me unmoved. We manage with ours all right, and often I let someone else have a ¼ lb. The

reduced soap ration for this period is a horse of another colour
though. But we do manage.

Friday, 29th. Well, we thought William Beveridge good last
night, and loved the way he sabotaged Churchill's speech two
nights before he makes it! We wish there were a Liberal here as
we'd vote for him or her. We vote Labour because otherwise we
would not vote at all.

JULY 1945

Thursday, 5th. Blazing sun for polling day. I went to the
village school a mile from here on my bicycle to vote. It is
the first vote I have had and I felt a sense of responsibility as I
put my cross. I voted for Vernon Bartlett [independent MP for
Bridgwater] because he is experienced in Parliament, a great
authority on foreign policy, progressive, with more striking
personality and more forceful speaker than other candidates
and independent of party whip system. I felt he would do
more good than the other candidates could possibly do, especially as he is a well-known figure.

Muriel Green

Friday, 6th. Well we both voted on our way to work yesterday,
both for AVA. It was a quiet affair through the day, and as it
was the finest day for months there should have been a heavy
poll. Girls at work who voted for first time, the two in my office
I mean, also voted on way to work. One got a thrill out of it,
other was very matter-of-fact.

Edie Rutherford

    Judging by the state of Berlin and other towns, the German
people should be so busy for years, building, and keeping
themselves fed, etc. that they should not have time to plan
wars. Hope it works out that way, for the sake of the world.

    Poor old Curtin gone.[91] A good chap. Funny to hear
BBC extol him, a lifelong Labourite, at a time when the

government here is calling Labour all the nasty things it can think up.

Tuesday, 10th. Talk about a total eclipse ... it started to rain about 2 p.m. and kept it up for hours. Ugh. This morn it is sunny again but with a wind – has summer gone? Delighted to hear in this morn's news about our extra heavy bombing of the Japs. I wish every Jap could be killed.

I sometimes wonder who did win this war. When one thinks of the way the Germans looted with each conquest and gloated publicly to the world about it, and then contrast it with a cut in rations which followed our victory ... Not that I want to swim in Danish butter ... but I doubt if we have learnt the lesson we needed to learn about how to deal with our enemy the Hun.

Kenneth Redmond   *Sunday, 15th.* St Swithin's Day – awoke to deluging rain. Was faced with the grave decision of 'pictures or museum' after lunch. I am beginning to wonder whether it is an advantage to have the cinemas and pubs open on a Sunday. It makes it so easy to think one is being happy or amused, and so easy to lose all ability to be able to amuse oneself. Outside my digs someone has stuck a candle in the streetlamp – probably trying to compensate for the deferred reinstatement of street lighting. That is one of the ridiculous things of the war – to have reintroduced street lighting while we were still fighting, and to have cut it out almost as VE Day was announced.

Edie Rutherford   *Monday, 23rd.* On the whole, the comments I hear about prefab. house on view in town are praiseworthy. All say it looks like a shed from outside, but inside is grand, and 'I would not mind living in one' is the general verdict. Given the right spot, we would not mind one, in fact we'd LOVE one – in the right spot.

Thursday, 26th. Today has been the most exciting day in the   Muriel Green
hostel we have had; even more exciting than VE Day, because
that was expected and the election results have been a staggering surprise. I was waiting for 12 to hear the first results. I was
in the lounge alone and simply jumped up and down with joy
and excitement at the obvious trend of the first results.

All were surprised at such a large majority especially for
Labour. The Tories certainly expected to have swept the country
with the Churchill figurehead, if there was any large majority
at all! At 1 p.m. E and I ran down to the lounge where about
15 people had assembled waiting. When the announcer gave
the result the general effect was a broad grin. I saw no visible
Conservatives present. I then left the lounge and made it my
business to phone the Town Hall for the local result. I was
answered promptly and could hardly write down the result for
excitement. Vernon Bartlett was in with a 2,000 majority.

One said on hearing result of Vernon Bartlett in for this
division, 'Votes for independent candidate are wasted because
he doesn't belong to any party.' I kept quiet, because I wasn't
being asked to do otherwise, but wished I had had the courage
to put a red ribbon in my hair before going on duty!

Friday, 27th. Well, well, well, who'd a thought it? Not I.   Edie Rutherford
Damn bad prophet me. But how GLAD I am. At last the people
will have a chance to govern. Pray God they get His help so
that they don't make colossal blunders. Theirs is the heaviest
task any government has ever faced in all our history. I would
not be anywhere but in England this day. Husband very pleased
and, like me, amazed and interested. We wonder now – mines
nationalised? Railways?

Saturday, 28th. Nice to have a prime minister whose wife does
some housework and her own shopping. I gather everyone is
suffering from shock about the election results – Tories from
shock of surprise at not getting in; others at shock of getting in.

I can't believe it myself yet entirely. Ah well, let us hope they get busy and DO something.

Muriel Green   *Tuesday, 31st.* Several people told me they have voted Conservative all their life before and this time they were so disgusted with the conditions pre-war, unemployment, etc., that they decided long ago to vote Labour at the next election. Most of them had voted for Bartlett in this area. Several said they have been unemployed, one man said he came out of the army after the last war and went on the dole for five years and he didn't want to see his sons do the same. There was no disrespect for Mr Churchill amongst them, but for the cronies and Municheers gathered around him.

I feel that at last the working classes of this country have begun to think for themselves and wake up. They have not been fooled by the bogey of voting 'National' or by Churchill's smiling face. They do not want to get back to 1939. The conscription and shortages here taught them democracy and that all men are really equal. I feel confident that a better world is going to be the result of this election and that the future in spite of so many difficulties is bright. Now is the chance of the Labour Party to show the world what they can do and what can be done. Churchill is an old man and as a war leader against Japan not irreplaceable. It is for the young people of this country to support the new government to success.

AUGUST 1945

Herbert Brush   *Tuesday, 7th.* News of the first atomic bomb dropped on Japan. What an awful weapon judging by the papers. Where should we be now if the Germans had made them first? It is probably a painless death to die by atomic bomb, and all your friends would be with you when you went into the unknown.

I wasted 6d to go into a waxwork exhibition in Oxford

Street, and when inside an extra charge of 6d was required to see the German concentration camp. I did *not* go into that, and the effigies of Hitler, Musso, Monty, etc., were so bad in the main part of the exhibition. However, the place was crowded with sightseers, and I guess that I was not the only one who thought that the sixpence was wasted.

Wednesday, 8th. I wonder whether the discovery of the atomic bomb has meant the end of civilisation. It is appalling to think that it might be so, that power has been discovered that if leased to a set of lunatics could end all our forefathers have built up. It is a terrifying thought because human nature has brought previous wars. They don't just happen by natural means, but are brought on by men and if they have brought on others unless human nature changes rapidly there might be fools who would bring about another, even if it would end everything. On the other hand, this new devastating weapon might have the reaction of keeping down war if it is controlled by men of peace. Another war would be too abominable for even the vilest of men to contemplate. We can only take that view if we look for optimism in life, the other is too depressing to ponder on. The new power might also be of use to aid civilisation, to fight disease and make life a more enjoyable place. Time will tell.

Muriel Green

Thursday, 9th. Russia's declaration of war on Japan came as a pleasant surprise. Not really a surprise, but as a good news item last night. Everything that will hasten the end of the war is good news. The sooner the fighting is over the better for all, foe as well as friend.

Thursday, 9th. Russia has come into this war as the Yanks came into the last one – in time for the end. Well, she had to do it to have a say in the peace. Japan gets her second atomic bomb. How many before she wakens? I brought up the subject of the

Edie Rutherford

new bomb at work yesterday. Horror of its power is definitely the chief reaction.

A boot and leather shop on the way to work, noted for its catchy phrases, has this week: NO SANDALS. NO PLIMSOLLS. NO KIDDING.

Muriel Green   *Friday, 10th*. The smashing news of Japan's sudden offer to surrender is simply a knock-out. I was rather stunned by the news because I didn't expect it so soon after VE Day. The atomic bomb and Russia's entry into the war has done it, but somehow I expected that the Japanese fanatical philosophy would make them hold out until nearly annihilated.

Herbert Brush   *Tuesday, 14th*. A dull, warm morning. Bar. [barometer] 29.48". Looks like more rain; there was a slight fall during the night. I wonder how much longer the Japs will fool about making up their minds whether the majority prefer to die rather than surrender. Another ato-bomb would hurry them up. I wonder whether we would have used an ato-bomb on Germany if the thing had been ready in time.

Edie Rutherford   *VJ Day, Wednesday, 15th*. Eight o'clock. We knew at midnight when the news came through – were fast asleep when suddenly a man's voice shouted, 'Jap war's over! Hurrah!' Both woke with a start which gave Husband a headache which he still has. I looked at clock and when I saw time realised what had been said on air. Recognised the shout as the voice of man in a flat on floor below ours.

Muriel Green   *VJ Day, Wednesday, 15th*. At last, at long last! The day we have waited for nearly six long years has come round. A new era has dawned in which it is up to the survivors and the young people to let it not happen again. A new people's parliament has opened and the world is ready for better things.

After lunch E and I cycled into town and went in the bar of

the leading hotel. It was not overcrowded and we were served with gin and orange at once. It was all very jolly. We met four of the other staff and stood in the square when general whoopee was being made. The church bells were ringing and crackers were going off right and left. Drunks were singing and about 30 people were dancing and doing the 'hokey-cokey' on the street. Records of light music were being played through a microphone and crowds of people were just standing watching the fun. I stayed until it was time for me to return for duty to the hostel.

We came back to the hostel and Mr C gave us another glass of port wine. Then we went for another walk and back to sit in the lounge for the King's speech and 9 p.m. news. Informal dance music from a piano and drums and several singing solos went on until midnight. It was all very orderly and as there was a shortage of men very boring. It wasn't really like a terrific celebration that it is. I retired to bed only thankful that the time we had fought and laboured for was here at last as we knew it would be one day. All bad things like all good things do not last for ever but now we must prolong the good things such as peace.

Friday, 24th. Hosts of people are arguing and will continue to argue about the use of the ato-bomb, but it is very certain that if either the Japs or the Germans had managed to make one of these bombs, it would certainly have been dropped in the heart of London and we, in Sydenham, would have had no further need to worry.

Herbert Brush

The secret of its manufacture is bound to leak out in time, especially if the energy can be applied to business in some way, but I don't think that it can be a simple process which the ordinary person will be able to understand. I dare say that someone will write a book and call it *Atomic Energy Simplified* for the man-in-the-street, but I don't imagine that I shall be alive to read the book.

Monday, 27th. 'Rem', the artist at St Martin's church, has put up a notice that all his collection of pictures on exhibition was destroyed during celebration on VJ Day. He had gone to lunch when I arrived so I left him a sandwich which I had saved from my lunch and dropped a few coppers in his box. I guess he will know who has been there when he sees the sandwich, though he does not know my name.

The mentality of some people on V-days is unexplainable as far as I can see. What possible good can it do anyone to destroy the pictures of a poor artist which he hangs on a churchyard fence to attract coppers. The poor old chap has had to use the pavement for a chalk picture. I guess that he can't get any more canvas now. His pavement picture is very good.

Nella Last   *Wednesday, 29th*. I'm tired tonight. I used to think when the war was over I'd be able to have lots more time for myself, but so far, only the shop closing has made any surplus and the garden takes up every spare half-hour I have. I baked bread and the pastry I had left in a bowl, made a plate tart and one on a saucer for my in-laws when rolled paper-thin and I put green gooseberry jam in them. I made a little custard and baked windfall apples and tidied up generally. I breathed a sigh of real gratitude when I saw what the butcher brought – 7d of corned beef, a good jelly bone, ¼ suet and ½ lb. sausage and simmered the jelly bone till the bones came out clean and minced the corned beef with the jellied sinew off the bone and I've good potted meat for two days – and a wee taste for my in-laws for tomorrow. Friday is their worst day for lunch. I've still my bacon to get. I feel no worries at all for meals till the end of the week. What a lot of women's time and thought goes on food nowadays and what a relief to know meals are assured a day or so ahead. I cooked sausage with tomatoes and runner beans, heated the remainder of the tinned soup from yesterday with tomatoes and a little macaroni I'd previously cooked, made Bird's custard enough for today and tomorrow to eat with gooseberry jam tart.

In between watching my oven I put the lawn-mower together and got a bit of weeding done and after I'd washed up I put my best tablecloths and napkins in to soak in soapy water and went out into the garden. I got the lawn cut but not rolled. I began to feel exhausted and knew it was time to stop, so I'll have to roll it on Friday morning if it's fine, that lawn is becoming my darling as I see weeds disappearing and only the twitch grass to fight and as I never pass a little 'bunch' of it when I walk on the lawn. I'll get rid of that. The dark heavy clouds that had hung about all day, grew darker and rain began to fall, so I put my tablecloths on the rack and went to lie down for half an hour before I made tea, as my husband had said he might be home early to go to the pictures. I had tea ready by 4.30, feeling irritated at the rush it entailed to go to the first house which starts at 5.30, which means we so rarely go, my husband has a queer 'fixative' about second houses. Tonight I told him flatly I refused to rush and scatter again – or to see him bolt an insufficient meal. There was a cheese salad, baked custard and apples, plain cake, apricot jam and wholemeal bread and butter, but neither of us ate much. It was a good picture ...

Friday, 31st. W dropped me at Camberwell Green this morning and I changed my book at Boots in Peckham. W asked me to buy her some cigarettes and I had to visit many shops and walk at least a mile before I managed to get a packet; then the man would let me have only one packet. I got another packet in another shop. This experience makes me glad that I don't smoke. The book I took out is *Göring, the Iron Man of Germany* by H. Blood-Ryan. I don't think that there will be much of his iron will left when his judges have finished with him.

W went to the hospital today to have her throat examined by a specialist. He says that there is not cause for worry and advised her to eat as much as she could and suck barley sugar all the time, but he did not tell her where to get all the food or

Herbert Brush

the barley sugar. She had to wait her turn for three hours, but the specialist's advice cost only one shilling. That is one of the advantages of paying 3d per week into the Hospital Saturday Fund.

SEPTEMBER 1945

Herbert Brush   *Sunday, 2nd.* A bright, warm morning. Bar. 29.7".

I did not sleep very well last night. A curious kind of nightmare which seemed to last a long time. The last I remember about it was that the world was to be destroyed in a few minutes and I did not care what happened. But it was not by an atomic bomb but by a solid body which was approaching from a direction opposite the sun, so there would be no chance of it being diverted from its course.

Monday, 3rd. I wonder what I was doing six years ago: it's too much trouble to look for my diary of that date, but I remember Chamberlain's lugubrious tones when he said, 'We are at war with Germany.'

A dull morning; looks like rain. Bar. 29.74".

GLOSSARY AND ABBREVIATIONS

AA, ack-ack	Anti-Aircraft (guns, gunfire)
All Clear	Single-note siren, signalling the end of an air raid
AFS	Auxiliary Fire Service (civilian support for the fire services)
Anderson shelter	Made of corrugated steel, they were erected in gardens and yards and often covered with soil
ARP	Air Raid Precautions
ATC	Air Training Corps
ATS	Auxiliary Territorial Service (women's sector of the army)
BEF	British Expeditionary Force
British Restaurant	Certain restaurants and cafés were in a government-sponsored scheme whereby they served good (unrationed) food at a subsidised price
Cert A	A training examination for army cadets
CO	Conscientious Objector
Conchie	Slang for Conscientious Objector
CSM	Company Sergeant-Major (British army)
DCM	Distinguished Conduct Medal
ENSA	Entertainments National Services Association
HG	Home Guard

HMS	His Majesty's Ship (or His Majesty's Service)
ILP	Independent Labour Party
Jerry	Slang name for Germans
Kitchen Front	A daily radio programme which extolled the virtue of cooking with simple nutritional ingredients
LPTB	London Passenger Transport Board
MO	Mass Observation
MOI	Ministry of Information
Morrison shelter	An indoor shelter named after the Home Secretary, Herbert Morrison
Mufti	Civilian clothes when worn by the military
Municheers	Those who had supported Chamberlain over the Munich Agreement in 1938
NAAFI	Navy, Army and Air Force Institute (ran canteens and shops for servicemen)
NCO	Non-commissioned Officer
NFS	National Fire Service
Poldi Hardness Tester	A mechanical device for measuring the hardness of metals
POW	Prisoner of war
PPU	Peace Pledge Union
QM	Quartermaster
RA	Royal Regiment of Artillery, usually shortened to Royal Artillery
RAF	Royal Air Force
RAMC	Royal Army Medical Corps
RAOC	Royal Army Ordnance Corps
RASC	Royal Army Service Corps

Red Caps	Military police
Reserved occupation	Not liable for conscription
Reveille	A magazine, popular in the forces
Sanatogen	Brand name for a popular 'nerve tonic'
SBAC	Society of British Aircraft Constructors
Tommy	Slang name for British soldier
VC	Victoria Cross medal
WAAF	Women's Auxiliary Air Force
WEA	Workers' Educational Association
WRNS	Women's Royal Naval Service
WVS	Women's Voluntary Service
YHA	Youth Hostels Association
YMCA	Young Men's Christian Association (provided sports facilities, cafés and other community services)

A NOTE ON THE SELECTIONS

Altogether around 500 people kept diaries for Mass Observation from 1939 to the end of the war in August 1945. Selecting diarists for this anthology from the many boxes of archive material was a challenging task. I wanted to convey a broad range of experience: a mix of male and female diarists of different ages, places of residence and occupations; and to reflect a range of writing styles. The selection could never be a 'representative' sample of the British population, nor could it hope to paint a complete historical picture of the period. The diarists were self-selecting, mainly from the South-East, mostly clerical workers, teachers, students, journalists and librarians. The diaries vary in their coverage, too. Some diarists wrote at the beginning of the war in September 1939 and are heard from no more, often because they were conscripted; others wrote for a short time, stopped, then returned months later; a few wrote regularly throughout the war and beyond.

In order to achieve a broad selection and provide a varied portrait of the war years, I decided to include some diarists whose work has been printed elsewhere, as well as featuring extracts previously unpublished. For example, Herbert Brush, Maggie Joy Blunt and Edie Rutherford are featured in Simon Garfield's *Our Hidden Lives* (2004), which covers the first three post-war years. Christopher Tomlin appears in Garfield's second anthology, *We Are at War* (2005), Muriel and Jenny Green in Dorothy Sheridan's *Wartime Women* (1990), and Nella Last in Richard Broad and Suzie Fleming's *Nella Last's War* (2006). George Springett, J. R. Frier, Frank Edwards, Peter Baxter, Kenneth Redmond and Doris Melling are all previously unpublished. I have also included two men who helped to shape Mass Observation: Henry Novy and Len England, young men in their 20s who were conscripted into the armed forces but kept up their reporting work. Henry Novy (1919–87) and his wife Priscilla (née Feare) were both paid investigators for Mass Observation. Henry Novy became one of the first trustees appointed to the Mass Observation Archive in the 1970s when the collection moved to the University of Sussex. Len England (1920–99) was interested in cinema-going and wartime humour and wrote reports on these subjects for Mass Observation. He continued to work for the organisation after the war, and in the 1950s became managing director of the market research company, MO (UK) Ltd.

Every effort has been made to trace the diarists and their families, but without much success. Those we have managed to contact were fully supportive of the project. I have preferred to use pseudonyms for most of the diarists to protect both their own identities and those of the people they refer to in their diaries. There are three exceptions: Nella Last's family gave permission for her real name to be published, and Len England and Henry Novy's names have also been used with their families' permission and because they were well-known staff at Mass Observation. Any reader who recognises their name or that of a relative as one of the diarists featured here should contact the publishers of this book.

DIARISTS' BIOGRAPHIES

The following brief biographies of the diarists represented in this book are based on the diaries themselves and on biographical information held by the Mass Observation Archive. Most diarists also answered themed Directive questions set by Mass Observation on topics such as food, rationing, clothes, money, morale, family and home life, politics, education and leisure activities.

PETER BAXTER

A Cambridge graduate born in 1917, Peter Baxter was a corporal based at RAF Padgate, Warrington, Lancashire, where he trained recruits during the war. He and his wife Dora lived in Blackpool, and his parents lived in Stamford Hill in London. He wrote continuous commentary on the events of the war in his diary for Mass Observation from May 1942 to February 1944.

MAGGIE JOY BLUNT

Maggie Joy Blunt was a writer living alone with her beloved cats in a cottage in Slough, Berkshire. In October 1941 she began working for an architectural journal based in London. She was a keen newspaper reader and kept herself informed of events both at home and abroad. She kept a sporadic diary for Mass Observation from 1939 to 1950.

HERBERT BRUSH

Herbert Brush lived in Forest Hill, south London with friends W and D. He was 70 years old and retired at the outbreak of war: he used to work in Dover as an electricity board inspector. A keen gardener, art lover, reader and writer of verse, he worked hard on his allotment and took 'Dig for Victory'

very seriously in between trips to the British Library reading
room and the National Gallery. He wrote his diary instalments
as 'diary letters' to his brother Caldwell, who sent them on
to Mass Observation. When Caldwell died in 1945, he re-
addressed his letters to his sister Nora. He wrote 'diary letters'
from September 1940 to March 1951, although instalments
for 1943 and 1944 are largely missing from the Mass Observation collection.

FRANK EDWARDS

Frank Edwards was 32 at the outbreak of war. A buyer for a
war factory in London, he was not conscripted to the forces,
but joined the Home Guard in September 1942 and was a fire-
watcher for his neighbourhood. He was an enthusiastic sup-
porter of the armed forces, particularly the RAF. He kept his
diary for the duration of the war.

LEN ENGLAND

In 1939, Len England was a young student living in Streatham,
London. After the Dunkirk evacuations he signed up for the
army. In January 1941 he joined the Royal Army Ordnance
Corps in Hinckley and became a non-commissioned officer,
posted to Donnington in March 1941. He kept diaries for
Mass Observation in September and October 1939, and from
January 1941 to January 1943. He worked for Mass Observation as a paid investigator and wrote many file reports from the
material collected by the organisation; he was responsible for
most of MO's research on cinema-going in wartime. He was
managing director of MO(UK)Ltd, when Mass Observation
became a market research organisation in the 1950s, and he
negotiated with Professor Asa Briggs to bring the early MO
papers to the University of Sussex in the 1970s. He died in
1999.

J. R. FRIER

A 19-year-old university student, J. R. Frier lived with his
parents and younger sister in London during vacations. He had
signed up to join the Royal Artillery by the end of 1939. His
girlfriend Pat was a student at London University. He knew
both French and German, and commented on the news broadcast from French and German radio stations. He kept a handwritten diary for Mass Observation from August to October
1939, and answered Directives sporadically until May 1944.

JENNY GREEN

Jenny Green, 25 when war was declared, worked in her family-
run garage business with their mechanic W in the village of
Snettisham in Norfolk. She lived with her widowed mother
and sister Muriel, who also wrote for Mass Observation and
worked in the garage. She handled the business accounts and
helped with the housework. She, like her sister, regularly
attended lectures at the local branch of the Workers' Educa-
tional Association, and attended summer schools run by the
University of Cambridge. She kept a diary for Mass Observation until August 1941, and answered Directive questions
from June 1939 to October 1942.

MURIEL GREEN

Jenny Green's younger sister Muriel was 19 years old when war
started. In 1941 she became a land girl and moved frequently
around the country: she was briefly a gardening apprentice in
manor-house gardens in Dorset, then worked in a garden in
the village of Empingham in Rutland in May 1941, and as
an under-gardener in Woodbridge in Suffolk. At the beginning of 1942 she moved to Huntley Manor in Gloucester,
and by the end of the war she was working in a hostel for war
factory workers near Taunton. She kept a handwritten diary for
Mass Observation throughout the war, and also responded to
Directives.

NELLA LAST

Nella Last was a housewife and mother who worked for the Women's Voluntary Service in the shipbuilding town of Barrow-in-Furness in north Lancashire (now in Cumbria). Her husband was a joiner and shopfitter. They had two sons: Cliff, who was called up for military service, and Arthur, who was a tax inspector – a reserved occupation: he responded to Directives for Mass Observation in 1943. Nella Last wrote persistently, and at length: she continued to send her diaries to Mass Observation until 1966, on thin paper in ink, each week carefully tied up with cotton thread. Entries for 1944 are missing. Nella Last was born in 1889 and died in 1968.

DORIS MELLING

Doris Melling, 22 at the start of the war, was a shorthand typist and hospital library assistant living in Liverpool with her parents. Her brother Herbert was called up to join the Royal Air Force. She was a member of a photographic society and a keen tennis player. She wrote for Mass Observation from August 1939 to May 1942.

HENRY NOVY

Henry Novy became a clerk in the Royal Army Medical Corps in Leeds in November 1940. When he turned 21 in December 1940 he married Priscilla Feare; both worked for Tom Harrisson as paid investigators for Mass Observation. He moved on a number of occasions in 1941: from the end of February he was at Catterick, Yorkshire; in April he moved to Shotley Bridge, County Durham; and was later posted to Woolwich in London. That same year Priscilla and he had their first child, Michael. He became one of the first appointed trustees of the Mass Observation Archive in the 1970s. He died in 1987.

KENNETH REDMOND

Kenneth Redmond was a civil servant who worked in Bridgend

in Wales and also in Bristol during the war. Aged 18 at the start of the war, he was an active member of his local youth club and Communist Party. His brother Tom was killed in action: this was a source of much grief to himself, his parents and sister Evaline. Evaline had a baby son, Roderick, in November 1944. Kenneth Redmond's family hosted evacuees in Swansea: a mother and daughter, Connie and Jennifer. He kept a diary for Mass Observation in 1944 and 1945.

EDIE RUTHERFORD

Edie Rutherford was an immigrant housewife from South Africa. An opinionated Socialist, she lived with her husband in a block of flats in Sheffield in Yorkshire. She was in her late thirties at the start of the war and was later called by the Ministry of Labour to work as a clerk. She typed a continuous diary for Mass Observation from August 1941 until December 1950.

GEORGE SPRINGETT

George Springett was a writer and conscientious objector lodging with a family in Bromley, Kent: the Robinsons with their daughter Violet. He was 29 when war was declared, and was determined to avoid conscription. He had sympathetic Communist friends, and was also close to a family called the Thompsons. His diary for Mass Observation was kept sporadically during 1941 and 1942, mostly written in flowing ink in small notebooks.

CHRISTOPHER TOMLIN

Christopher Tomlin, 28 at the start of the war, was a paper salesman living in Fulwood, Preston, with his parents; his brother Dick was stationed in France. At the end of 1940 he trained at RAF Padgate for the RAF Volunteer Reserve. He kept his Mass Observation diary from September 1939 to December 1940, typed at the start, then handwritten in capital letters.

THE MASS OBSERVATION ARCHIVE

The Mass Observation Archive began with the papers from Mass Observation, a British social research organisation formed in the late 1930s with the aim of accumulating a written record about the everyday life of ordinary people in the UK. Mass Observation ran from 1937 until the early 1950s and provided an especially rich historical resource on civilian life during the Second World War. The Mass Observation Archive came to the University of Sussex in 1970 at the invitation of Lord Briggs, who was then the university's Vice-Chancellor. Were it not for Len England, and two social historians, Angus Calder and Paul Addison, the papers might have been left forgotten in the basement of the offices of MO (UK) Ltd.

Today, a major autobiographical project is run from the Archive itself, based at the University of Sussex library. Hundreds of volunteers respond to regular requests to write in both diary form and in reports on themes about themselves, their families, workplaces and communities. This material has been gathered since 1981 and so far over 3,000 people have volunteered to be contributors. The greater part of it is available for research and teaching. The Mass Observation Archive collaborates with researchers from academia, the media or any member of the public to set themes to which the volunteers will respond. Recent topics have included the London bombings, genetics and cloning, football, public mourning, sexuality, homes, ethical shopping, domestic violence, gardening and the smoking ban of 2007.

The Mass Observation Archive is a charitable trust and runs a Friends scheme to finance its work. For more information about the scheme, see the website www.massobs.org.uk, email moa@sussex.ac.uk, or write to The Mass Observation Archive,

Special Collections, University of Sussex Library, Brighton
BN1 9QL, UK.

DOROTHY SHERIDAN
Director, Mass Observation Archive

ENDNOTES

1   A liner torpedoed off the coast of Ireland with the loss of 112 passengers.

2   The first British warship to be lost during the war, the aircraft carrier *Courageous* was sunk on 17 September with the loss of over 500 crew.

3   Following hard on the heels of Stalin's annexation of eastern Poland, the two Baltic states were forced, on 5 and 10 October respectively, to allow the establishment of Soviet military bases within their borders.

4   A secret treaty, signed in 1915, by which Britain and Russia agreed to partition the Ottoman Empire at the end of the First World War.

5   On 14 October the battleship HMS *Royal Oak* was torpedoed by the German submarine U-47 and sank at the British Home Fleet naval base in Scapa Flow, Orkney, Scotland, with the loss of nearly 900 crew.

6   Twenty-two drowned when the Mersey pilot boat *Charles Livingston* ran aground in a gale early on the morning of 26 November.

7   Soviet forces invaded Finland when the Finns rejected Stalin's aggressive territorial demands. Despite mounting a fierce resistance, the Finns were forced to cede territory in the peace treaty of March 1940.

8   The cargo liner *Doric Star* was sunk off St Helena by the pocket battleship *Admiral Graf Spee* rather than her sister ship, the *Admiral Scheer*.

9   There was an earthquake on Wednesday 27 December, in which whole towns and villages over a wide area of northern and north-eastern Anatolia were destroyed. Hundreds of thousands of people were killed, injured or rendered homeless.

10 Leslie Hore-Belisha was dismissed as Secretary of State for War on 4 January.

11 Danish resistance collapsed within twenty-four hours. On the same day Germany invaded Norway, and rapidly secured the strategically important ports which would give the German navy and air force access to the Atlantic and the North Sea.

12 The IRA had launched a bombing campaign in Britain in 1939.

13 Germany invaded Holland and Belgium on 10 May; both countries surrendered by the end of the month.

14 France fell to the Germans, and on 22 June an armistice was signed at Compiègne, in the railway carriage used in 1918 for Germany's surrender.

15 Franklin D. Roosevelt defeated Republican candidate Wendell Willkie in the US presidential election on 5 November.

16 Italy, which had entered the war in June 1940, invaded Greece through Albania on 28 October. The Greeks counter-attacked and drove back the Italians some 15 miles into Albania.

17 Marshal Rodolfo Graziani's 10th Army advanced from Libya into Egypt as far as Sidi Barrani, but were routed by British and Commonwealth forces under General Wavell in a counter-offensive which began on 9 December. In Cyrenaica, a province of Libya, the Allied campaign against the Italian forces was widely reported in Britain. Within two months, the Italian threat in North Africa was averted.

18 The Allies drove Italian divisions back past Benghazi in north-east Libya on 6 February.

19 US Congress did not pass the long debated Lend-Lease Act until March 1941, enabling Franklin D. Roosevelt to authorise the lend or lease of arms and equipment to states 'whose defence the President deems vital to the

defence of the United States'. This included Britain, China and, later, Russia.

20 At the end of March 1941, British naval forces – including the First World War battleship HMS *Warspite* – successfully fought the Italian fleet off Cape Matapan in southern Greece.

21 Germany invaded Yugoslavia and Greece on 6 April. British forces were called in to help Greek troops, but the German assault overwhelmed them; many soldiers were captured or evacuated.

22 The Libyan port of Tobruk was held by British, Australian and Polish troops for most of 1941, isolated and besieged by Italian forces and the German General Rommel's Afrika Korps. In November, the new British commander-in-chief, Auchinleck, launched Operation Crusader, whose main objective was to push through Cyrenaica and relieve Tobruk. This campaign was partially successful, but in January 1942 Rommel launched a counter-attack.

23 Hitler's deputy, Rudolf Hess, was reported to have crashed a Messerschmitt 110 in a field near Glasgow on 13 May. There were many speculations about the reason for his strange visit to Britain. He was imprisoned in the Tower of London, then placed under secure psychiatric care.

24 HMS *Hood* was sunk on 24 May by the *Prinz Eugen* and the *Bismarck*. The loss of the navy's flagship with 1,400 crew caused deep despair at home. Three days later the British retaliated and the *Bismarck* was crippled and sunk in the North Atlantic.

25 William Joyce, an Irish-American Fascist who fled from Britain to Germany in 1939, broadcast propaganda from Radio Hamburg. Allied forces were evacuated from mainland Greece to Crete in April. On 20 May German parachutists and gliders landed in western Crete.

Despite heavy casualties, they managed to consolidate
their position. Allied troops were forced to withdraw
over the mountains to the south coast, where they were
evacuated to Egypt.

26   Syria, mandated to the French in 1920, was now
      controlled by Vichy France, the collaborationist
      government of unoccupied France since the Franco-
      German armistice of June 1940. Allied forces entered
      Syria in May 1941, and crushed the Vichy French
      resistance within three weeks.

27   In Operation Barbarossa, Germany invaded Russia on
      several fronts, from the Baltic to the Black Sea.

28   The aircraft carrier HMS *Ark Royal* was torpedoed by
      German submarine U-81; the crew were evacuated
      before it sank near Gibraltar.

29   The retired admiral of the fleet and Conservative MP
      from 1934 to 1943, Sir Roger Keyes had been appointed
      Director of Combined Operations by Churchill in June
      1940. He was replaced in September 1941 following
      the rejection of his ambitious plans and breakdown of
      relations with the chiefs of staff.

30   On 7 December, Japanese planes attacked the US naval
      base at Pearl Harbor in Hawaii. Next day the Japanese
      attacked Hong Kong, which fell on Christmas Day.

31   Amidst appalling conditions, on 5 December, the
      Red Army under General Zhukov launched a counter-
      offensive that finally halted, and then drove back, the
      German advance from the outskirts of Moscow.

32   Manila fell to the Japanese on 2 January 1942. As well
      as the Philippines, Japanese forces attacked Burma,
      Malaya and the Dutch East Indian islands of Borneo,
      Sumatra, Java and Timor. By the end of the month they
      had swept down the Malay Peninsula towards Singapore.

33   Singapore fell to the Japanese on 15 February, along
     with 130,000 British, Australian and Empire prisoners
     of war.

34   The battleships *Scharnhorst*, *Gneisenau* and heavy cruiser
     Prinz Eugen sailed through the English Channel on their
     way to Norway from the French port of Brest on 11 and
     12 February. This was humiliating for both the RAF and
     Royal Navy, who were caught off guard.

35   As the Japanese took Singapore and Rangoon, the
     British in India were under great threat. Churchill sent
     Sir Stafford Cripps to India in March 1942 to negotiate
     with Indian political leaders over the future status of
     the country (India had been offered dominion status).
     He was unsuccessful. Nehru and Jinnah knew that
     they could agree to nothing without the agreement of
     Gandhi – and Gandhi would accept nothing less than
     independence.

36   The 1,400-strong Australian garrison on the
     strategically important south-west Pacific island of New
     Britain (now part of Papua New Guinea) was quickly
     defeated by a much larger Japanese force, which then
     massacred over 150 prisoners of war.

37   Fears that Japan might occupy Madagascar and use it as
     a forward base led British forces to land on the Vichy-
     held island on 5 May. French resistance ended within 48
     hours.

38   Sir Arthur Harris, commander-in-chief of the RAF's
     Bomber Command, ordered three 'thousand-bomber
     raids' on the German cities of Cologne, Essen and
     Bremen. The aim was to damage German morale, but
     the raids were actually less effective than was claimed at
     the time.

39   Rommel's panzer divisions had been advancing east
     across Libya since January 1942. In late May, as the
     Italians attacked the Allied defences at Gazala, the

German tanks drove deep into the desert to outflank the British in Tobruk, which fell on 21 June. Nearly 40,000 prisoners were taken, and by the end of June the Axis forces had reached El Alamein in Egypt, where the British Eighth Army under Claude Auchinleck had established a defensive position. Rommel's attempt to break through was halted in the first battle of El Alamein.

40 The Dieppe raid on 19 August was planned to test the potential of a full-scale invasion of France by sea. It was a fiasco, with Canadian and British troops suffering heavy casualties.

41 In August 1942 Churchill had replaced Auchinleck with General Harold Alexander as commander-in-chief in North Africa and the Middle East, and General Bernard Montgomery took over the Eighth Army. On the night of 23 October, a massive artillery bombardment was the prelude to the second battle of El Alamein. The Axis forces were gradually pushed back deep into Libya. Allied war planners had long debated opening a second front to relieve the pressure on Russia. Eventually they agreed to develop the North African campaign into a Mediterranean front. On 8 November, in Operation Torch, Allied forces – mostly American – landed in Morocco and Algeria.

42 Vichy French Admiral Jean Darlan was given political control of French North Africa in exchange for collaboration with the Allies. He was assassinated in late December.

43 The bitter fighting for Stalingrad had continued since mid-August. On 19 November a Soviet pincer movement encircled the German Sixth Army positions in and around the city.

44 Churchill broadcast to the nation after the second battle of El Alamein. Although this was perhaps 'the end of

the beginning', he promised a long struggle ahead:
'Remember that Hitler with his armies and his secret
police holds nearly all Europe in his grip. Remember
that he has millions of slaves to toil for him, a vast mass
of munitions, many mighty arsenals and many fertile
fields. Remember that Goering has brazenly declared
that whoever starves in Europe it will not be the
Germans.'

45 In January 1943, the Allies held a conference at
Casablanca in French Morocco, at which Churchill,
Roosevelt, the joint chiefs of staff and Generals
Eisenhower and Alexander discussed the future direction
of the war. Stalin, preoccupied with the Stalingrad
campaign, was unable to attend. The conference agreed
to seek unconditional surrender from Germany, Italy and
Japan. Despite continuing Russian pressure for a second
front in western Europe, the British view that this
would be premature prevailed.

46 At the end of January the German Sixth Army finally
surrendered at Stalingrad.

47 There was a small article in *The Times* on the following
day about the massacre of Jews. It referred to a report
received by the British section of the World Jewish
Congress from central Europe that the extermination of
Jews in occupied Europe by massacre and starvation had
speeded up.

48 The campaign in North Africa continued during 1943,
with setbacks to the Allies in February when Rommel
attacked the US Second Corps in southern Tunisia at the
Kasserine Pass. British reinforcements helped to impede
the German advance, and Rommel was forced back.

49 On 12 April German military authorities reported
the discovery of a mass grave of 4,000 Polish officers
murdered by Soviets in Katyn Forest, near Smolensk.

This signalled a final breakdown of Polish–Soviet relations during the war.

50 On 16 May, the British 617 Squadron of RAF Bomber Command, led by Wing Commander Guy Gibson, destroyed major dams supplying power and water to the Ruhr valley in western Germany. Although the attack, which became known as the 'Dambusters raid', was a great propaganda coup, the long-term disruption to the region's industrial output was relatively limited.

51 On that day there was a letter in *The Times* from Pope Pius XII written in response to the bombing of Rome by the US military in daylight. The Pope expressed his sorrow at the failure of his efforts to prevent the bombing of the city.

52 Having been recaptured by the Germans in February 1943, Kharkov was finally taken by the Russians in the aftermath of the battle of Kursk, on 23 August, by which time three-quarters of the city had been destroyed.

53 Here Churchill and Roosevelt, with their diplomatic and military advisers, discussed the war in the Far East and agreed plans to land in France the following spring. Meanwhile, following the invasion of Sicily on 10 July and the fall of Mussolini two weeks later, Allied forces would attack the Italian mainland from the south.

54 In the largest raid so far on Berlin, more than 700 RAF bombers dropped 1,700 tons of bombs during the night of 23–4 August, killing more than 5,000.

55 On 3 September the 13th Corps of Montgomery's Eighth Army crossed the Straits of Messina from Sicily to mainland Italy. The Allies established themselves in Reggio, and six days later a major force was landed at Salerno, south of Naples.

56 Italy capitulated on 8 September. A representative of Marshal Badoglio, Italy's prime minister since the

downfall of Mussolini at the end of July, had signed an
unconditional armistice with the Allies in secret on 3
September. Mussolini was rescued by a German airborne
operation on the 12th.

57   German troops, landed from the Italian mainland, had
     delayed Montgomery's advance on Messina in north-east
     Sicily.

58   After rescuing Mussolini, the Germans installed him as
     head of a renegade republic in northern Italy.

59   Correctly Arthur Aaron. Despite his severe injuries the
     21-year-old piloted his bomber back to base following a
     raid on Turin on 12 August.

60   In November 1943, the Home Secretary, Herbert
     Morrison, ordered the release of Sir Oswald Mosley,
     founder of the British Union of Fascists, and his wife,
     Lady Diana Mosley. The couple had been interned since
     May and June 1940 respectively under Regulation 18B
     of the Emergency Powers Act.

61   The Allied leaders met in Teheran on 28 November to
     formulate a co-ordinated strategy.

62   On 26 December the *Scharnhorst* was sunk off North
     Cape, after careful plotting by the Royal Navy.

63   By January 1944 Allied troops had still not reached
     Rome, as the German forces under Marshal Kesselring
     put up a stiff resistance and entrenched themselves
     behind the defensive Gustav Line which stretched across
     central Italy. In an attempt to breach this line, the Allies
     landed at Anzio, south of Rome, and bombed the heavily
     defended Monte Cassino to the south-east, where the
     1,400-year-old Benedictine monastery was destroyed.

64   Rome was liberated on 4 June, two days before the
     D-Day landings in Normandy.

65   The First World War Russian air ace Alexander
     Prokofiev de Seversky emigrated to the USA, where he

became an influential advocate of strategic bombing through the development of intercontinental aircraft.

66   Between 13 June 1944 and the beginning of March 1945 more than 10,000 V1 flying bombs were launched. More than 6,000 civilians, mostly in London, were killed.

67   A group of disillusioned German officers plotted to kill Hitler at his East Prussian headquarters, but he escaped with minor injuries when the bomb – left under a conference table by Colonel von Stauffenberg – exploded. Von Stauffenberg was arrested and shot, and his co-conspirators were hanged after a show trial.

68   The advance through the difficult Normandy countryside had been slow and costly. The Allies finally broke through into more open country eight weeks after the D-Day landings.

69   In Operation Dragoon, Allied troops landed in south-eastern France by sea and air, tying up German forces badly needed in the north. The French Resistance was increasingly active, blowing up rail tracks to delay the transportation of German troops and armaments.

70   With help from the French Resistance, Marseilles fell to the Allies on 23 August. King Michael of Rumania signed an armistice with the Russians and declared war on Germany.

71   Sixty-one men, women and children were killed when an American bomber crashed during bad weather into a school and neighbouring buildings in the Lancashire village of Freckleton.

72   At the beginning of August, the Russian advance through eastern Europe had almost reached Warsaw. The Polish underground forces, loyal to the exiled Polish government in London, rose against their German occupiers, expecting the Russians to arrive within days.

But the Russians did not move, and the uprising was crushed.

73   On 17 September, in Operation Market Garden, British and American troops were parachuted into the Netherlands. The plan was to cross the Meuse at Grave, the Waal at Nijmegen and the Rhine at Arnhem, with a view to opening a way into the Ruhr. The Americans took Bridges at Nijmegen and Eindhoven, but after heavy fighting the British troops at Arnhem were forced to surrender, the Allies having seriously underestimated German strength in the area.

74   General Kazimierz Sosnkowski was commander-in-chief of the Polish government in exile's armed forces after the death of General Sikorski. Sosnkowski's criticism of the Allies for failing to support the Warsaw uprising led to him being relieved of his command.

75   As German forces withdrew from Greece, British troops were despatched there to hold the peace between rival resistance groups. As in Yugoslavia, the leftist groups had gained the upper hand and in Allied circles there was concern that the largely Communist EAM/ELAS forces would move to seize power in Greece. This was the prelude to a civil war in Greece that would continue until 1949.

76   The US presidential election was held on 7 November 1944 and was won by Franklin D. Roosevelt, the only US president to be elected to a fourth term.

77   Churchill received the freedom of Paris on 11 November, to the acclaim of the crowds who saw him parade along the Champs-Elysées with Charles de Gaulle.

78   Greek police had fired on a leftist demonstration in Athens in early December, and British troops had become involved in subsequent skirmishes between leftist and royalist factions. Churchill and Eden flew to

Athens on Christmas Eve in an attempt to negotiate
a constitutional solution. The Labour Party in Britain
was critical of the use of British troops in what they
considered a purely Greek affair.

79   The fighting that had flared up in Athens in December
1944 was brought to an end by an uneasy ceasefire
between the commander of British forces and the
leftist factions. Sporadic outbursts of localised violence
continued throughout 1945.

80   Churchill, Roosevelt and Stalin met at Yalta in the
Crimea in the second week of February 1945 to discuss,
among other things, the political settlement of Eastern
Europe. The Poles felt they had been betrayed when it
became clear that Poland would effectively come under
Soviet control.

81   American army private Gustav Hulten and his
accomplice 18-year-old English waitress Elizabeth Jones
were arrested for several murders in 1944. Both were
found guilty; Hulten was hanged on 8 March 1945, and
Jones imprisoned.

82   The battles of Mandalay and Meiktila in South-East Asia
resulted in British victory. The retreat of Japanese armies
ensured a safe passage to Rangoon and the recapture of
Burma.

83   The San Francisco conference, 25 April–26 June 1945,
concluded with 50 nations signing the Charter of the
United Nations.

84   After long-term ill health, Franklin D. Roosevelt
suffered a cerebral haemorrhage and died on 12 April;
Harry S. Truman was sworn in as US president.

85   Shortly after the Hammer and Sickle was hoisted over
the Reichstag, Hitler committed suicide in his bunker
in Berlin on 30 April 1945. German forces in Berlin
finally surrendered on the afternoon of 2 May.

86   The German army in Italy capitulated on 2 May, four days after Mussolini, his mistress and close associates had been caught and killed by Italian partisans.

87   Germany surrendered unconditionally on 7 May and Victory in Europe Day, VE Day, was announced for the following day.

88   In an election campaign speech on 4 June Churchill had said that a Labour government would need to rely on 'a form of Gestapo'. This infuriated many people.

89   The Labour leader Clement Attlee broadcast a dignified and considered response the day after Churchill's speech, culminating in a plea to rise above traditional party divisions and look to the future: 'It is for us to help to re-knit the fabric of civilised life woven through the centuries, and with the other nations to seek to create a world in which free peoples living their own distinctive lives in a society of nations co-operate together, free from the fear of war.'

90   King Leopold III had ordered the capitulation of the Belgian army in 1940. He refused to abdicate and remained unpopular in Belgium.

91   The Australian prime minister, John Curtin, died from heart disease on 5 July, aged 60.

SELECTED FURTHER READING

PUBLISHED MASS OBSERVATION DIARIES AND ANTHOLOGIES, AND HISTORIES OF MASS OBSERVATION

Broad, Richard and Suzie Fleming (eds), *Nella Last's War* (London, 2006).

Calder, Angus and Dorothy Sheridan (eds), *Speak for Yourself: A mass observation anthology* 1937–1949 (London, 1984).

Cockett, Olivia, *Love and War in London: A woman's diary* 1939–1942, ed. Robert W. Malcolmson (Waterloo, Ont., 2005).

Garfield, Simon (ed.), *Our Hidden Lives: The everyday diaries of a forgotten Britain* 1945–1948 (London, 2004).

—— *We Are at War: The diaries of five ordinary people in extraordinary times* (London, 2005).

——*Private Battles: How the war almost defeated us* (London, 2006).

Gilles, Midge (ed.), *Waiting for Hitler: Voices from Britain on the brink of invasion* (London, 2006).

Hubble, Nick, *Mass Observation and Everyday Life* (London, 2006).

Jeffrey, Tom, *Mass Observation: A short history*, Mass Observation Archive Occasional paper no. 10 (Brighton, 1990).

Jolly, Margaretta, 'Historical Entries: Mass Observation diarists 1937– 2001', *New Formations*, no. 44 (Autumn 2001).

Malcolmson, Robert and Peter Searby (eds), *Wartime Norfolk: The diary of Rachel Dhonau* 1941–1942 (Norwich, 2004).

Sheridan, Dorothy (ed.), *Among You Taking Notes: The wartime diary of Naomi Mitchison* (London, 1985).
——*Wartime Women: An anthology of women's wartime writing for mass observation* (London, 1990).
Sheridan, Dorothy, Brian V. Street, and David Bloome: *Writing Ourselves: Mass observation and literacy practices* (Cresskill, NJ, 2000).
Stebbing, Edward, *Diary of a Decade* 1939–50 (Lewes, Sussex, 1998).

BOOKS PUBLISHED BY MASS OBSERVATION 1937–1945
(in order of date first published)

Madge, C. and T. H. Harrisson, *Mass Observation* (London, 1937).
Jennings, H. and C. Madge, with T. O. Beachcroft, J. Blackburn, W. Empson, S. Legg and K. Raine, *May the Twelfth: Mass observation day surveys* (London, 1937).
Madge, C. and T. H. Harrisson, *First Year's Work* (London, 1938).
——*Britain by Mass Observation* (London, 1939).
——*War Begins at Home* (London, 1940).
Mass Observation, *Clothes Rationing Survey* (London, Advertising Service Guild Bulletin 1941), Change no. 1.
——*Home Propaganda* (London, Advertising Service Guild Bulletin, 1941), Change no. 2.
——*A Savings Survey* (London, Advertising Service Guild Bulletin, 1941), Change no. 3.
——*People in Production: An enquiry into British war production* (London, 1942).
——*War Factory* (London, 1943).
——*People's Homes* (London, Advertising Service Guild Bulletin, 1943), Change no. 4.
——*The Pub and the People: A worktown study* (London, 1943).

——*The Journey Home* (London, Advertising Service Guild, 1944).

——*Britain and her Birth-rate* (London, 1945).

SELECTED HISTORIES OF BRITAIN IN THE SECOND WORLD WAR

Calder, A., *The People's War* (London, 1969).

Donnelly, M., *Britain in the Second World War* (London, 1999).

Gardiner, J., *Wartime Britain* 1939–1945 (London, 2004).

Longmate, N., *How We Lived Then: A history of everyday life during the Second World War* (London, 1971).

Ziegler, P., *London at War* 1939–1945 (London, 1995).

RELATED WEBSITES

Mass Observation Archive
www.massobs.org.uk

University of Sussex Library Special Collections
www.sussex.ac.uk/library/speccoll

BBC History
www.bbc.co.uk/history/worldwars/wwtwo

The People's War
www.bbc.co.uk/ww2peopleswar

The National Archives
www.nationalarchives.gov.uk

Imperial War Museum
www.iwm.org.uk

Churchill Speech interactive
www.churchillspeeches.com

ILLUSTRATIONS

1. A crowd watching Big Ben strike eleven o'clock, London. Photographer unidentified, 3 September 1939. (*Hulton Archive/Getty Images*)

2. A child waiting to be evacuated, London. Photograph by Bert Hardy, 1942. (© *Hulton-Deutsch Collection/CORBIS*)

3. Men queuing outside a Royal Navy recruiting station. Photographer unidentified, 1939. (*Mirrorpix*)

4. Clearing up after a bombing raid, London. Photographer unidentified, August 1940. (*Hulton Archive/Getty Images*)

5. Bomb damage at the corner of Tottenham Court Road and Oxford Street, London. Photographer unidentified, October 1940. (*popperfoto.com*)

6. The Mackenzie family in their Anderson shelter during a raid. Photograph by Hans Wild, 1940. (*Time Life Pictures/ Getty Images*)

7. 'Business as usual', Oxford Street, London. Photograph by George Rodger, 1940. (© *George Rodger/Magnum Photos*)

8. Bidding farewell to loved ones at Paddington Station, London. Photograph by Bert Hardy, 23 May 1942. (*Hulton Archive/Getty Images*)

9. RAMC stretcher drill, Leeds. Photographer unidentified, c.1940. (*Wellcome Library, London*)

10. Wartime bookselling, London. Photograph by George Rodger, 1940. (© *George Rodger/Magnum Photos*)

11. A mother cradling her newborn baby, both wearing their gas masks. Photographer unidentified, c.1941. Neg. no. D3918.(*The Trustees of the Imperial War Museum, London*)

12. A member of the ATS standing in front of a recruiting poster. Photographer unidentified, 2 April 1942. (*Hulton Archive/Getty Images*)

13. Allotment holders hard at work on their plots, Clapham Common, London. Photographer unidentified, 30 March 1940. (© *Hulton-Deutsch Collection/CORBIS*)

14. A simple ceremony on Remembrance Day. Photographer unidentified, 11 November 1941. (*popperfoto.com*)

15. Women queuing for horse meat. Photographer unidentified, c. 1943. (*Mirrorpix*)

16. A victim of a V1 flying bomb in Aldwych, London. Photographer unidentified, 1944. (*popperfoto.com*)

17. Children playing as air-raid wardens, London. Photographer unidentified, 1941. (*Mirrorpix*)

18. A queue waiting to see the RAF film *Journey Together*. Photographer unidentified, 1944. (*Hulton Archive/Getty Images*)

19. German POWs marching to their internment. Photograph by R. H. Clough, 20 August 1944. (*Hulton Archive/Getty Images*)

20. A bomb crater beside a garden air-raid shelter, London. Photographer unidentified, c. 1940. (*Mirrorpix*)

21. A V1 flying bomb about to land on a residential area, southern England. Photographer unidentified, 22 June 1944. (© *CORBIS*)

22. Dancing and singing on VE Day in Fleet Street, London. Photographer unidentified, 8 May 1945. (*popperfoto.com*)

23. A family in their back yard waving at trains carrying soldiers returning home. Photographer unidentified, c. 1945. (© *Hulton-Deutsch Collection/CORBIS*)

INDEX